The Rehnquist Court

THE REHNQUIST COURT

Understanding Its Impact and Legacy

David L. Hudson Jr.

Foreword by John R. Vile

PRAEGER

Westport, Connecticut
London

Library of Congress Cataloging-in-Publication Data

Hudson, David L., 1969–
The Rehnquist Court : understanding its impact and legacy / David L. Hudson Jr. ; foreword by John R. Vile.
p. cm.
Includes bibliographical references and index.
ISBN 0–275–98971–2 (alk. paper)
1. United States. Supreme Court—History. 2. Rehnquist, William H., 1924–2005. 3. Constitutional history—United States. I. Title.
KF8742.H78 2007
347.73'26—dc22 2006028064

British Library Cataloguing in Publication Data is available.

Library of Congress Catalog Card Number: 2006028064
ISBN: 0–275–98971–2

First published in 2007

Praeger Publishers, 88 Post Road West, Westport, CT 06881
An imprint of Greenwood Publishing Group, Inc.
www.praeger.com

Printed in the United States of America

The paper used in this book complies with the Permanent Paper Standard issued by the National Information Standards Organization (Z39.48–1984).

10 9 8 7 6 5 4 3 2 1

To John R. Vile, a great scholar,
and David L. Hudson Sr., a great father.

CONTENTS

FOREWORD

The last two years have been momentous for the U.S. Supreme Court. After 11 years without a single vacancy—the second longest such period in U.S. history—Justice Sandra Day O'Connor tendered her pending resignation in 2005, contingent on confirmation of a replacement. Before the Senate had begun hearings on John Roberts, the gifted former trial attorney and appellate judge whom President George W. Bush had nominated as her successor, Chief Justice William J. Rehnquist died. Bush subsequently proposed that the Senate confirm Roberts for the position of chief justice and nominated another appellate judge, Samuel Alito, Jr., to replace Justice O'Connor. In relatively short order the Senate confirmed Roberts in September 2005 and Alito in early February 2006, and the era of the Roberts Court had begun.

David Hudson was in the fortuitous position of having already done much of his work on this volume on the Rehnquist Court before anyone knew that its time in the sun was about to set so abruptly. This will accordingly be one of the first books, if not *the* first, to assess this era in which Rehnquist served as chief in its totality. I have been privileged to read the chapters as David has written them. As expected, his wide experience in analyzing Supreme Court decisions, in teaching both undergraduate and law students, and in explaining Court rulings in both speeches and books to diverse audiences has insured that his contribution will be accessible to a wide variety of audiences. His numerous interviews with key attorneys who argued before this Court and clerks who worked for its justices as well as his absolute fair-mindedness further guarantee that readers, having heard from both Rehnquist supporters and critics, will have the information they need to form their own conclusions.

REHNQUIST'S BACKGROUND AND APPOINTMENT TO THE SUPREME COURT

William Hubbs Rehnquist was born in Milwaukee, Wisconsin, and earned his law degree from Stanford University, where he was a classmate of Justice Sandra Day (O'Connor), another high-achieving student. After clerking for U.S. Supreme Court justice Robert Jackson (where he authored a memorandum on *Brown v. Board of Education* that has haunted him ever since), Rehnquist moved to Phoenix, Arizona, and quickly rose in the law profession, where his work for Republican candidates got the attention of the Nixon administration. It named him to its Office of Legal Counsel, where, in addition to serving as the attorney general's counsel, he helped review and vet Supreme Court nominees.

In the opening chapter of this book David Hudson describes the improbable set of circumstances under which Richard Nixon appointed Rehnquist to a position on the Burger Court. Unlike most contemporary justices, albeit consistent with some of the greatest justices of the past, Rehnquist did not have prior judicial experience when President Nixon nominated him as an associate justice. Nixon hoped that Rehnquist, who had been a critic of the Warren Court, would help reverse the rising liberal tide that it had initiated. Even though he was not the first Nixon appointee, Rehnquist's voice was often a lonely one during his early years—I remember a colleague who once consistently called him "the wrench," as though his primary function was that of hindering the otherwise smooth operation of that body. Justices who were less sure of themselves might have yielded to peer pressure and retreated, but Rehnquist relished his role as a gadfly, playfully sporting a figurine of the Lone Ranger that his clerks had given him on his desk at the Supreme Court and perhaps savoring presidential election returns that gave Republican presidents an increasing number of judicial nominations.

REHNQUIST'S ELEVATION AS CHIEF JUSTICE

After Burger stepped down from the Court to head celebrations of the bicentennial of the U.S. Constitution, President Reagan elevated Rehnquist to the chief's position and added an associate justice, Antonin Scalia, the quintessential "stealth candidate" who flew in under almost everyone's radar, who would tilt the Court even further to the right. Rehnquist came increasingly to occupy a position of influence. Although scholars have observed that Justices Sandra Day O'Connor and Anthony Kennedy often cast the critical fifth vote in key cases (and references to an O'Connor or Kennedy Court, like earlier references to a "Brennan Court," serve as reminders of the inadequacy of designating a Court by the name of its chief), the Court majority increasingly included the chief justice. Just as Justice William Brennan is often credited with the ability to reach across partisan divides, so, too, Rehnquist reached out to those with whom he often disagreed. It is perhaps as significant that Rehnquist genuinely appeared to like ideological rivals Brennan and Thurgood Marshall as that they appeared to like him.

It may be years before scholars have enough first-hand materials to be able definitively to establish that Rehnquist was simultaneously an effective task and social leader for the Court, but the information available to this date appears to confirm that he was both efficient in administering Court business and affable with, and fair to, his colleagues. Rehnquist's tenure is notable as a time when the Supreme Court arguably kept, and perhaps increased, its influence on American institutions, while cutting back significantly on the number of cases that it accepted for oral argument.

REHNQUIST'S SUCCESSES AND FAILURES

The Rehnquist Court will always be known for a number of firsts. It was the first Court to see the appointment of not one, but two, women (and only the second to see the appointment of an African American). It was the first Court to see the appointment of an Italian American. More controversially, it was the first Court directly to intervene in a case that helped determine the outcome of a presidential election. Although the Court continued to resist pressures to televise its proceedings, it was the first Court, again in the case of *Bush v. Gore,* to release oral transcripts of its arguments on the same day that it heard them.

Rehnquist undoubtedly wished for other firsts. He clearly hoped, at least in the early years, that the Court would reverse, rather than merely trim, *Miranda v. Arizona* (1966) and other liberal rulings respecting the rights of criminal defendants. As one of only two dissenters in the 1973 decision in *Roe v. Wade* (Byron White was the other), Rehnquist undoubtedly hoped that his Court would not only curtail, but also reverse, the judicial recognition of a federal right to an abortion. He probably hoped that the Court would further widen its interpretation of the Tenth Amendment and extend greater protections to states' rights than it did. He was surely disappointed that the Court did not reverse, rather than merely continue to limit, the use of racial classifications in university admissions. Although helping to beat back attempts to recognize a broad constitutional "right to die," he was likewise disappointed that the Court added homosexuality to the list of classifications other than race and gender to which it gave increased scrutiny. While resisting attempts to declare that the death penalty was in and of itself unconstitutional, Rehnquist continued to protest against decisions that limited its application and that continued to spread appeals over decades, making a mockery of the idea of swift punishment.

And yet, over time, Rehnquist and some of his conservative colleagues were remarkably successful in inaugurating major changes in constitutional thinking. Under Rehnquist, the Court exercised a power, once frequently employed but kept in abeyance for 40 years, to strike down a law that Congress had justified under its power to control interstate and foreign commerce. The Court thus affirmed that the Constitution not only limits the national government through explicit constitutional restrictions but also by limiting the powers vested in it. Under Rehnquist, the Court (regrettably in this author's judgment) modified long-standing doctrine relative to the free exercise clause of the First Amendment. Under Rehnquist, the Court reasserted some fairly dormant maxims of judicial restraint while from time to time asserting that it would have the final say on key matters of constitutional interpretation.

Impatient critics from the right continue to bemoan the Court's inability to reverse many major precedents, albeit with the sobering recognition that Reagan failed to get Robert Bork (a well-published conservative) confirmed to the U.S. Supreme Court and that George H. W. Bush had a close call with Justice Clarence Thomas's confirmation (where allegations of sexual harassment magnified concerns over his conservative views). Apprehensive critics from the left have bemoaned every change as though it were the fatal stab to the body politic. Prognostications from both sides, who often tailor their criticisms to the propaganda of interest groups whose advertising thrives on overstatement, have often been bleak. Critics have excoriated the Court for departing from precedent and for adhering too closely to it; for exercising too little activism and too little restraint; for being too result oriented and not cognizant enough of the effects of its decisions. If Charles Dickens were still alive, he could note that it was both the best and worst of times, depending on whom one consulted.

The Burger Court years have often been described as "the constitutional revolution that wasn't." The Rehnquist Court might receive a similar appellation. Rehnquist was enough of an iconoclast that he once had the temerity to question the idea of a "living Constitution," but ironically, the defenders of the idea have often been the most resistant to changes that Rehnquist and his colleagues have sought to initiate. Whereas many previous Courts have established themselves for breaking new judicial paths, with some notable exceptions, many of which Rehnquist himself opposed, the Rehnquist Court may have best established itself for returning to older ones, confident that the people themselves would hew their own new paths if they became dissatisfied with the old ones.

WHAT HUDSON'S BOOK HAS TO OFFER

Individuals who are interested in the Rehnquist Court could have a no more readable or fairer introduction to the subject than this. Hudson has shown an amazing ability to keep sight of the big picture while describing individual cases. Although one can read the book profitably from cover to cover, Hudson has so organized it that readers can pick out chapters that detail Rehnquist's own life and pivotal role in the Court, learn about the lives and views of the justices that collectively composed the Rehnquist Court, and examine particular areas of the law that interest them. While he puts Rehnquist era decisions within the context of traditional liberal and conservative categories, Hudson's nuanced treatment convincingly shows that these labels have often done more to obscure than to illumine the Rehnquist Court.

It will take years, if not decades, to know how long Rehnquist-era precedents will last, but there can be little doubt that the Rehnquist Court played a vital part in American politics and that Chief Justice Rehnquist's own vision was an important influence. With seven current justices having spent most of their time on the Rehnquist Court, and with the current chief having served as a clerk to Rehnquist, Rehnquist's influence is likely to endure well into the Roberts Court. Readers who want to understand the current Court can hardly do better than by beginning with its predecessor, and few starting points will prove more profitable than this book.

John R. Vile

Chapter 1

EARLY CAREER TO SUPREME COURT CONFIRMATION

> During a four-year term, the President of the United States, sitting at this desk, in this historic room, makes over 3,000 major appointments to various government positions. By far the most important appointments he makes are those to the United States Supreme Court.
>
> —President Richard Nixon in television address to the nation (October 21, 1972)

> So just be as mean and rough as they said you were.
>
> —President Richard Nixon to William Rehnquist (1971)

When William Rehnquist was a young boy, one of his schoolteachers at Atwater Elementary School asked him his future plans. Legend has it that the young Rehnquist boldly proclaimed, "I'm going to change the government."[1] Years later, this young boy from Wisconsin would occupy the highest seat in the federal judiciary—Chief Justice of the United States Supreme Court—for 19 years. He served more than 33 years on the high court. He changed or moved the Court's jurisprudence in many areas and guided with a steady hand the federal courts as the chief administrator. He accomplished the goal he articulated as an elementary school child.

Born in Milwaukee in 1924, Rehnquist grew up in a stable, two-parent home in the Milwaukee suburb of Shorewood. His father, William Benjamin Rehnquist, a Swede, served as a wholesale paper broker, while his mother,

Margery Peck Rehnquist, spoke four languages and supplemented the family income as an interpreter. His parents were conservative, opposing many of the policies of the administration of Franklin Delano Roosevelt and his New Deal program. Rehnquist attended the all-white Shorewood High School, where he excelled academically without great effort, displayed a love of history, dabbled in acting, and worked on the school newspaper. Even as a youngster, classmates remember him as a conservative—as were most people in Shorewood.

A young Rehnquist won a scholarship to Kenyon College in Ohio, but his education was interrupted by his service in World War II. He enlisted in the Army Air Corps in a meteorology program and was stationed mainly in North Africa. After the war, he attended Stanford University on the G.I. Bill, where he obtained his undergraduate and master's degrees. Rehnquist then attended Harvard, where he obtained a master's degree in government. Then Rehnquist returned out West to Stanford in 1950 for law school. Rehnquist excelled in his legal studies, graduating first in his class. While there, he befriended a female classmate and fellow law review member named Sandra Day. The two briefly dated but remained friends for many years. Of course, Sandra Day was none other than the future U.S. Supreme Court justice Sandra Day O'Connor, the first woman appointed to the high court.

Rehnquist graduated first in his class from Stanford Law School in 1952. In the summer of 1951 his administrative law professor, Phil Neal, asked Rehnquist if he would like to interview with Supreme Court Justice Robert Jackson. Neal, who had clerked for Jackson a few years earlier, informed Rehnquist that Justice Jackson was coming to the law school for the dedication of the university's new law school building. In his book on the Supreme Court Rehnquist recalled that "the suggestion came out of a clear blue sky, but of course I said yes."[2]

Rehnquist's interview with Jackson went well, but the young Rehnquist did not expect to land the prestigious clerkship position. To his surprise, Jackson informed him by letter in November 1951 that he had the job beginning February 1, 1952, until June 1953. Rehnquist served as a clerk for Justice Jackson when the justices heard oral arguments in several cases that later became consolidated at the Supreme Court and known collectively as *Brown v. Board of Education.*[3] Rehnquist authored a memo—which became controversial years later—in which he wrote that the Court should not overrule *Plessy v. Ferguson,* the 1896 Supreme Court decision that ruled that separate public facilities based on race are constitutional as long as they are substantially equal. Rehnquist later claimed that he wrote the memo as a suggestion of Jackson's views.

After his Supreme Court clerkship, Rehnquist moved to Arizona and began the private practice of law in Phoenix, Arizona, in 1953. He joined the law firm of Evans, Kitchel, and Jenckes. He became politically active in the Republican Party and even gave speeches criticizing some liberal decisions of the Warren Court. He also served as local counsel for the Arizona Republican Party.

After a few years, Rehnquist formed a partnership with Keith Ragan, who used to be the president of the Phoenix Young Democrats. In 1957, he moved to the law firm Cunningham, Carson, and Messenger. Afterward, he formed a partnership with James Powers, a self-described liberal Democrat.

During his time of private practice Rehnquist also found time to criticize publicly the Warren Court. In December 1957, he published an article in *U.S. News & World Report* in which he talked about the growing influence of liberal law clerks on the justices. He said that the clerks on the Court when he was clerking for Jackson showed "extreme solicitude for the claims of Communists and other criminal defendants."[4] He called Chief Justice Earl Warren and Associate Justices Hugo Black and William Douglas "left wing philosophers." Rehnquist also wrote letters to the editor expressing his opposition to a Phoenix public accommodations law and a school integration plan. In June 1964, Rehnquist spoke against the public accommodations law at the city council. These letters would also prove to be juicy fodder for his opponents during confirmation.

Rehnquist campaigned heartily for the U.S. senator from Arizona Barry Goldwater in his failed bid for the 1964 presidential election. During the campaign Rehnquist became connected with Richard G. Kleindienst, who worked on the Goldwater campaign and later on Richard Nixon's successful 1968 presidential campaign.

"THE PRESIDENT'S LAWYER'S LAWYER"

Rehnquist's connection with Kleindienst proved vital to his career path when Kleindienst became President Nixon's deputy attorney general. Kleindienst appointed Rehnquist to the Justice Department's Office of Legal Counsel. Rehnquist's job was to serve, in the later words of President Nixon, as the "President's attorney's attorney"—the attorney for Attorney General John Mitchell. From this position Rehnquist examined the constitutionality of presidential executive orders and other constitutional law questions that arose in the executive branch.

Rehnquist continued his criticism of the Warren Court during his time in the Office of Legal Counsel. He criticized Vietnam War protestors as the "new barbarians" who "care nothing for our system of government and law." In his official capacity Rehnquist advocated many pro-law enforcement positions that gave short shrift to the constitutional rights of criminal defendants. In September 1971—one month before his surprise nomination to the Supreme Court—Rehnquist testified in front of a Senate subcommittee that criminal defendants should be convicted on less than unanimous jury verdicts. Traditionally, in federal cases and in most states, defendants can only be found guilty by a unanimous jury. Rehnquist testified that defendants should be convicted based on 10–2 or 9–3 votes.[5] In what would become a familiar role when he became a justice, he also vented that inmates were abusing the writ of habeas corpus by continuously challenging their underlying convictions with several petitions in federal court: "Within the past generation, the federal habeas corpus has been interpreted to permit repeated attacks on final judgments of conviction, even though those judgments have long since run their course through the prescribed trial and appellate review."[6]

Rehnquist also emphasized that the administration was justified in its attempts to protect people from crime rather than worry too much about what caused people to commit those crimes. At a December 1970 speech at the University of Hawaii, Rehnquist said, "No one denies the paramount importance of getting at the root causes of crime, whatever these may be and however they may be gotten—a matter upon which many individuals agree. But to suggest that this is the only problem is to entirely overlook the equally important problem of dealing with those who are now committing criminal acts, whatever the reasons for their antisocial behavior.... It is little consolation to a woman who is mugged on the street of a large city to be told that the person who mugged her grew up in an urban ghetto."[7]

However, Rehnquist impressed many—ideological allies and foes—with his substantial legal abilities. Attorneys in the Justice Department before the Nixon administration admired his "ability to pull back from a close legal call and summarize both sides of the issue."[8]

A SURPRISE CHOICE

The name of William Rehnquist was not even on the radar screen when the names of possible Supreme Court nominees were discussed by President Nixon and Attorney General John Mitchell. Kleindienst, in his memoirs entitled *Justice,* wrote, "That William Hubbs Rehnquist of Arizona found himself on the nation's highest court, however, was the product of many seemingly unrelated factors. So many, in fact, that the likelihood of their coming together again to produce a similar result is beyond probability."[9]

Ironically, during his time at the Office of Legal Counsel Rehnquist reviewed, or vetted, the individuals that President Nixon and Attorney General Mitchell were considering nominating to the U.S. Supreme Court.

There were several vacancies at the U.S. Supreme Court after the retirement of Chief Justice Earl Warren, the resignation of Justice Abe Fortas, and the retirements of Justices John M. Harlan and Hugo Black.

President Nixon had made the Supreme Court an issue in his successful 1968 presidential campaign, promising to restore the Court with law and order justices. Warren Burger, a conservative jurist on the U.S. Court of Appeals for the District of Columbia, fit the bill perfectly. Nixon had trouble filling Justice Fortas's seat as the U.S. Senate rejected the president's first two choices, Clement F. Haynsworth, Jr. of South Carolina and G. Harrold Carswell from Florida.

Haynsworth had served on the U.S. Court of Appeals for the Fourth Circuit since the 1950s. However, his nomination triggered great opposition in the Senate, particularly after Associate Justice Abe Fortas—President Lyndon Baines Johnson's choice to replace Earl Warren as chief justice—resigned after improprieties surfaced. Several Democratic senators, including Indiana's Birch Bayh, were less than pleased with the Fortas situation and vowed to give Nixon's nominees a close examination.

Haynsworth had the misfortune of being President Nixon's first choice to fill the Fortas vacancy at a time when political battles were being waged fiercely in the Senate. It also did not help that Haynsworth had voted in two cases involving companies in which he owned stock. Civil rights groups also opposed Haynsworth on ideological grounds. In November 1969, the Senate rejected him by a vote of 55–45. The next choice was Carswell, who had served as a Federal District Court judge in Florida and then for a brief time on the U.S. Court of Appeals for the Fifth Circuit. The die was cast negatively for Carswell after it was discovered that in 1948, he said, "Segregation of the races is proper and the only practical and correct way of life in our states. I have always so believed and I shall always so act." The Senate rejected Carswell by a vote of 51–45. In his memoirs, Deputy Attorney General Kleindienst wrote that the Senate was justified in rejecting Carswell.[10]

The president then nominated Warren Burger's close friend and best man at his wedding, little-known Harry M. Blackmun, who was a judge on the U.S. Court of Appeals for the Eighth Circuit. Because he was the president's third choice (after Haynsworth and Carswell), Blackmun also referred to himself as "good ole number three."

Then President Nixon received the news that Justices Hugo Black and John Marshall Harlan were retiring for health reasons. With the next two vacancies Nixon had the chance to change the composition of the Court quite dramatically. He could replace Justice Black, who was a liberal on many constitutional issues, with a diehard conservative. Harlan was the grandson of a Supreme Court justice, John Marshall Harlan, known as "the

Great Dissenter" for his lone dissent in the Court's 1896 decision *Plessy v. Ferguson,* which upheld a racial segregation law in Louisiana. The grandson believed in judicial restraint and dissented in many of the Warren Court decisions, believing that the Court had gone too far. Ironically, his place was taken by a justice—William Rehnquist—who had even stronger thoughts about the misdirection of the Warren Court.

President Nixon initially considered U.S. Congressman Richard Poff from Virginia, who initially was receptive but dropped out for family reasons. Nixon then considered a host of candidates, including Herschel Friday, a prominent Arkansas attorney; Robert Byrd, the senator from West Virginia; and a female California jurist named Mildred Lillie. However, the American Bar Association gave unfavorable ratings to both Friday and Lillie, Nixon's top two choices. Rehnquist's role in this process was to defend the records of those judges or nominees considered by the administration. For example, Rehnquist defended Judge Lillie's record as a member of the California Court of Appeals against criticisms that her opinions were reversed at a high rate by the California Supreme Court. Rehnquist conducted a thorough study of her opinions and compiled statistics showing that overall, her record of reversals was not very alarming or unusual.[11]

The president then considered Lewis Powell, a 64-year-old, well-respected attorney from Richmond, Virginia, who was a past president of the American Bar Association and had held other prominent positions, and Senator Howard Baker from Tennessee. Powell accepted, but Baker waffled on his decision. In the meantime, several administrative officials—unbeknown to William Rehnquist—recommended Rehnquist. In his book *The Rehnquist Choice,* John W. Dean, associate deputy attorney general in the Department of Justice, claims he was the first one to recommend Rehnquist.[12] Dean claims that on October 4, 1971, "in a seemingly innocuous conversation," he mentioned the name of William Rehnquist to Richard Moore, special counsel to the president. "The president has a perfect candidate right under his nose," Dean said to Moore.

Two days later, Senator Goldwater urged President Nixon to consider Rehnquist. The president knew who Rehnquist was, but his recall was faulty on the correct pronunciation of his name. A transcript of a White House conversation of July 1971 revealed Nixon saying "you remember the meeting we had when I told that group of clowns we had around there. Renchburg and that group. What's his name? … Yeah Renchquist."[13]

By all accounts Rehnquist was unaware that he was under consideration. He had said earlier in response to a question from a friend about his chances: "None at all, because I'm not from the South, I'm not a woman, and I'm not mediocre." White House aide Richard Moore, who had supported the idea of Rehnquist as justice to President Nixon, recalled years later that he went to Attorney General Mitchell's office on October 20, 1971, and saw a dazed William Rehnquist sitting down in a chair. Moore asked Mitchell, "What's the matter with him?" Mitchell informed Moore that Rehnquist had just been told that he could be nominated to the U.S. Supreme Court.[14]

President Nixon surprised the nation on October 21, 1971, when he announced his two picks were Powell and Rehnquist. He praised both candidates for their superb legal careers and abilities. "William Rehnquist has been outstanding in every intellectual endeavor he has undertaken," Nixon told the nation. "He is, in effect, the President's lawyer's lawyer."[15]

CONTENTIOUS CONFIRMATION HEARINGS

Initial reaction to the nominees was surprise. The headline the next day in the *Chicago Tribune* summed it up well: "Surprise Choices for the Court."[16] Several senators responded that at least the two nominees appeared better qualified than the president's previous picks.

Some senators quickly galvanized against Rehnquist, given his intimate connection to President Nixon. Democratic senator Birch Bayh from Indiana expressed concerns about Rehnquist's testimony before Senate subcommittees in which he advocated very conservative positions. "I am concerned with some of the attitudes expressed by Mr. Rehnquist before the Senate constitutional rights subcommittee of which I am a member," he said. [17] Bayh expressed particular concern about Rehnquist's testimony regarding the administration's broad powers to conduct domestic surveillance, which the senator viewed as anathema to individual liberty and privacy.

In early November the Senate Judiciary Committee interrogated Rehnquist about many conservative positions he had taken in his writings and testimony before congressional subcommittees. During the hearings the American Bar Association—the largest professional association of attorneys—revealed that both Powell and Rehnquist had received the group's highest rating. Powell received the endorsement unanimously 12–0, while Rehnquist received a favorable vote of 9–3.

At his confirmation hearings, allegations surfaced that Rehnquist had challenged the legality of certain African American voters at the polls. The National Association for the Advancement of Colored People (NAACP) spoke loud and clear against Rehnquist. Civil rights leader Roy Wilkins blasted Rehnquist's record on civil rights, arguing that the "Rehnquist doctrine would return the nation to pre-1954 practices" and "permit segregation by race, both by private individuals and by government."[18] Similarly, Vernon Jordan questioned whether a nominee with a "consistent record of opposition to civil rights bills … is really what is needed in a Supreme Court justice in this time of racial tension."[19] The American Civil Liberties

Union publicly opposed a Supreme Court nominee for the first time when they called Rehnquist "a dedicated opponent of individual liberties."

However, many supported Rehnquist during his confirmation. James Powers, a law partner of Rehnquist from 1960 to 1969 and a liberal Democrat, said that Rehnquist opposed racism of any form. Powers said that Rehnquist's opposition to the public accommodations law in Phoenix was based on constitutional grounds.[20] Herbert Ely, the Arizona Democratic chairman, wrote a letter to the Senate Judiciary Committee arguing that Rehnquist should be confirmed. Ely did acknowledge that if he were president, he would not nominate the conservative Rehnquist. John P. Frank, an Arizona Democratic attorney who successfully argued the famous *Miranda* case before the U.S. Supreme Court on behalf of defendant Ernesto Miranda, also said that Rehnquist was a less than ideal appointment but should be confirmed. "His character is absolutely unimpeachable," Frank told the *Washington Post.* "I have no serious doubts that he should be confirmed. On the other hand, given my premises, he is enough of an extreme conservative that it is a deplorable appointment."[21]

During his testimony Rehnquist said that he had changed his mind about the Phoenix public accommodations law, saying he was wrong to elevate the freedom of businesspersons over minorities' equal access rights to places of public accommodation. "I would not have the same feeling now," he testified.

On November 23, 1971, the Senate Judiciary Committee approved Powell 16–0 and Rehnquist 12–4. The four senators voting against Rehnquist were four Democrats: Bayh, Edward Kennedy, Philip Hart, and John V. Tunney. The Senate judiciary majority issued a 40-page brief to the full Senate explaining why Rehnquist should be confirmed. The majority report noted that Rehnquist had shown a "deep and unwavering commitment to the Constitution" and "professional competence, open-mindedness and a sense of fairness."[22] The four dissenting members of the Senate Judiciary Committee issued their minority report, contending that Rehnquist was "outside the mainstream of American thought." They focused on Rehnquist's 1967 opposition to a school integration plan in Phoenix and quoted Rehnquist's statement that "we are no more dedicated to an 'integrated' society than we are to a segregated society—instead, we are dedicated to a free society."[23] The minority report claimed that Rehnquist's record shows "a dangerous hostility to the great principles of individual freedom under the Bill of Rights and equal justice for all people."

This action meant that the full Senate would consider the nominees. The Rehnquist confirmation became even more contentious after *Newsweek,* in early December 1952, published a Supreme Court memo addressed to Justice Robert Jackson from then law clerk Rehnquist while the Court was considering the question of segregation of public schools in *Brown v. Board of Education.* The memo, which bore Rehnquist's initials, "WHR," sent shock waves through certain segments of society and provided plenty of ammunition to his critics. The memo concluded, "I realize that it is an unpopular and unhumanitarian position, for which I have been excoriated by 'liberal' colleagues, but I think Plessy v. Ferguson was right and should be re-affirmed." The memo certainly seemed to provide instant legitimacy to those in the civil rights community who opposed Rehnquist.

Rehnquist responded to the surfaced memo by writing a letter to Senator James O. Eastland, the chairman of the Senate Judiciary Committee. Rehnquist stated he wrote the memo at Justice Jackson's request to be a rough draft of Jackson's views on the case. "As best I can reconstruct the circumstances after some 19 years, the memorandum was prepared by me at Justice Jackson's request; it was intended as a rough draft of a statement of his views at the conference of the Justices, rather than as a statement of my views," Rehnquist wrote.[24]

Rehnquist denied that he held the view that *Plessy v. Ferguson* should be reaffirmed in *Brown v. Board of Education.* "In view of some of the recent Senate floor debate, I wish to state unequivocally that I fully support the legal reasoning and the rightness from the standpoint of fundamental fairness of the Brown decision," he wrote.

Rehnquist's fellow law clerk, Donald Cronson, stepped to his former colleague's defense when he told newspaper reporters that Rehnquist opposed segregation. Cronson, who was an international lawyer based in London in the early 1970s, said that both he and Rehnquist "personally thought at the time that the 1896 decision, Plessy v. Ferguson, was wrong."[25] Cronson also said that he wrote much of the memo that bore the initials "WHR," saying that he recognized his own "purple prose."

Bayh, who strongly opposed Rehnquist, called the nominee's explanation "self-serving" and sought to prevent a full vote on the nominee. Senator Kennedy also lambasted Rehnquist, saying "never in the course of American history have so few taken so much from so many, and William Rehnquist was there every step of the way."[26]

Bayh asked his colleagues to delay a vote on the nominee so that there could be more time to evaluate the entire record. He called for a vote to delay the confirmation vote until January 1972, but his proposal was rejected 70–22.

Some senators accused Bayh of filibustering and filed a motion for cloture, which would have closed off further debate on Rehnquist. Even though the cloture motion failed to garner the necessary two-thirds vote, the majority of the Senate agreed with the president that the Senate should vote on the nominee. On December 10, 1972, the Senate voted to confirm

Rehnquist 68–26. Rehnquist received favorable votes from 38 Republicans and 30 Democrats. Three Republicans and 23 Democrats voted against him. One of those three Republicans voting against Rehnquist was African American senator Edward W. Brooke from Massachusetts, who was critical of Rehnquist's record on civil rights issues—particularly his public opposition to the school desegregation plan in Phoenix.[27] The other two dissenting Republicans were Jacob K. Javits from New York and Clifford Case from New Jersey.

Meanwhile, the Senate voted to confirm Powell by a vote of 89–1. Rehnquist gave a short statement, thanking the Senate for confirmation, the president for the nomination, and giving thanks "to the many people in and out of the Government without whose support the outcome might have been quite different."[28]

Opponents were dismayed by Rehnquist's elevation to the Court. The *Chicago Daily Defender* opined in an editorial that "it is a disaster to have such a man on the nation's highest court."[29]

A SUPREME COURT JUSTICE

On December 30, 1971, Justice Harlan—whose resignation led to Rehnquist becoming a member of the Supreme Court—died of bone cancer. All of the sitting justices and others, including soon-to-be justices Powell and Rehnquist, attended the funeral. Harlan's replacement was sworn in a week later along with Powell on January 8, 1972, in a closed, 10-minute ceremony. With signs on the court building stating "Building Closed Until Noon Except by Invitation," Chief Justice Burger delivered the oath to the two new justices in a courthouse full of friends, relatives, and government officials. Among the visitors in the courtroom were William and Margery Rehnquist. It was the first time that two justices were sworn in together in 60 years, when Willis Van Devanter and Joseph Lamar were sworn in jointly in 1911. Rehnquist was designated as the Court's most junior justice because his signed commission from President Nixon was signed December 15, 1971, while Powell's was signed December 9, 1971. The two newest justices then took their places at the respective ends of the bench, the so-called freshman seats. "We look forward to many years of work with you in our common calling," Burger told the two men.[30] After the brief ceremony, Powell and Rehnquist joined their colleagues in the Court's private Friday conference to discuss which cases the Court might hear the remainder of the term.

Rehnquist survived the process to become a member of the U.S. Supreme Court. Though they lost the confirmation battle, Democratic senators Bayh and Tunney were partly prescient in their comments. "Here we are talking about a Supreme Court nominee who is going to be on the court for a quarter century or perhaps three decades," Bayh said. "We should have adequate time to answer the questions that have been raised."[31] Similarly, Senator Tunney expressed no regret about probing Rehnquist's philosophy and past statements, saying that a person of Rehnquist's age could still be sitting on the Court in 2000.

Bayh and Tunney were both right. Rehnquist served more than three decades on the Court, and he sat on the Court past the year 2000, until his death in September 2005.

Chapter 2

LONE RANGER ON THE BURGER COURT

> I came to the court sensing, without really having followed it terribly closely, that there were some excesses in terms of constitutional adjudication during the era of the so-called Warren Court. And I felt that I probably would disagree with some of these decisions.... So I felt that at the time I came on the Court, the boat was kind of keeling over in one direction. Interpreting my oath as I saw it, I felt that my job was, where those sort of situations arose, to kind of lean it the other way.
>
> —Justice William Rehnquist (1985)[1]

Justice Rehnquist began his Court work the same day, January 8, 1972, that Chief Justice Burger swore him and Justice Powell to their oaths of office. Rehnquist proved to be an effective conservative voice on the Burger Court, articulating a constitutional vision that differed greatly from the vision of Justices William Brennan and Thurgood Marshall, two stalwart liberals, and Warren Court veterans who remained on the Court.

THE WARREN COURT

The Warren Court signifies the period of time when Chief Justice Earl Warren served as the head of the Court from 1953 to 1969. The Warren Court changed constitutional law dramatically. In the words of Supreme Court scholar Bernard Schwartz, it "rewrote much of the corpus of American constitutional law,"[2] issuing numerous landmark rulings, including *Brown v. Board of Education,*[3] which struck down segregated public schools; *New York Times Co. v. Sullivan,*[4] which forced state libel laws to meet First Amendment constitutional guarantees and ensured that there should be a "profound national commitment to the principle that debate on public issues should be robust, uninhibited and wide-open"; *Engel v. Vitale,*[5] which invalidated school-sponsored prayer in public schools; *Gideon v. Wainwright,*[6] which gave indigent criminal defendants in state court charged with felonies the right to an attorney; *Miranda v. Arizona,*[7] which required the police to issue warnings to suspects to prevent involuntary confessions; *Baker v. Carr,*[8] which ruled that legislative reapportionment presented a constitutional question reviewable by the courts; and *Mapp v. Ohio,*[9] which ruled that the exclusionary rule, prohibiting the introduction of evidence seized unlawfully, applied to state court defendants.

These were just a few of the Court's decisions that breathed strong life into many protections found in the Bill of Rights. The Warren Court seemed to view itself as the grand protector of civil liberties, the moral compass of the nation. Former solicitor general, federal appeals court judge, and law clerk to Chief Justice Burger, Kenneth Starr writes that "the Warren Court brought about a revolution in what is known as 'criminal procedure.'"[10]

Earl Warren was a former Republican candidate for president and governor of California. In one of the great historical ironies of the twentieth century, Warren as California governor spoke out strongly in favor of interning Japanese Americans on the West Coast for security reasons during World War II. This supporter of internment—an egregious violation of civil rights—became the primary mover behind a Court that insured the success of the Civil Rights Movement, revolutionized criminal procedure, and acted as the moral compass for the country.

Many, including a young lawyer in Phoenix named Bill Rehnquist, believed that the Warren Court was an activist Court that acted more like a super-legislature than a court. As a Phoenix attorney in the private sector, Rehnquist had railed against the excesses of the Warren Court, particularly in the criminal justice arena. He specifically named the trio of Chief Justice Warren, Brennan, and Douglas as the primary culprits of legislating from the bench with a left-wing bias.

President Nixon and other conservatives hoped that Chief Justice Burger would be able to lead a counterrevolution on the Court, curtailing the excesses of the Warren Court: "Implicit in Nixon's agenda was the creation of a new Court that would not extend the [Warren Court] revolution in criminal procedure and might even roll it back."[11] William Rehnquist was nominated to the Court in large part because of his conservative judicial philosophy. In many respects the Burger Court was a disappointment for those who wished to turn back the clock on the Warren Court precedents. The Burger Court extended the right of privacy in its famous 1973 decision *Roe v. Wade,* holding that privacy included a woman's right to choose whether to have an abortion. The Burger Court extended the *Gideon v. Wainwright* right to counsel to all state court defendants facing imprisonment—whether by felony or misdemeanor—in *Argesinger v. Hamlin.*[12] A majority of the Burger Court even effectively invalidated the death penalty nationwide with its 1972 decision in *Furman v. Georgia.*[13]

THE LONE RANGER

Unlike others on the Burger Court, William Rehnquist was not a disappointment to conservatives. He generally advocated his conservative judicial philosophy forcefully and articulately, whether in the majority or the dissent. He was considered "the Court's most dynamic member."[14] Supreme Court historian Bernard Schwartz wrote that Rehnquist filed 54 solo dissents as an associate justice on the Burger Court.[15] Political scientist Harold Spaeth writes that Rehnquist wrote 62 lone dissents during his time on the Burger Court—60 of which he characterizes as conservative.[16] Whatever the exact number, Rehnquist's frequent lone dissents earned him the moniker "the Lone Ranger." His clerks even presented him with a Lone Ranger doll to celebrate his penchant for striking out on his own in many opinions.

One of his more notable dissents took place in the Court's 1973 decision in the school desegregation case *Keyes v. School Dist. No. 1, Denver.*[17] The case involved allegations that Denver school board officials had persisted in a pattern of insuring segregated schools. The case did not involve a state law, present or in the recent past, that mandated racial segregation of the schools. Instead, the plaintiffs alleged that the school board officials had manipulated student attendance zones and the location of schools to insure that there was segregation of schoolchildren. The majority held that "a finding of intentionally segregative school board actions in a meaningful portion of a school system, as in this case, creates a presumption that other segregated schooling within the system is not adventitious."[18]

Justice Rehnquist filed a solo dissent, accusing the majority of taking "a long leap in this area of constitutional law" by equating the alleged segregation of schools in places like Denver with areas of the country where segregation was mandated by law. Rehnquist wrote that if the plaintiffs could prove that school officials had deliberately engaged in techniques designed to create segregated schools, then the minority students "are undoubtedly deprived of their constitutional right to equal protection of the law." However, he said the majority opinion ignored "significant differences between the proof" required in such a case with the proof required in a case where there was a state law mandating "total segregation."[19]

Even more dramatic was Rehnquist's split from his colleagues in *Taylor v. Louisiana,* a highly watched decision involving gender and juries.[20] Louisiana had a law that allowed women to serve on juries only if they specifically wrote a letter to government officials declaring their willingness to serve on juries. The net effect of such a "volunteer rule" meant that women were significantly underrepresented on juries.

Criminal defendant Billy J. Taylor, who was convicted by an all-male jury of kidnapping charges, contended that he was entitled to a new trial because his Sixth Amendment rights to an impartial jury were denied. Taylor's attorneys argued that the selection of a trial jury from a representative cross section of the community is an essential element of the right to an impartial jury. The majority of the Burger Court agreed, writing that "the fair-cross-section requirement is violated by the systematic exclusion of women."[21] Justice Byron White wrote for the majority, "If it was ever the case that women were unqualified to sit on juries or were so situated that none of them should be required to perform jury service, that time has long since passed."[22]

Rehnquist dissented, pointing out that defendant Taylor did not show that at his trial he "had been unfairly treated or prejudiced in any way by the manner in which his jury was selected."[23] Rehnquist pointed out that only 13 years before the Warren Court, the Court had rejected a constitutional challenge to a similar jury system in Florida.[24] Rehnquist criticized what he termed "the complete swing of the judicial pendulum."[25] He admitted that Louisiana's jury statute may be an "anachronism" but said the majority overreached by imposing its "perception of modern life" into its constitutional analysis.[26]

Rehnquist often dissented alone in equal protection cases. A prime example was the Court's 1972 opinion in *Weber v. Aetna Casualty & Surety Company.*[27] The case involved a Louisiana workman's compensation statute that denied recovery to illegitimate, unacknowledged children. When their father died, his five children sought to recover workers' compensation benefits. The four legitimate children recovered but not his illegitimate child. The majority characterized this as discriminatory, noting that both the legitimate and illegitimate children lived in the same home. The state contended that it had a strong interest in protecting legitimate family relationships. However, the majority concluded that "imposing disabilities on the illegitimate child is contrary to the basic concept of our system that legal burdens should bear some relationship to individual responsibility or wrongdoing."[28]

Rehnquist dissented, accusing his colleagues of "doing nothing less than passing policy judgments upon the acts of every state legislature in the country."[29] He reasoned that the Louisiana law may have been part of a larger legislative scheme to "discourage formation of illicit family relationships." To Rehnquist, this was not an irrational way for the state to accomplish its goals. The Court, according to Rehnquist, had no business determining whether this was the best or wisest course for the legislature. He also argued that the Court's analysis had strayed very far away from the purposes of the Fourteenth Amendment and had caused an "invitation for judicial exegesis over and above the commands of the Constitution."[30]

The next year, the Burger Court struck down a New Jersey law that prohibited public assistance benefits for the care of illegitimate children in *New Jersey Welfare Rights Organization v. Cahill.*[31] The law, called the Assistance to Families of the Working Poor, provided welfare benefits to households with a married couple who have at least one minor child. The law operated to deny benefits to illegitimate children but granted benefits to legitimate children. Relying on its *Weber* decision, the majority determined that the law violated equal protection by singling out illegitimate children. The court reasoned that "there can be no doubt that the benefits extended under the challenged program are as indispensable to the health and well-being of illegitimate children as to those who are legitimate."[32]

Justice Rehnquist dissented, finding that the statute was a reasonable way for the New Jersey legislature to protect the married family unit: "It does not seem to me irrational in establishing such a special program to condition the receipt of such grants on the sort of ceremonial marriage that could quite reasonably be found to be an essential ingredient of the family unit that the New Jersey Legislature is trying to protect from dissolution due to the economic vicissitudes of modern life."[33]

Rehnquist often dissented alone in criminal law cases, finding no constitutional violation when his colleagues did. A prime example was the Court's decision in *Green v. Georgia.*[34] The state charged Roosevelt Green and codefendant Carzell Moore with capital murder for the rape and death of a convenience store clerk. Moore was tried first and convicted of capital murder. At Moore's trial the state used the testimony of another man who testified that Moore told him that he had killed the woman, shooting her after he sent Green to the store on an errand.

At his trial Roosevelt Green sought to introduce the testimony of this man. The trial court judge disallowed this evidence, ruling that the man's testimony in Moore's trial was inadmissible hearsay. Perhaps because of this evidence, a jury sentenced Green to death. On appeal, the U.S. Supreme Court reversed, finding that the state could not use its hearsay rule to defeat justice. The majority pointed out that the evidence was reliable as the State had used it in a prior case. The majority also noted that the testimony was "highly relevant to a critical issue" in the case. The majority concluded that the exclusion of this evidence violated Green's due process rights.[35]

Rehnquist disagreed, accusing the majority of "embalming the law of evidence in the Due Process Clause of the Fourteenth Amendment to the United States Constitution."[36] He accused the majority of running roughshod over the state's interests and choices in its criminal law. He wrote, "Nothing in the United States Constitution gives this Court any authority to supersede a State's code of evidence because its application in a particular situation would defeat what this Court conceives to be 'the ends of justice.'"[37]

In *Ake v. Oklahoma* the Burger Court ruled 8–1 that the Constitution requires states to provide indigent criminal defendants access to psychiatric assistance.[38] The case involved the prosecution of Glen Burton Ake, who murdered a couple and wounded their two children. Ake apparently was a paranoid schizophrenic, whose competency to stand trial was questioned. After taking enough antipsychotic drugs to become competent to stand trial, Ake stood trial, though he did not have the funds for a psychiatrist to testify as to his sanity or lack thereof at the time of the murders. The Court majority determined that "when a defendant has made a preliminary showing that his sanity at the time of the offense is likely to be a significant factor at trial, the Constitution requires that a State provide access to a psychiatrist's assistance on this issue if the defendant cannot otherwise afford one."[39] The majority did not limit its rule to capital cases.

Rehnquist fulfilled his role as the lone dissenter, arguing that the "constitutional rule announced by the Court is far too broad."[40] He would limit the rule to capital cases and would limit defendants to "an independent psychiatric evaluation, not to a defense consultant."[41] He also questioned whether a state even has to make an insanity defense available to a defendant in the first place.

In the First Amendment context Rehnquist certainly had no problem filing solitary dissents. In one of his very first opinions Rehnquist wrote a dissenting opinion in a case involving the claims of Texas inmate Fred A. Cruz, who claimed that prison officials discriminated against him because he was a Buddhist. In *Cruz v. Beto* the Court ruled 8–1 that the lower courts erred in summarily dismissing Cruz's constitutional claims, including his First Amendment right to freely exercise his right to practice his religion.[42] "If Cruz was a Buddhist and if he was denied a reasonable opportunity of pursuing his faith comparable to the opportunity afforded fellow prisoners who adhere to conventional religious precepts, then there was palpable discrimination by the State against the Buddhist religion, established 600 B.C., long before the Christian era," the Court wrote in a per curiam opinion.[43]

Rehnquist disagreed, emphasizing Cruz's inmate status and the fact that he was serving 15 years for robbery. He reasoned that prison policies should be reviewed under a very deferential standard: "Absent a complaint alleging facts showing that the difference in treatment between petitioner and his fellow Buddhists and practitioners of denominations with more numerous adherents could not reasonably be justified under any rational hypothesis, I would leave the matter in the hands of prison officials."[44]

Rehnquist's pattern as a lone ranger surfaced often in First Amendment cases, as his views of free expression often bowed to his pro-majoritarian, pro-government views. In *Virginia Pharmacy Board v. Virginia Consumer Council,* the Court ruled 7–1 that the state of Virginia could not prohibit truthful price advertising by pharmacists. The Court's decision established that commercial speech, advertising, received First Amendment protection.[45] Rehnquist criticized the majority in his solitary dissent, bemoaning the fact that advertisers now had free-speech protections. He also proved prescient when he wrote: "Under the Court's opinion the way will be open not only for dissemination of price information but for active promotion of prescription drugs, liquor, cigarettes, and other products the use of which it has previously been thought desirable to discourage."[46]

Rehnquist continued to dissent from the Court's protection of other types of commercial speech, including attorney advertising. The Burger Court first ruled in 1977 that at least some attorney advertising was protected by the First Amendment. In *Bates v. State Bar of Arizona* the Court ruled 5–4 that two Arizona attorneys had a First Amendment right to place an ad listing prices for low-cost legal services in the *Arizona Republic.* Rehnquist was one of the four dissenters. The very next year, the Court confronted a pair of lawyer solicitation cases. In one case from Ohio, attorney Albert Ohralik went to the hospital room of a young woman laid up in traction after an auto accident to attempt to get her to sign a legal representation agreement. In the other case, *In re Primus,* South Carolina attorney Edna Smith Primus was reprimanded for sending a letter to a woman on Medicaid that had been sterilized.[47] Primus hoped to challenge a policy for the American Civil Liberties Union (ACLU) in which women allegedly were compelled to undergo sterilization to keep their Medicaid benefits. The Burger Court unanimously ruled that the invasive, enterprising activities of Albert Ohralik could be prohibited but ruled 7–1 that attorney Primus's inquiring efforts on behalf of the ACLU could not be disciplined.

Justice Powell, writing for the majority, reasoned that Primus did not solicit for money but was merely offering the legal services of the ACLU. "And her actions were undertaken to express personal political beliefs and to advance the civil-liberties objectives of the ACLU, rather than to derive financial gain," Powell wrote.[48]

Once again, Rehnquist filed the only dissent, reasoning that he saw no "principled basis" for distinguishing the actions of Albert Ohralik from Edma Smith Primus. In colorful language he wrote, "If we were given the latitude of novelists in deciding between happy and unhappy endings for the heroes and villains of our tales, I might well join in the Court's disposition of both cases. We can, of course, develop a jurisprudence of epithets and slogans in this area, in which 'ambulance chasers' suffer one fate and 'civil liberties lawyers' another."[49] Rehnquist believed that the First Amendment did not prohibit either state from disciplining these attorneys.

The Burger Court ruled 7–1 in *Richmond Newspapers, Inc. v. Virginia* that the press and the public had a qualified First Amendment right to attend criminal trials.[50] The case began after a trial judge excluded everyone other than the trial participants from the fourth murder trial of defendant John Paul Stevenson. In his plurality opinion Chief Justice Burger wrote that "the right to attend criminal trials is implicit in the guarantees of the First Amendment"[51] and that "absent an overriding interest articulated in the findings, the trial of a criminal case must be open to the public."[52]

Rehnquist dissented with a memorable beginning—a citation to the Gilbert and Sullivan operetta *Iolanthe,* in which the Lord Chancellor says, "The Law is the true embodiment of everything that's excellent, / It has no kind of fault or flaw, / And I, my Lords, embody the Law."[53] He quoted his former Supreme Court boss Justice Robert Jackson's famous line: "We are not final because we are infallible, but we are infallible only because we are final."[54] Rehnquist believed that his colleagues were acting like the Lord Chancellor character in the opera—believing that they were the embodiment of Law. To Rehnquist, the U.S. Supreme Court should not interfere with the functioning of state court systems. He argued that the Court's decision represented another example of the Court reading too much into the Constitution and imposing on state government. He wrote that the proper framing of the issue in the case was "whether any provision in the Constitution may fairly be read to prohibit what the trial judge in the Virginia state-court system did in this case."[55]

In a victory for the press the U.S. Supreme Court ruled 8–1 in *Cox Broadcasting Corp. v. Cohn* that a television station could not be held liable for invasion of privacy for revealing the name of a deceased minor rape victim.[56] The father of the deceased minor sued the station after one of its reporters revealed her name, which he obtained from indictments of six youths charged with the rape and death of the girl. A Georgia law prohibited the press from reporting the names of rape victims. The majority ruled in favor of the press, emphasizing the fact that the press obtained the minor victim's name from a public record. "Once true information is disclosed in public court documents open to public inspection, the press cannot be sanctioned for publishing it," Justice Byron White wrote for the majority.[57] Justice Rehnquist filed a solitary dissent without discussing the merits of the case. He believed that the Court did not have jurisdiction because there was further litigation in the case before the state courts.

Rehnquist fulfilled his "Lone Ranger" function in commercial speech and advertising cases. In *Village of Schaumberg v. Citizens for a Better Environment* the Court struck down a town law that prohibited door-to-door solicitation by groups not using at least 75 percent of their receipts for "charitable purposes."[58] The village had argued that the measure was necessary to protect the public from fraud, crime, and undue annoyance. The majority determined that the village's "legitimate interest in preventing fraud can be better served by measures less intrusive than a direct prohibition on solicitation."[59] The majority also reasoned that there was no rational reason to think that groups who use less than 75 percent of their revenues for charitable purposes would be more invasive of residential privacy than other charitable solicitors. For this reason the Court determined that the law swept too broadly and violated the First Amendment.

Justice Rehnquist filed a "Lone Ranger" dissent, writing that the majority's "decision relegates any local government interested in regulated door-to-door activities to the role of Sisyphus."[60] (Sisyphus was a mortal in Greek mythology who was forced to roll a rock up a hill and then have it roll back down continuously.) Rehnquist added that a "simple request for money lies far from the core protections of the First Amendment."[61]

In 1980, the U.S. Supreme Court established a test for commercial speech regulations in *Central Hudson Gas & Elec. Corp. v. Public Service Commission of New York* that it still uses more than 25 years later.[62] Applying this test, eight members of the Court determined that a complete ban on promotional advertising by electrical utilities violated the First Amendment. The state contended that the ban served a substantial state interest in energy conservation. However, the majority wrote that "to the extent that the Commission's order suppresses speech that in no way impairs the State's interest in energy conservation the Commission's order violates the First and Fourteenth Amendments and must be invalidated."[63]

Justice Rehnquist accused the majority of "improperly" substituting its own judgment over that of a state in determining the breadth of an advertising ban on state-owned utilities. He said the ban was "more accurately viewed as an economic regulation"[64] and that "a State has broad discretion in determining the statements that a public utility may make."[65]

The Burger Court struck down a Massachusetts law that allowed churches and schools to veto businesses' applications for liquor licenses located within 500 feet. The majority, in an opinion in *Larkin v. Grendel's Den, Inc.* by Chief Justice Burger, reasoned that the law "enmeshes churches in the processes of government and creates the danger of political fragmentation and divisiveness on religious lines."[66] The Court concluded that because of this church-state entanglement, the law violated the establishment clause of the First Amendment.

Rehnquist dissented in an opinion marked by sarcasm and literary allusions. Referring to prior Court opinions that great and hard cases make bad law, Rehnquist added, "Today's opinion suggests that a third class of cases—silly cases—also make bad law."[67] He thought the majority exaggerated the connection the law had to the advancement or establishment of religion: "The heavy First Amendment artillery that the Court fires at this sensible and unobjectionable Massachusetts statute is both unnecessary and unavailing."[68]

MAKING HIS MARK ON THE BURGER COURT

Rehnquist made his mark on the Burger Court with far more than his interesting lone dissents. Over the course of his 14 years on the Burger Court, he wrote his share of opinions both in the majority and in the dissent. One of the first major cases Rehnquist participated in was the Court's landmark 1972 decision *Furman v. Georgia.* In that decision the Court invalidated Georgia's death penalty by a narrow 5–4 vote. Three justices—Brennan, Marshall, and Douglas—viewed capital punishment as a per se violation of the Constitution, while Justices Potter Stewart and Lewis Powell argued that the particular death penalty statutes did not give juries enough guidance to determine which defendants should be subjected to the ultimate punishment. Because of this opinion, no inmates were executed until 1977—one year after the Supreme Court reinstated the death penalty in *Gregg v. Georgia.*[69] Rehnquist dissented in *Furman* and joined the majority in *Gregg.*

Rehnquist was one of two justices—along with Byron White—to dissent from the Burger Court's landmark opinion in *Roe v. Wade,* which invalidated a Texas antiabortion law.[70] Rehnquist did not just dissent in cases. He seemed to write his dissenting opinions with an eye to the future: "When most Justices seem to consider each opinion in terms of the case at hand, Justice Rehnquist sows the seeds of future opinions in cases that will embody similar issues. This approach gives a tactical advantage to one who would move the Court in a particular direction."[71]

Early in his tenure, Rehnquist made his mark in another way—one that would nearly come back to haunt him years later. In the words of one Supreme Court reporter, "It did not take Justice Rehnquist long to become the subject of a virtually unprecedented Court controversy."[72]

In *Laird v. Tatum* the U.S. Supreme Court had to decide whether to hear a constitutional challenge filed by antiwar activists to the Pentagon's surveillance program.[73] Rehnquist, in his capacity as head of the Office of Legal Counsel, had testified about the program and even offered his opinion that the plaintiffs had no standing to bring the suit. Despite prior comments on the issue, Rehnquist did not recuse, or disqualify, himself from the case. Instead, he cast the deciding vote that effectively dismissed the lawsuit. Rehnquist then broke Court tradition by writing a 15-page memorandum opinion that explained why he felt no need to recuse himself from the case. He wrote that just because a judge has expressed an opinion on an issue before coming to the bench does not mean that the judge must recuse himself. "None of the former justices of this court ... have followed a practice of disqualifying themselves in cases involving points of law with respect to which they had expressed an opinion or formulated policy prior to ascending to the bench."[74]

Rehnquist's conservative jurisprudence drew the attention of law professors. In 1976, Harvard law professor David Shapiro wrote a 64-page law review article examining Rehnquist's opinions for his first four terms. He identified "three basic propositions" that guide his jurisprudence:

> Conflicts between the individual and the government should be resolved against the individual.
>
> Conflicts between state and federal authority should be resolved in favor of the states.
>
> Questions of the exercise of federal jurisdiction should be resolved against such exercise.[75]

During his time on the Burger Court Rehnquist published a law review article that explained some of his views on constitutional law. The article, published in the *Texas Law Review,* was entitled "The Notion of a Living Constitution."[76] Rehnquist attacked the broad notion of a "living Constitution" that asked courts to serve as the "voice and conscience of contemporary society" and to act as a "roving commission second guessing Congress." To Rehnquist, this notion of a living Constitution flouted the values of a democratic society committed to popular government and majority rule. To Rehnquist, change in society should come primarily through the popularly elected democratic branches of government rather than through the judiciary. If people want change, they should attempt to urge the legislature to pass new laws.

However, Rehnquist did write opinions that favored individuals and was not always on the side of government or employers. For example, he wrote the Supreme Court's first sexual harassment opinion, which held that an employer could violate Title VII's prohibition against sex discrimination by creating a sexually hostile work environment. In *Meritor Savings Bank v. Vinson* Rehnquist wrote that the "language of Title VII is not limited to 'economic' or 'tangible' discrimination."[77] He concluded that "a plaintiff may establish a violation of Title VII by proving that discrimination based on sex has created a hostile or abusive work environment."[78]

Rehnquist also determined that the state of Georgia could not classify the movie *Carnal Knowledge,* starring Jack Nicholson and Candice Bergen, as obscene. In *Jenkins v. Georgia* Rehnquist wrote that "there are occasional scenes of nudity, but nudity alone is not enough to make material legally obscene."[79]

Rehnquist also wrote the opinion for the Burger Court ruling in favor of an African American Mississippi schoolteacher who claimed she was terminated by school officials for complaining about racial discrimination. In *Givhan v. Western Line Consolidated School District* Rehnquist wrote that a public employee does not lose her First Amendment rights simply because she speaks about an important public issue only to her principal behind closed doors.[80] Rehnquist wrote that the Court's public employee free speech cases "do not support the conclusion that a public employee forfeits his protection against governmental abridgement of freedom of speech if he decides to express his views privately rather than publicly."[81]

"Neither the Amendment itself nor our decisions indicate that this freedom is lost to the public employee who arranges to communicate privately with his employer rather than to spread his views before the public," Rehnquist wrote. "We decline to adopt such a view of the First Amendment."[82] The case still remains an important public employee free speech case which insures that not every public employee loses constitutional protection when he speaks out against injustices at work.[83]

Perhaps more importantly than his jurisprudence, Rehnquist was a breath of fresh air on the Court, a man who was able to get along with other justices—even those to whom he was ideologically opposed. When he first arrived on the Court, his closest friend was William O. Douglas, perhaps the Court's most liberal member. He got along well with Brennan and Marshall. Bob Woodward and Scott Armstrong wrote in their exposé on the Burger Court, *The Brethren,* that "the liberals found it hard not to like the good-natured, thoughtful Rehnquist."[84] Rehnquist became known as a justice with a good sense of humor and friendliness toward law clerks and Court personnel.

CONCLUSION

William Rehnquist stood out on the Burger Court for his consistent conservative judicial philosophy. He advocated greater autonomy for state laws, less protection for criminal defendants, and generally interpreted the Bill of Rights in a less expansive way than his colleagues. He was unafraid to write for the entire Court or for himself. It did not matter as much to him whether he was in the majority as whether he was articulating the constitutional vision that he fervently believed was correct.

"Bill is a slick article," said one of his unnamed Supreme Court colleagues to a *New York Times* reporter. "Even when you disagree with him, you have to concede that he has brought a touch of class to the Court. He may never make Chief, but he's not going to be one of those men who slip onto the Court and then off unnoticed. Everybody will know he was here."[85] The unnamed Supreme Court justice was only partly correct. Rehnquist did not "slip onto the Court and then off unnoticed." But he did become chief justice.

Supreme Court reporter Jim Mann was more prescient when he wrote in 1981, "But for now Rehnquist appears to be emerging as the man history will regard as the most influential figure on the Supreme Court in the final quarter of the 20th century."[86] Rehnquist became one of the most influential justices—and chief justices—in history.

Chapter 3

BECOMING THE CHIEF

> Justice Rehnquist is outside the mainstream of American constitutional law and American values, and he does not deserve to be chief justice of the United States.
>
> —Senator Edward Kennedy (July 29, 1986)

> The bottom line is that William Rehnquist has the academic background and the judicial experience to justify his elevation to chief justice. The quality of his opinions amply demonstrates judicial competence.
>
> —Justice Stanley Mosk (July 30, 1986)[1]

TABBED AS THE SUCCESSOR TO CHIEF JUSTICE BURGER

In late May of 1986, 78-year-old Warren Burger had served as chief justice for 17 years. He had improved the administration of the federal judiciary in many ways by creating the National Institute for State Courts, the Institute for Court Management, and the National Institute for Corrections. He also started the Supreme Court Fellows program, which allows talented individuals to work for the Court, the Federal Judicial Center, and the Administrative Office of the Courts for one year.

However, Burger was not nearly as effective as a leader of the Court. He did not garner the same level of respect among his colleagues as had Earl

Warren. Allegations surfaced that Burger was less than fair in doling out opinion assignments. There also was some perception on the Court that Burger was less than fully prepared for conference meetings.

On May 27, 1986, Burger informed President Reagan that he wanted to step down from his judicial post so that he could concentrate on his role as chairman of the upcoming bicentennial celebration of the Constitution. The Burger retirement gave President Reagan a golden opportunity to reshape the Court. The president and three of his closest advisors—Chief of Staff Donald T. Regan, Attorney General Edwin Meese III, and White House Counsel Peter J. Wallison—focused on finding a replacement for the 78-year-old Burger. These three advisors made of list of about a dozen possible replacements, all of them judges. The advisors examined their judicial opinions.[2]

The trio of advisors next met with the president on June 9, 1986, and informed him of the potential replacements. The president then said that he would like to meet with one of the judges on the list—Associate Justice William Rehnquist. Three days later, on June 12, the president met with Rehnquist and, after a 30-minute interview, decided that the associate justice was his man. The president apparently asked Rehnquist about his health, and the associate justice informed the president that he recently had been given a good bill of health from his physician.

President Reagan obviously came away impressed with Rehnquist as he decided to pick a chief justice from the ranks of associate justice—something done only a handful of times in Supreme Court history. For example, Earl Warren and Warren Burger were not associate justices when they were made chief justice. Only Edward White, Charles Evans Hughes, and Harlan Stone had served as associate justices before becoming chief justice.

Reagan announced on June 17, 1986—the same day as the official announcement of Burger's retirement—that he was nominating William Rehnquist as chief justice to replace Burger and Judge Antonin Scalia of the U.S. Court of Appeals for the District of Columbia to replace Rehnquist as associate justice. The announcement of Burger's retirement and the nominations of Rehnquist to chief and Scalia to Rehnquist's spot came from the White House briefing room. The press conference was announced before a live, national television audience, whose viewers saw President Reagan flanked by Burger, Rehnquist, and Scalia.

"Justice Rehnquist has been an associate justice of the Supreme Court since 1971, a role in which he has served with great discretion and skill," Reagan said. "He is noted for the intellectual power, the lucidity of his opinions and the respect he enjoys among his colleagues."[3] The president also mentioned his other nominee, Scalia, who also was rated highly by his trio of advisors. Scalia was widely acclaimed for his brilliance and fiery conservative opinions. "His great personal energy, the force of his intellect, the depth of his understanding of our constitutional jurisprudence uniquely qualify him for elevation to our highest court," the president said.[4] Reagan also made history with his nomination of Scalia—the first Italian American ever to serve on the nation's high court.

Attorney General Edwin Meese explained that the president and his committee evaluated the candidates based on three criteria, including intellectual capability, integrity, and a "commitment to the interpretation of the law, rather than being a lawmaker."

The newly nominated chief justice added a touch of his characteristic humor to the important announcement when he told the country, "I wouldn't call it the culmination of a dream, but it's not everyday when you're 61 years old that you get to take on a new job."[5] Before he could take that new job, however, Rehnquist had to survive another bruising round of confirmation hearings—a process that would last three months.

ANOTHER CONFIRMATION BATTLE

Once again, Rehnquist had been nominated with another justice, and once again, Rehnquist attracted the attention. Much as Lewis Powell had glided through nomination in 1971, the same could be said for Scalia in 1986. Each time, many Senate Democrats locked their barrels at the chest of William Rehnquist. He became the lightning rod of controversy that distracted all focus away from Scalia. Several senators praised the Rehnquist nomination immediately. "Justice Rehnquist is a great justice on the Supreme Court," said Senator Russell Long from Louisiana.

Democratic senator Edward Kennedy from Massachusetts, an opponent of Rehnquist during the 1971 hearings, was even more vocal during the 1986 hearing. "Mainstream or too extreme, that is the question," Kennedy said before the Senate Judiciary Committee. "By his own record of massive, isolated dissent, Justice Rehnquist answers that question—he is too extreme on race, too extreme on women's rights, too extreme on freedom of speech, too extreme on separation of church and state, too extreme to be chief justice."[6]

Republican senator Orrin Hatch from Utah, who emerged as Rehnquist's chief defender during the hearings, responded, "Some of these assertions here are quite ridiculous." He derided the attacks on Justice Rehnquist as a "Rehnquisition." In Congress Republican senator Robert Dole from Kansas also dismissed the attacks, saying "fortunately, the President's candidate is so well qualified that the arguments we heard yesterday will not amount to a hill of beans."[7] Dole continued, "I do not believe that anybody on the Judiciary Committee has a hunting license, but I know there will be efforts to dredge up a lot of things that happened 25, 30 years ago."[8]

Rehnquist also received the support, ironically, of liberal California Supreme Court justice Stanley Mosk, who wrote an editorial published in the *Los Angeles Times:* "If I were in the Senate, I would vote to confirm the nomination of Justice Rehnquist," he wrote. Mosk noted that Rehnquist had written an opinion for the Supreme Court in *Pruneyard Shopping Center v. Robins* that recognized the ability of the California Supreme Court to provide greater protection for individual liberties than are provided for in the U.S. Bill of Rights.[9] Rehnquist reasoned that the Constitution "does not limit the authority of the state to exercise its police power or its sovereign right to adopt in its own Constitution individual liberties more expansive than those conferred by the federal Constitution." Mosk called this "true federalism."

Many of the charges against Rehnquist were similar to the charges leveled against him in 1971—that he harassed minority voters in the early 1960s in Phoenix; that he was less than truthful about the 1952 *Plessy v. Ferguson* memo; and that he harbored views that were out of the mainstream, particularly with regard to civil rights.

The Jackson memo still reared its head, even though it was written more than 30 years before the latest confirmation hearings. Justice Jackson's secretary, Elise H. Douglas, wrote a letter to Senator Edward Kennedy, once again disputing Rehnquist's version of the memorandum. "As I said in 1971 when this question first came up, that is a smear of a great man," she wrote. "Justice Jackson did not ask law clerks to express his views."[10] Rehnquist's former law clerk colleague, Donald Cronson, described the 1952 memo issue as "silly" and "very much res judicata a matter already decided."[11] The 1952 memo will always be linked to Rehnquist. His critics continue to insist that he lied during both of his confirmation hearings. In his book *The Rehnquist Choice,* John Dean concludes, "It is now quite clear to me what happened: Rehnquist lied."[12]

The voting issue took center stage during the Senate judiciary hearings, even more time than the 1952 memo. At the Senate judiciary hearings in late July and early August, several witnesses testified that Rehnquist had harassed minority voters at the polls in Arizona in the early 1960s. The charges came from individuals such as the Reverend Snelson W. McGriff of Phoenix and Charles W. Pine, Arizona's Democratic chairman for several years in the 1970s. These individuals said that they had seen Rehnquist question minority voters about their qualifications. This testimony was bolstered by San Francisco–based attorney James J. Brosnahan, a former U.S. attorney who went to Phoenix to investigate claims of alleged voter harassment. Brosnahan said that on election day in 1962 he saw Rehnquist at a Phoenix polling place, although he did not personally see Rehnquist harassing any voters. Rather, Brosnahan, in his capacity as U.S. attorney, heard others complain about Rehnquist's allegedly harassing and annoying activities toward minority voters.

Several Republican senators questioned Brosnahan about his testimony 24 years later, but the former federal prosecutor insisted on his recollections. Under a line of questioning from Senator Hatch, Brosnahan responded, "If I wasn't absolutely sure that I interviewed Bill Rehnquist because voters pointed him out, do you think Senator, I would do that? Because I assure you, I assure you that if it was even close, if it was even close, I would be home having my Friday afternoon lunch at Jack's and I would not be here in front of you. I'm telling you my recollection."[13] Brosnahan's retort engendered applause in the hearing room. For his part Rehnquist testified under heavy interrogation at the hearing that he had never "harassed or intimidated" voters and that he had not personally challenged the qualifications of any voters.[14]

There also was a new charge related to his refusal to disqualify himself in *Laird v. Tatum,* the case challenging the military's surveillance program. Senator Patrick Leahy said, "Everything points to his sitting on the case so he could cast a vote for the Administration he just left."[15]

Many law professors, including ethics experts, expressed their opinion that Rehnquist should have disqualified himself from the case. In a reply letter to Senator Howard Metzenbaum, Professor Stephen Gillers wrote, "In conclusion, because Justice Rehnquist had previously expressed an opinion on how the legal requirement of standing should operate in the case of Laird v. Tatum, it was improper for him to participate in an opinion that that applied the standing rule in that very case."[16] Respected legal ethics expert Geoffrey C. Hazard, Jr. of Yale Law School, a Republican, also wrote that Rehnquist should have disqualified himself from the case and may have violated ethics rules, including one mandating a "duty of candor to the Senate" in answering questions about the case.[17]

In a letter to the editor, Christopher Pyle—one of the attorneys in the army surveillance case and a professor of constitutional law at Mount Holyoke College—explained why Rehnquist should not have sat on the case. He went even further in his allegations against Rehnquist, writing that Rehnquist "had a substantial personal and political interest in preventing the lawsuit from going forward."[18] Pyle explained that if the U.S. Supreme Court had allowed the lawsuit to go forward against the government, the plaintiffs may have uncovered the roles played by Attorney General John Mitchell, Deputy Attorney General Richard Kleindienst, and Rehnquist. Attorneys for the plaintiffs in the *Laird* case then filed a motion in the U.S. Supreme Court asking the Court to reopen the case because Justice Rehnquist should have recused himself. Critics charged that Rehnquist was not truthful in his testimony when he responded that he had no personal knowledge of the evidentiary issues in *Laird v. Tatum* when he worked for the Office of Legal Counsel.

More than 100 law professors entered the fray by submitting a letter to the Senate. The letter identified a "common thread" that repeatedly surfaced in charges against Rehnquist. That thread, according to the professors' letter, "pertains to the integrity and ethical standards of the nominee."[19]

Rehnquist received some hopeful news during the midst of his grilling before the Senate Judiciary Committee from the American Bar Association (ABA). The group, on July 30, 1986, reported to Congress that Rehnquist was "well qualified," the highest rating the organization gave. ABA spokespersons indicated that a survey had been done of the other members of the Court, who largely gave positive testimony about Rehnquist. The only negative comments concerned his strong conservative judicial philosophy. One justice said that Rehnquist could "pull this court together."[20] On August 14, 1986, the Senate Judiciary Committee voted 13–5 in favor of Rehnquist. Meanwhile, the panel voted unanimously to confirm Judge Antonin Scalia. Senator Kennedy said of Scalia, "He is a conservative, not an extremist."[21]

The fight continued over Chief Justice Rehnquist. Even in early September, civil rights leaders vowed to continue the fight over the nominee, whom they viewed as hostile to minorities, women, and the Civil Rights Movement. Ralph Neas, executive director of the Leadership Conference on Civil Rights, said that confirmation was not a certainty and that there was potentially enough momentum to derail the confirmation. Neas added that Carswell and Haynsworth were rejected by the full Senate after surviving a vote from the Judiciary Committee. Similarly, Joseph Rauh, the group's counsel and a former U.S. Supreme Court law clerk, spoke in very strong language against Rehnquist, saying that his nomination was a "desecration of everything this country stands for and it ought to be stopped."[22]

Senator Dole told his colleagues that if one cut through all the legalese, "the case boils down to one simple fact: Those who would torpedo these nominations are liberal, and the President's nominees are conservative."[23] A few days later, Democratic senator Paul Sarbanes from Maryland spoke for a considerable amount of time, recounting the allegations against the chief justice, some of which he termed "very disturbing." He emphasized the 1952 *Brown v. Board of Education* memorandum; the ballot security program in Arizona, where some alleged Rehnquist challenged minority voters; allegations by Rehnquist's brother-in-law regarding a trust; the refusal to recuse himself in *Laird v. Tatum;* and his conservative judicial philosophy. Sarbanes focused on Rehnquist's "limited, pinched view of the Constitution when it comes to the protection of individual rights."[24] He concluded that Rehnquist's career spoke of "judicial implacability" and "an intellect in the service of a closed and narrow mind."[25]

Democratic senator Howard Heflin from Alabama explained that he would vote for Rehnquist, even though he respected the opinions of many of his fellow Democrats who deeply opposed Rehnquist. Heflin said the "persuasive" factor for him was the respect that Rehnquist had earned among his colleagues on the Supreme Court. He explained,

> I know that there are those who question Justice Rehnquist's sensitivity to civil rights of minorities and women. I do not agree with every opinion of Justice Rehnquist. In fact, I find myself in disagreement with many. But I do not believe those opinions are so extreme as to be unreasonable. Every stream has a right bank and a left bank. There is no question that Justice Rehnquist's views are always close to the right boundary of the stream, but they are nonetheless within the mainstream of modern judicial thought.[26]

Numerous editorials urged the Senate to reject Rehnquist, including ones published in the *New York Times,* the *Evening Sun,* and the *Baltimore Sun.* Civil rights protestors interrupted a speech that Rehnquist gave at Indiana University as part of the dedication for the university's new law school building.[27]

On September 17, 1986, the full Senate confirmed Rehnquist by a vote of 65–33. Forty-nine Republicans and 16 Democrats voted for Rehnquist, while 31 Democrats and 2 Republicans voted against him. Senators Charles Mathias (from Maryland) and Lowell P. Weicker, Jr. (from Connecticut) were the only two Republicans to cast a vote against Rehnquist. The Mathias vote was interesting because as a member of the Senate Judiciary Committee, he had voted to approve Rehnquist. Mathias said he changed his mind after becoming more troubled by Rehnquist's failure to disqualify himself in *Laird v. Tatum* in 1972.

The 33 negative votes against Rehnquist were the most for any nominee that survived the confirmation process up to that point (a record later broken by Justice Clarence Thomas in 1991). Previously, three justices—Mahlon Pitney in 1911, Charles Evans Hughes in 1930, and Rehnquist himself in 1971—had all received 26 negative votes.[28] Ironically, the Senate voted 98–0 in favor of Justice Scalia, who proved to be a more conservative jurist than Rehnquist. "The difference in the handling of the two nominations was dramatic," wrote Linda Greenhouse of the *New York Times.* "The Judiciary Committee report on Justice Rehnquist was 114 pages long. The committee's report on Justice Scalia consisted of 76 words."[29]

President Reagan praised the outcome in the Senate but chastised Congress for the contentious confirmation hearings. "This vote in the full

Senate is a bipartisan rejection of the political posturing that marred the confirmation hearings," the president said. "It is clear to all now that the extraordinary controversy surrounding the hearings had little to do with Justice Rehnquist's record or character—both are unassailable and unimpeachable. The attacks came from those whose ideology runs contrary to his profound and unshakable belief in the proper constitutional role of the judiciary in this country."[30] He added that "William Rehnquist will prove to be a Chief Justice of historic stature."[31]

For his part William Rehnquist appeared unfazed after surviving the confirmation ordeal. He declined to address the confirmation process other than to say that he was "glad" that the process "had finally run its course" and that he was "gratified" that the Senate had confirmed his nomination. He added that he was "looking forward to the future" and would do his best "to be a good chief justice."[32]

Chief Justice Rehnquist and Associate Justice Scalia took their oaths of office on Friday, September 26, 1986. The nation now had its 16th chief justice, a man who would sit atop the Court for nearly 20 years. He would guide the Court in a way that impressed even his ideological opponents. On his passing in September 2005 his former nemesis Edward Kennedy stated, "Chief Justice Rehnquist served this country with the greatest distinction, and I respected his leadership of the federal judiciary and his strong commitment to the integrity and independence of the courts."[33]

Chapter 4

JUSTICES ON THE REHNQUIST COURT

> William Rehnquist has been a lucky man. Eight Justices have joined the Court since he took his seat on January 7, 1972. Four of those eight—Justices O'Connor, Kennedy, Scalia, and Thomas—have provided him with a working majority on many issues.
>
> —Linda Greenhouse (2003)[1]

Fourteen justices served on the Court during the 19 years that William Rehnquist held the position of chief justice. In addition to Rehnquist, in order of appointment, they included William Brennan, Byron White, Thurgood Marshall, Harry Blackmun, Lewis Powell, John Paul Stevens, Sandra Day O'Connor, Antonin Scalia, Anthony Kennedy, David Souter, Clarence Thomas, Ruth Bader Ginsburg, and Stephen Breyer. These justices spanned the careers of six presidents and the ideological gamut. They featured the only two female justices in the history of the Court, the only two African American justices in the history of the Court, and the first Italian American justice. They featured justices with varying methods of constitutional interpretation—originalists, textualists, pragmatists, and modernists.

During its first eight years, from 1986 until 1994, the Rehnquist Court saw great change in the Court's membership with the retirements of Justices Powell, Brennan, Marshall, White, and Blackmun. These retirements led to the additions of Justices Kennedy, Souter, Thomas, Ginsburg, and Breyer. In 1994, when Justice Breyer replaced Harry Blackmun, the Court enjoyed a stability of membership for more than 11 years—the second longest in Supreme Court history.

WILLIAM BRENNAN

When Rehnquist first assumed the mantle of chief justice, the Court held a formidable lineup of liberal justices anchored by Warren Court appointee William Brennan, who was appointed by President Dwight D. Eisenhower in 1956. Eisenhower selected Brennan, a little-known jurist from New Jersey, in part because he was Catholic and a politically inactive Democrat. He had thought Brennan would be a moderate justice. Instead, he appointed the future liberal craftsman of the Warren Court. Later, Eisenhower would regret the nomination. When asked what mistakes he had made, the president allegedly replied that two of them sit on the U.S. Supreme Court, referring to Chief Justice Warren and Justice Brennan.

Brennan obtained his law degree from Harvard University, studying under Supreme Court justice Felix Frankfurter, who was known on the Court as a practitioner of judicial restraint. Once, when asked about his former pupil, Frankfurter said he had encouraged his students to think for themselves but that Brennan had taken it too far. Brennan was appointed to the New Jersey Superior Court in 1949, the Appellate Division of the Superior Court in 1950, and the New Jersey Supreme Court in 1952. When Justice Sherman Minton retired, President Eisenhower apparently wanted to appoint a state court jurist who was a Democrat, a moderate, and a Catholic. William Brennan seemed to fit the bill, and he received the nomination of a lifetime.

Eisenhower appointed Brennan to the bench in October 1956, when the Senate was in recess (not in session), allowing Brennan to take his seat on the high court before confirmation. The Senate confirmed him in March 1957 with one dissenter—Senator Joseph McCarthy, who was famous, or infamous, for his extreme efforts to ferret out communists in America.

Brennan served nearly 34 years on the Court; many scholars considered him to be the leading intellectual force of the Warren Court. He believed strongly in a living Constitution and used his position on the Court to sway many of his colleagues to his positions. Even when he was a member of the more conservative Burger and Rehnquist Courts, Brennan was a formidable ideological foe. Brennan effectively led the Court, in part because of his intelligence, but perhaps more so because of his magnetic personality and persuasive powers. He got along well with his colleagues—even those with whom he disagreed. Rehnquist wrote in his book on the Supreme Court, "Bill Brennan and I disagreed with each other about a lot of constitutional issues, but his buoyant outlook on life and friendly warmth toward his colleagues ensured that disagreements about the Constitution would not mar personal relationships."[2]

Brennan authored some of the Court's landmark decisions, from the ruling in *Baker v. Carr,*[3] in which the Court entered the "political thicket" and claimed jurisdiction over legislative reapportionment claims, to the libel case *New York Times Co. v. Sullivan,*[4] to the leading free exercise of religion opinion in *Sherbert v. Verner.*[5] Brennan's magnetic personality endeared him to his colleagues, and he became a master at obtaining five votes. A lasting testament to his persuasive powers was that in 1990, he managed to obtain five votes to uphold an affirmative action policy at the Federal Communications Commission, even though the Court the year before had invalidated a similar affirmative action policy in Richmond, Virginia. Brennan retired from the Court shortly after the 1989–1990 term because of a stroke.

Brennan and Rehnquist—though they often disagreed on legal matters—were both legal giants. "Brennan and Rehnquist were the two modern masters of manipulating precedents in U.S. Reports," says constitutional law scholar Thomas Baker. "They both possessed an encyclopedic knowledge of the law and facile, plastic minds."[6]

BYRON WHITE

In 1962, President John F. Kennedy nominated his deputy attorney general Byron R. White to the Supreme Court. White was unique among the annals of the high court as he was famous in athletics long before embarking on a legal career. He was an all-American running back from the University of Colorado and later led the National Football League in rushing his rookie year. His athletic accomplishments led to his place among the pantheon of gridiron greats in the College Football Hall of Fame.

Born in Fort Collins, Colorado, White obtained his undergraduate degree from the University of Colorado and his law degree from Yale Law School, though his schooling was interrupted by service in World War II. He graduated as a member of the prestigious Order of the Coif from Yale and then clerked for U.S. Supreme Court justice Fred Vinson. When White became a member of the Supreme Court, he became the first justice to have previously served as a U.S. Supreme Court law clerk.

After his clerkship, White entered private practice in Colorado. He was active in politics in his home state for the presidential campaign of John F. Kennedy. When Kennedy entered the White House, Robert F. Kennedy—the U.S. attorney general—selected White as a deputy attorney general.

In 1962, White became the surprise choice to replace retiring justice Charles Whittaker on the Supreme Court.

He believed that a justice's job was to decide particular cases rather than advocate and pursue an overarching constitutional vision. When asked during his confirmation hearings what the job of a Supreme Court justice was, he replied, "To decide cases."[7] The Senate confirmed him by voice vote, and he served on the Court for more than 30 years, until the end of the 1992–1993 term. He was known as fierce questioner from the bench.

White was not a liberal in the true sense of the word and became one of the more conservative members of the Warren Court, particularly in criminal cases. He dissented in *Miranda v. Arizona,*[8] rejected the idea of a reporter's privilege in *Branzburg v. Hayes,*[9] and severely limited high school students' First Amendment rights in *Hazelwood School Dist. v. Kuhlmeier.*[10] White also wrote the majority opinion in *Bowers v. Hardwick,* upholding a Georgia antisodomy law.[11]

THURGOOD MARSHALL

Thurgood Marshall—similar to his colleague Byron White—was famous long before he became a U.S. Supreme Court justice. President Lyndon Baines Johnson made history by nominating Marshall as U.S. solicitor general in 1965 and then to the U.S. Supreme Court in 1967. President Johnson said, when nominating Marshall to the high court, "I believe he already has earned his place in history."

Marshall had earned his place in history by serving as lead counsel for the NAACP and as the architect behind the legal challenges that led to the U.S. Supreme Court's historic 1954 decision in *Brown v. Board of Education,* which declared that segregated public school facilities were unconstitutional. Marshall won 29 of 32 cases that he argued before the U.S. Supreme Court. His legendary advocacy on behalf of racial justice earned him the moniker "Mr. Civil Rights."

Johnson appointed Marshall to a federal judgeship on the Second U.S. Circuit Court of Appeals in 1961. He then appointed him as solicitor general and two years later elevated him to the U.S. Supreme Court. Marshall found an immediate ally in Brennan, and they voted together on many cases throughout their long careers. Marshall found himself in dissent for most of his career after the end of the Warren Court. He stayed on the Court until the end of the 1990–1991 term. When he announced his retirement to his colleagues in conference, Chief Justice Rehnquist surprisingly stood up and hugged him. Justice O'Connor cried. He died of heart failure in 1993.

Rehnquist called Marshall the Court's "raconteur." In an interview with author Juan Williams, Rehnquist said of his colleague, "Thurgood Marshall stood for the broadest interpretation of almost all the provisions of the Constitution. He was a very stout champion of individual rights. And he was an equally stout champion of minority rights."[12]

HARRY BLACKMUN

President Nixon nominated the little-known Harry Blackmun to the U.S. Supreme Court in 1970 after the Senate had rejected his first two nominees—Clement F. Haynsworth, Jr. and G. Harrold Carswell. Blackmun, who grew up in Minnesota, was a childhood friend of Chief Justice Warren Burger, who told President Nixon that Blackmun would make a fine Supreme Court justice.

Blackmun obtained his undergraduate and law degrees from Harvard University. On graduation he clerked for Federal Appeals Court judge John Sanborn of the Eighth Circuit. He then settled into private practice in Minneapolis for 16 years before he became counsel at the famous medical center, the Mayo Clinic, in 1950, where he remained for nine years. In 1959, President Eisenhower tabbed him to fill the spot vacated by his former boss Judge Sanborn on the Eighth Circuit.

After the Senate had rejected Haynsworth and Carswell, Burger urged Nixon to appoint his friend Blackmun. Because he was the president's third choice, Blackmun referred to himself as "good ole number three." He was unanimously confirmed 94–0, and he took his seat next to his best friend, Warren Burger. The press dubbed Burger and Blackmun "the Minnesota Twins." Early in his career, Blackmun did vote often with Chief Justice Burger, but he gradually moved to the left throughout the course of his career in one of the more remarkable evolutions. For example, on the Court, Blackmun originally was a supporter of capital punishment. However, in one of his last opinions in 1994, Blackmun famously wrote, "From this day forward, I shall no longer tinker with the machinery of death."[13]

Blackmun was most famous for his majority opinion in *Roe v. Wade,* the 1973 decision finding that the constitutional right of privacy included a qualified right to an abortion.[14] Over the years, Blackmun forcefully and personally defended his famous opinion in later cases. He also was a pioneer on the Court in terms of protecting commercial speech—a type of speech that the Court for decades had said was entitled to no First Amendment protection.

On the Burger Court, Rehnquist sat next to Blackmun for 14 years, where they shared an interest in geographical trivia, which "helped to lighten an occasional dull moment" on the bench, according to Rehnquist.[15]

LEWIS POWELL

Lewis Powell was a moderate conservative nominated to the bench by President Nixon jointly with William Rehnquist in 1971. A Virginian, Powell obtained his undergraduate and law degrees from Washington and Lee University in Lexington, Virginia. He later obtained an advanced law degree (an LLM) from Harvard, where he studied under Justice Felix Frankfurter, among others.

Powell then began a long and distinguished career in private practice in Richmond. He served as president of the ABA in 1964–1965 and as president of the American College of Trial Lawyers in 1968–1969. Though he was a Democrat, President Nixon liked Powell's relatively conservative views on criminal justice and knew that the Senate would confirm him. Powell thought his age (64) would be a problem, but he accepted the appointment.

He served on the Court until the end of the 1986–1987 term, which meant that he served only one term on the Rehnquist Court. However, Powell left his mark on the Court as he often served as the key swing vote in many cases. Ken Starr writes that the Burger Court was often the Powell Court because of his moderate views at the center of the Court. He wrote the Court's opinion in the landmark affirmative action case *Regents of the University of California v. Bakke.*[16]

Rehnquist described him as "the ultimate southern gentleman, in the very best sense of that term." On Powell's death Rehnquist said that Powell "was the very embodiment of judicial temperament, receptive to the ideas of his colleagues, fair to the parties to the case, but ultimately relying on his own seasoned judgment."[17]

JOHN PAUL STEVENS

In 1976, President Gerald R. Ford made his only nomination to the high court—John Paul Stevens. Born in Chicago, Stevens obtained his undergraduate degree from the University of Chicago and his law degree from Northwestern, where he finished first in his class. Stevens then clerked for U.S. Supreme Court justice Wiley Rutledge, becoming the third justice (after his colleagues Byron White and William Rehnquist) to serve as both a Supreme Court law clerk and justice.

After his clerkship, Stevens entered private practice in Chicago, where he specialized in antitrust law. In 1970, President Nixon appointed him to the U.S. Court of Appeals for the Seventh Circuit. When Justice William Douglas retired, President Ford considered many replacements. Stevens was a well-respected jurist who was viewed as a moderate. Ford's White House counsel Philip Buchen said four years after Stevens was on the bench that "we didn't have any feeling whether he'd be liberal or conservative."[18] What they got was a maverick wild card with a strong independent streak. The Senate unanimously confirmed Stevens 98–0 in December 1975.

At the time of his appointment, some critics warned that Stevens would be a consistent conservative. They were wrong. In a very prescient column Jerald terHorst wrote in December 1975, just after Stevens's confirmation, "There is something about the man that suggests he is capable of holding strong views and holding them independently, if need be. And with spark."[19] The *New York Times* accurately wrote in 1976 that Stevens "is willing to take the liberal position as well as the conservative."[20]

Stevens has proven to be as independently minded a justice as ever in the history of the Supreme Court, setting records for writing separate concurring and dissenting opinions. He became a wild card and a maverick on the Burger Court, and this pattern continued into the Rehnquist Court. For example, in 1985, Stevens criticized the comments of President Reagan's attorney general Edwin Meese, who had questioned the Court's jurisprudence on church-state issues and had questioned whether many of the provisions of the Bill of Rights should be applied to the states. Stevens said that Meese's view "overlooks the profound importance of the Civil War and the postwar amendment, and particularly upon the relationship between the Federal Government and the separate states."[21] Then, in 1987, Stevens publicly supported conservative Supreme Court nominee Robert Bork, stating, "I personally regard him as a very well-qualified candidate and one who will be a very welcome addition to the Court."[22]

Throughout his long career—which has extended more than 30 years through the entire period of the Rehnquist Court—Stevens has never been afraid to march to the beat of his own constitutional drummer. In 1978, he wrote the Court's majority opinion in *F.C.C. v. Pacifica Foundation,* holding that the FCC could fine a radio station for broadcasting indecent material during daytime hours.[23] Nearly two decades later, however, Stevens wrote the Court's majority opinion in *Reno v. ACLU,* holding that Congress's attempt to regulate indecent material on the Internet violated the First Amendment.[24]

On Court matters he has proven independent as well. He employs only three law clerks, instead of the usual four. He also refuses to allow his law clerks to join in the so-called cert. pool—a process first suggested by Justice Powell, in which the justices pool their law clerks together to make recommendations on which cases should be granted review. Stevens's clerks conduct their own independent review of all cases. "His nonparticipation in the cert. pool is a prime example of his independence," says attorney Jeffrey Fisher, who clerked for Stevens in the October 1998–1999 term. "He greatly values independent thinking and is suspicious of groupthink. He believes strongly in the value of dissent and independent analysis."[25]

"His persona evolved from an independent-minded centrist to one of the more liberal members of the Supreme Court," Fisher says. "His views did not change that much, but the Court moved to the right. I think his views did not change as much as the Court changed around him."

SANDRA DAY O'CONNOR

The most recognizable member of the U.S. Supreme Court over the past 30 years was none other than its first member of the distaff side—Sandra Day O'Connor. Born in El Paso, Texas, O'Connor was raised on a ranch in Arizona named the Lazy B. She obtained her undergraduate and law degrees from Stanford University. At law school she became friends with classmate and fellow law review member William Rehnquist. The two even went to a few movies together.

Even though she graduated third in her class (Rehnquist graduated first), law firms would not hire a female attorney. One prominent law firm in Los Angeles would only offer her the job of legal secretary. She became a deputy attorney for San Mateo County, California. She then entered private practice in Arizona and became active in local politics. In 1965, O'Connor became the first woman to be an assistant attorney general for the state of Arizona. Her interest in politics continued, and she served as an Arizona state senator from 1969 to 1971.

In the Arizona senate she spoke on the floor and elsewhere in support of Rehnquist, whom President Nixon had nominated for the Supreme Court. On October 22, 1971, she even made the bold prediction on the Senate floor that one day, Rehnquist could become chief justice of the U.S. Supreme Court.[26] She began a campaign of her own to help Rehnquist's confirmation. Rehnquist later sent her a note on Court stationary: "Words are inadequate to convey my appreciation for what you have done for me in connection with the nomination to the Supreme Court."[27]

O'Connor served in the Arizona Senate until 1975, including a stint as majority leader. In 1978, she successfully campaigned for the Maricopa County Superior Court, a trial judge position that she held for four years. In 1979, Democratic governor Bruce Babbitt appointed O'Connor to the Arizona Court of Appeals. While on the Arizona court, O'Connor was introduced to Chief Justice Warren Burger, who was very impressed with her and her legal knowledge. When President Nixon and his staff had raised the idea of nominating California jurist Mildred Lillie, Burger had not been pleased. It would be different with O'Connor a few years later.

During the 1980 presidential election Republican challenger Ronald Reagan announced that one of his moves if elected would be to appoint the first woman to the U.S. Supreme Court. The U.S. Supreme Court justices responded in November 1980 by dropping their official salutation of "Mr. Justice" and replacing it with simply "Justice." When asked why the change, Justice Stevens replied, "You can probably guess."[28]

In 1981, Reagan fulfilled his campaign promise by nominating O'Connor. Chief Justice Burger recommended her to White House officials. Others were recommending federal appeals court judge Cornelia Kennedy from the Sixth Circuit. Former president Ford, a Michigan native, recommended Kennedy, who had served in the Michigan state court system and a federal district in the state before being elevated to the Sixth Circuit.

O'Connor impressed Reagan at their July 1981 meeting, and that was enough to insure her legacy in American history. After meeting O'Connor, Reagan declined to meet with any other potential nominees.[29] On August 19 Reagan made the historic announcement. O'Connor's nomination did not please some, who feared she might support abortion rights. Moral Majority president Jerry Falwell allegedly said, "All good Christians should oppose O'Connor," which brought a famous retort from a famous Arizonan and former presidential candidate, Barry Goldwater, who said, "All good Christians should kick him [Falwell] in the ass."[30]

On September 21, 1981, the Senate confirmed O'Connor by a vote of 99–0. Rehnquist later wrote that he was "overjoyed at her appointment to the Supreme Court."[31] On the Court O'Connor voted with Burger and Rehnquist in some cases but gradually moved to the center. By the end of her career in early 2006, many commentators referred to it as the "O'Connor Court." She certainly became one of the most influential justices of the Rehnquist Court.

ANTONIN SCALIA

In 1986, Ronald Reagan created for himself the rare opportunity to fill two vacancies with the retirement of Chief Justice Warren Burger. He did so by nominating Associate Justice Rehnquist to chief justice, which left him an associate justice position. He filled it with the first Italian American, Antonin Scalia.

Born in Trenton, New Jersey, Scalia obtained his undergraduate degree from Georgetown and his law degree from Harvard. After graduation, Scalia entered private practice with a prominent firm in Cleveland, Ohio. He left that position to teach law at the University of Virginia. In 1971, he entered public service as the general counsel to the White House's Office of Telecommunications Policy. In 1974, he became an assistant U.S. attorney general in charge of the Office of Legal Counsel—the same position Rehnquist held before his unexpected elevation a few years earlier.

Scalia then continued law teaching at Georgetown, Chicago, and Stanford law schools before President Reagan nominated him to the federal D.C. Circuit Court of Appeals in 1982. There, the conservative Scalia displayed his creative, biting style of writing that had endeared him to conservatives and earned the wrath of liberals. Though Scalia at times vigorously disagreed with his colleagues on the D.C. Circuit, they enjoyed sitting on the bench with him. Judge Patricia Wald, a more liberal jurist on the D.C. Circuit, said that Scalia was "fun to work with" and has "an open mind."[32] Judge Abner Mikva, another liberal justice on the D.C. Circuit, said, "He's got a good sense of humor, lots of human qualities, an uproarious laugh—he's a good storyteller."[33]

In 1986, when President Reagan nominated both Rehnquist and Scalia, opposition centered on the future chief justice, leaving Scalia an easy path to confirmation. "Two men owe at least some of the ease of their confirmations to William Rehnquist—Lewis Powell and Antonin Scalia," says constitutional law professor Thomas Baker. "In both of these nominations, it was Rehnquist who was the lightning rod both times.[34] Even Massachusetts senator Edward Kennedy, who deeply opposed Rehnquist, said of Scalia, "On most issues, it is difficult to maintain that Judge Scalia is outside the mainstream.[35] Scalia sailed through with a vote of 98–0, and Scalia later said that if the other two senators were present, they would have voted for him too. It is hard to imagine in the current political climate that a justice like Scalia would be confirmed easily, much less unanimously. "Scalia would not be confirmed 98–0 in the current climate of judicial confirmations, which has changed radically since the Bork affair," says Baker. "That changed things radically in the way the Senate operates.[36]

On the Court Scalia proved more conservative than William Rehnquist. He considers himself a textualist, someone who focuses on the text of the Constitution and statutes to ascertain their meaning. A series of lectures he delivered in 1995 formed a 1997 book entitled *A Matter of Interpretation: Federal Courts and the Law.*[37] In his book he explains that textualism is often confused with strict constructionism: "A text should not be construed strictly, and it should not be construed liberally; it should be construed reasonably, to contain all that it fairly means."[38] Scalia dismisses legislative history as an authoritative source of guidance for a law's meaning. He criticizes the notion of a "living Constitution" for providing "no chance of agreement, upon what is to be the guiding principle of the evolution."[39] In a speech at the University of Mississippi in Oxford, Scalia said the idea of a living Constitution is "a lovely thought, a lovely phrase, but it will destroy us or destroy the Supreme Court as we've known it."[40]

Scalia has forcefully advanced his theories of constitutional interpretation in his distinctive writing style, which continues to attract many supporters and detractors. "The best writing stylist on the Court is Nino Scalia," Baker says. "He has a vivid, personal style in his writing. He can turn a phrase. He is a writer's writer. Whether one views him as Saint Nino or as the spawn of the devil, everyone has to admit that his opinions are the most fun to read. Reading a Scalia opinion is like watching a prizefight, while by contrast reading an opinion of some of his colleagues is like watching paint dry."[41]

Although he writes well, Scalia had had limited success in persuading his colleagues to follow his positions. Rather, he appears quite comfortable playing the role of the fiery dissenter who lambastes his colleagues for judicial overreaching. Most often, he has sparred with Justices Stevens, Souter, and Breyer. For example, in an important Sixth Amendment criminal opinion, *Apprendi v. New Jersey,* Scalia differed with Breyer over constitutional interpretation. In his concurring opinion Scalia wrote, "Justice Breyer proceeds on the erroneous and all-too-common assumption that the Constitution means what we think it ought to mean. It does not; it means what it says."[42]

Scalia's ire has not always been confined to his colleagues on the bench. Occasionally, he will vent publicly at reporters who write about the Court. In 2000, Scalia lambasted a column from well-respected Supreme Court reporter Tony Mauro as "gossipy, titillating and thus characteristically Mauronic copy." The article for *Legal Times* indicated that Scalia had complained about the rule limiting justices' outside income from speeches and that he had considered resigning from the Court.[43]

"Scalia is bombastic and very opinionated and does not like criticism very much," Mauro says. "He also loves wordplay and the clever turning of a phrase."[44] Scalia never apologized for the third-grade name-calling but did write a nice note to Mauro a few years later, when Mauro wrote a nice story that included comments from Scalia's son Matthew, who was serving in Iraq.

ANTHONY KENNEDY

In 1987, Justice Powell—who often held the center of the court—retired. President Ronald Reagan, fresh from his successful nominations of William Rehnquist to chief justice and Antonin Scalia to associate justice, sought to nominate well-known conservative jurist and scholar Robert Bork to replace Powell. Bork was considered very well qualified from a legal and scholarship standpoint, but he aroused tremendous opposition from civil rights groups and others. Bork had criticized the Supreme Court decisions of *Roe v. Wade* and *Griswold v. Connecticut* as reading into the Constitution a right of privacy. Senator Edward Kennedy famously fired the devastating warning shot on Bork: "Robert Bork's America is a land in which women would be forced into back alley abortions, blacks would sit at segregated lunch counters, rogue police could break down citizens' doors in midnight raids, schoolchildren could not be taught about evolution." In October 1987, the Senate rejected Bork's nomination 42–58.

Reagan then nominated former Harvard law professor Douglas Ginsburg, who was serving on the federal D.C. Circuit Court of Appeals. Ginsburg withdrew his nomination after allegations of a financial conflict of interest arose. Allegations also surfaced that Ginsburg had smoked marijuana while on the Harvard law faculty. These allegations doomed his nomination, leaving President Reagan to turn to his third choice: fellow Californian Anthony Kennedy. A letter to the editor in the *Los Angeles Times* summed up the process from Bork to Kennedy: "Appointing Judge Anthony Kennedy to the Supreme Court is a wise, sensible decision. Going from Bork to Ginsburg to Kennedy is like going from Goliath to David to Solomon."[45]

Earlier in his career as a private attorney, Kennedy had impressed Edwin Meese, then a lobbyist for the California District Attorneys Association. Kennedy also caught the eye of then governor Reagan for his work in helping draft a ballot initiative that would cut state spending. Those contacts paid off in 1975, when Reagan and Meese recommended Kennedy for the Ninth U.S. Circuit Court of Appeals. Kennedy held that judicial post for more than 13 years, until his elevation to the high court. President Reagan and his attorney general Meese remembered Kennedy for his faithful and diligent work in the 1970s. Kennedy, who amassed a moderate to conservative record on the Ninth Circuit, sailed through confirmation by a vote of 98–0.

Early in his career, conservatives rejoiced at Kennedy's conservative voting record on the Court. A leader of the conservative National Legal Center for the Public Interest said that the "conservatives got more of what they were looking for ideologically than they would have gotten with Bob Bork." A Supreme Court reporter for the *Washington Post* wrote in 1989 that "Kennedy is as conservative as any justice nominated by President Ronald Reagan."[46] *New York Times* reporter Linda Greenhouse described the Court's first full term with Kennedy as "the year the court turned right" and that Kennedy provided a "consistent conservative vote."[47]

However, the pundits and press were not entirely accurate about Justice Kennedy, who moved to the center of the Court on many issues. For the later years of the Rehnquist Court Kennedy moved to the center and became a First Amendment champion. In 2003, he wrote the Court's opinion in *Lawrence v. Texas*, striking down a law that criminalized same-sex sodomy acts as a violation of personal liberty.[48] In 2005, in *Roper v. Simmons,* Kennedy wrote the Court's opinion for a five-member majority that held that executing criminal defendants who committed murders as juveniles violated the Eighth Amendment ban against cruel and unusual punishment.[49]

Kennedy occupied the center of the Rehnquist Court for many years with Justice O'Connor, so much that some experienced Supreme Court watchers called it the "Kennedy Court." Georgetown law professor Mark Tushnet said, "The Constitution is what Anthony Kennedy says it is."[50] Others speculate that Kennedy will occupy an even more crucial role in the Roberts Court as the ultimate swing justice on many constitutional issues.[51]

DAVID SOUTER

Little was known about David Souter when President Bush tabbed him as the unlikely successor to William Brennan. Alabama senator Howard Heflin dubbed him a "stealth" candidate, a moniker picked up by many commentators.[52] The lack of a paper trail concerned many on the right and the left. President George H. W. Bush said that he had no idea how Souter would rule on many issues. It turns out that President Bush told the truth.

The Massachusetts-born Souter was the only child of a bank official and homemaker. He obtained undergraduate and law degrees from Harvard University and also earned a Rhodes Scholarship at Oxford. After law school graduation, he took a job in the private sector at a well-respected firm in Concord, New Hampshire. In 1968, he took a job as an assistant state's attorney general. The state's attorney general Warren Rudman picked Souter as his lead deputy in 1970. In 1976, Souter was selected as Rudman's successor. In 1978, he was selected for the Superior Court judgeship. During his career in New Hampshire Souter also befriended state governor John Sununu, a friendship that would prove crucial to his judicial career.

In 1983, Sununu nominated Souter to the New Hampshire Supreme Court, where he served until 1990. Rudman, now a U.S. senator, persuaded President George Bush to appoint Souter to the federal bench on the U.S. Court of Appeals for the First Circuit. He was sworn in by none other than the chief judge of the First Circuit, Stephen Breyer—his future colleague on the U.S. Supreme Court.

When Justice Brennan retired, Rudman mentioned to President Bush that Souter would make an excellent choice for the high court. Souter apparently told Rudman, "What have you done to me now?" President Bush narrowed his selection to four candidates: Souter, Edith Jones of the Fifth Circuit, and two judges from the D.C. Circuit Court of Appeals, Clarence

Thomas and Laurence Silberman. With backing from Rudman and Sununu, now Bush's chief of staff, Souter had a chance, though he was the least well known of the four finalists. President Bush apparently was impressed enough with his face-to-face interview with Souter to nominate him.

Sununu had written that Souter's nomination to the high court was a "home run" for conservatives, a prediction that would prove inaccurate.[53] The Senate Judiciary Committee approved Souter's nomination 13–1, and the full Senate confirmed him by a vote of 90–9. Thurgood Marshall publicly admitted that neither he nor William Brennan had ever heard of Souter. They were not alone, though it is fair to say that Marshall would probably be pleasantly surprised if he had lived long enough to see Souter's voting record on the Court. Souter biographer Tinsley Yarbrough writes that "David Souter would figure prominently in the partial failure of the Reagan-Bush Supreme Court agenda."[54]

Perhaps it was not that unusual that Souter proved to be a disappointment to conservatives. During his confirmation hearings, when asked about the *Miranda* decision relating to the rights of criminal defendants, he replied, "I personally have looked at Miranda as a pragmatic decision intended to protect a right."[55] Souter evolved from a justice who voted more with the conservatives to a justice who is considered moderate to liberal. He joined Kennedy and O'Connor in 1992 in an unusual per curiam opinion that upheld "the central holding" of *Roe v. Wade.*[56]

He also is the rare justice who will admit that he made a mistake in an earlier ruling. For example, in *Barnes v. Glen Theatre, Inc.*,[57] Souter provided the fifth vote to uphold a ban on nude performance dancing. Souter reasoned that the ban was not designed to suppress an unpopular form of free expression but to address harmful secondary effects associated with nude dancing. The problem was that cities would claim secondary effects and enact many types of onerous restrictions on adult businesses without any evidence that the businesses or the content of the dances cause any such harmful effects. In 2000, the majority of the Court upheld another ban on nude dancing in *City of Erie v. Pap's A.M.*[58] Justice Souter dissented and acknowledged what he believed to be his earlier mistake in *Barnes:* "I may not be less ignorant of nude dancing than I was nine years ago, but after many subsequent occasions to think further about the needs of the First Amendment, I have come to believe that a government must toe the mark more carefully than I first insisted. I hope it is enlightenment on my part, and acceptable even if a little late."[59]

Souter dissented in *Bush v. Gore,* the 2000 decision that effectively decided the presidential election between George W. Bush and Al Gore.[60] He has consistently dissented in the Rehnquist Court's federalism decisions that struck down many federal laws as invasions of state authority. Yarbrough concludes, "It is thus a supreme irony that the first President Bush, in nominating a 'stealth candidate' and thereby attempting to avoid the controversy Robert Bork's nomination had provoked, chose a justice who has proven to be the very antithesis of Bork and most of the Reagan-Bush appointees to the Court."[61] Even Souter's backer to the Supreme Court, John Sununu—who had called him a "home run" to conservatives—admitted years later that Souter had been a disappointment to conservatives: "There's been a lot of disappointment in where David Souter has ended up on the court," Sununu said. "I would have rather seen him as an ally of Justice (Antonin) Scalia."[62]

CLARENCE THOMAS

Perhaps no member of the Supreme Court in recent memory has been maligned more than Clarence Thomas, a man who rose from abject poverty in Pin Point, Georgia, to the highest court in the land. He ascended to the bench amid great controversy after law professor Anita Hill, who worked under Thomas at the Equal Employment Opportunity Commission (EEOC), revealed that Thomas allegedly sexually harassed her years ago. Though Hill never complained, she brought the charges on the eve of Thomas's confirmation.

The issue of Hill's veracity often depended on people's political leanings. Those who disagreed with Thomas's jurisprudence seemed to believe Hill, while those on the right tended to support Thomas. In any event, Thomas survived the charges by a narrow 52–48 confirmation vote.

Thomas obtained his undergraduate degree from Holy Cross and his law degree from Yale University. After his graduation in 1974, he worked as an assistant attorney general in Missouri under the state's attorney general John Danforth, who would later become a U.S. senator and Thomas's chief backer. At the age of 32 Thomas became the assistant secretary of education for civil rights and then the next year became chair of the EEOC—a position he held for eight years. Under Thomas, the EEOC did not pursue many class action suits but focused on cases in which individuals suffered egregious discrimination. Average settlements rose dramatically under Thomas's leadership.[63]

In 1990, President Bush nominated Thomas to the federal D.C. Circuit Court of Appeals, a court often seen as the grooming arena for future Supreme Court justices. He served on the D.C. Circuit Court for only a short time because in 1991, President Bush selected Thomas to replace the recently retired Thurgood Marshall. The Thomas-Hill confirmation controversy degenerated into a soap opera affair with moments of high drama. Perhaps the most memorable line came when Thomas thundered at the table during his hearing, "And from my standpoint, as a black American, as far as I am concerned, it is a high-tech lynching for uppity blacks who in any way deign to think for themselves, to do for themselves, to have different ideas." Thomas biographer Ken Foskett called it "one of the most memorable lines in American judicial history."[64]

On the bench Thomas has proven to be a strong originalist, focusing on the Constitution as it was written in 1787, rather than what some may wish it to be. Former federal appeals court solicitor general and independent counsel Ken Starr writes that Thomas is the "Rehnquist Court's most original thinker."[65]

Thomas has staked out positions, particularly in his concurring and dissenting opinions, that establish his independence and original thinking on the Court. In *United States v. Lopez* the Rehnquist Court invalidated a federal gun law, finding that Congress did not have the authority under the Constitution's commerce clause to pass such a law related to a local, criminal problem.[66] In his concurrence Thomas called on the Court to reevaluate its jurisprudence on the commerce clause and return to the Founders' original understanding of the clause. He wanted the Court to adopt "a standard that reflects the text and history of the Commerce Clause without totally rejecting our more recent Commerce Clause jurisprudence."[67]

He has been an unexpected defender of the First Amendment in certain areas, including the Court's most forceful advocate for commercial speech.[68] In another concurring opinion, this time in 1996, Thomas wrote that truthful commercial speech should be entitled to as much protection as noncommercial speech, such as political expression.[69]

Thomas is most known for his reticence at oral argument, many times not asking a single question during oral argument. Other times, he has been labeled wrongly as a Scalia clone. He has earned the respect of his colleagues on the Rehnquist Court. Justice Kennedy says that Thomas has a "photographic" memory of details about specific cases and the record before the court.[70]

RUTH BADER GINSBURG

Ruth Bader Ginsburg became the second woman appointed to the U.S. Supreme Court in 1993 and was President Bill Clinton's first nominee to the high court. Born in Brooklyn, Ginsburg graduated from Cornell and then attended two years at Harvard Law School before transferring to Columbia for her final year of law school. Despite her impeccable credentials, gender discrimination prevented her from landing a job with top private law firms. She taught law school at Rutgers and then Columbia Law School.

She became the director of the ACLU's Women's Rights Project. In that capacity she distinguished herself as a national defender of gender equality, arguing six cases before the U.S. Supreme Court and winning five. For her trailblazing advocacy against gender discrimination she was often called the "Thurgood Marshall of gender equality law." In 1980, President Jimmy Carter nominated her to the U.S. Court of Appeals for the District of Columbia, where she served for more than 13 years, until Clinton elevated her to the Supreme Court.

She compiled a record of a moderate jurist rather than a liberal extremist. On the D.C. Court, she became close friends with fellow jurists and future Supreme Court colleagues Antonin Scalia and, later, Clarence Thomas. She was somewhat conservative in the criminal justice arena. During her confirmation hearings she even quoted Chief Justice Rehnquist on the issue of judicial restraint. Though she favored a woman's right to choose, she has criticized the Court's 1973 decision in *Roe v. Wade.* In a 2005 talk at the University of Kansas she said that that historic decision of the Court "seemed to me not the way courts generally work."[71]

"Her advocacy in gender equality cases on the national stage helped her come to the attention of President Clinton," says Baker. "She was an able Supreme Court advocate, a professor and scholar and a veteran and well-respected judge. She is a proceduralist and will often write the Court's opinion on 'case or controversy' issues, like standing and subject matter jurisdiction."[72] Like her friend Justice Scalia, she is a very active questioner at oral arguments. Sitting at her first argument on the high court in 1993, Ginsburg asked 17 questions alone during the first hour.[73]

Jeffrey Rosen writes that outside of the gender discrimination arena, "she appears to be the most restrained Justice on the Court."[74] She has taken a leading role on the Court on gender equality issues. She authored the Court's majority opinion in *United States v. Virginia,* holding that Virginia Military Institute violated the equal protection clause by denying admission to women.[75] She wrote that the school failed to establish an "exceedingly persuasive justification" for its males-only admissions policy.

STEPHEN BREYER

President Clinton appointed Stephen Breyer to fill the seat vacated by Justice Harry Blackmun in 1994. Breyer had been a front-runner for the seat occupied by Justice Ginsburg. Born in San Francisco, Breyer obtained an undergraduate degree from Stanford University and a law degree from Harvard. He then served as a law clerk to Justice Arthur Goldberg of the U.S. Supreme Court. After his clerkship, Breyer held several positions in the federal government, including assistant attorney general, assistant special prosecutor in the Watergate investigation, and chief counsel to the Senate Judiciary Committee.

It was the position of chief counsel to the Senate Judiciary Committee that led Breyer to key contacts with politicians on the right and the left. He later served as a leader of the U.S. Sentencing Commission, which drafted the federal sentencing guidelines. He was known to be pragmatic and effective, endearing himself to politicians on the left and the right. His experience enabled him to sail through the Senate Judiciary Committee.

While working for the government, Breyer taught administrative law at Harvard Law School. In 1980, President Jimmy Carter nominated him to the U.S. Court of Appeals for the First Circuit, a position he held until his high court appointment in 1994. From 1990 until his elevation Breyer served as chief judge of the First Circuit.

On the Court Breyer has voted often with Stevens, Souter, and Ginsburg in the Court's federalism cases, which examine the boundaries of authority between the federal and state governments. However, Breyer is a pragmatic moderate at heart and, like Justice O'Connor, has gravitated toward the middle of the Court. For example, in June 2005, the Rehnquist Court issued two split decisions involving the posting of 10 Commandments monuments on government property. The Court upheld a display in a Texas public park and rejected displays in two Kentucky courthouses by 5–4 votes.[76] The difference between the two cases was Justice Breyer, who was the swing vote in both decisions.

Breyer also has become an intellectual challenger to Justice Scalia. Unlike Scalia, who focuses on the text of the Constitution and its original meaning, Breyer often focuses on original purpose and context. Linda Greenhouse wrote of the two in 2002, "Not since the Roosevelt era, when Justice Hugo L. Black (text) and Justice Felix Frankfurter (context) battled over the meaning of the Bill of Rights, has the court had two justices willing to engage each other—and the public—in a debate over basic principles."[77]

In 2005, Breyer published *Active Liberty: Interpreting Our Democratic Constitution,* laying out his general judicial philosophy of interpreting the Constitution and its various provisions.[78] In his book Breyer writes of textualism, "I do not believe that textualist or originalist methods of interpretation are more likely to produce clear, workable rules."[79] In his concluding chapter Breyer warns that textualist and originalist theories can undermine democratic freedom: "For any and all of these reasons, I hope that those strongly committed to textualist or literalist views—those whom I am bound not to convince—are fairly small in number. I hope to have convinced some of the rest that active liberty has an important role to play in constitutional (and statutory) interpretation."[80]

CONCLUSION

The Rehnquist Court featured many legal giants, including Rehnquist, Brennan, and Marshall. In its early years the Court tackled many important constitutional social issues, such as affirmative action and abortion. Rehnquist often found himself in dissent on his own Court. The early years of the Court also featured many membership changes with the retirements of Powell, Brennan, and Marshall and then later the retirements of White and Blackmun. With these retirements the Court entered its second phase with a distinct membership. The changes in membership also enabled William Rehnquist to advance his visions of federalism—a subject addressed in the next chapter.

Rehnquist Court Justices

Justices	Years on the Court	Years on Rehnquist Court
William Brennan	1956–1990	1986–1990
Byron White	1962–1993	1986–1993
Thurgood Marshall	1967–1991	1986–1991
Harry Blackmun	1971–1994	1986–1994
Lewis Powell	1972–1987	1986–1987
William Rehnquist	1972–2005	1986–2005
John Paul Stevens	1976 to present	1986–2005
Sandra Day O'Connor	1981–2006	1986–2005
Antonin Scalia	1986 to present	1986–2005
Anthony Kennedy	1988 to present	1988–2005
David Souter	1990 to present	1990–2005
Clarence Thomas	1991 to present	1991–2005
Ruth Bader Ginsburg	1993 to present	1993–2005
Stephen Breyer	1994 to present	1994–2005

Chapter 5

FEDERALISM

> The powers delegated by the proposed constitution to the federal government are few and defined. Those which are to remain in the State governments are numerous and indefinite .... The powers reserved to the several States will extend to all the objects which, in the ordinary course of affairs, concern the lives, liberties, and properties of the people, and the internal order, improvement, and prosperity of the State.
>
> —James Madison in *The Federalist* no. 45

> Surely there can be no more fundamental constitutional question than that of the intention of the Framers of the Constitution as to how authority should be allocated between the National and State Governments.
>
> —Associate Justice William Rehnquist (1975)[1]

Associate Justice William Rehnquist believed that the federal government had become all-encompassing to the point of encroaching on the autonomy of individual states. This was not a vision of states' rights in the mode of Southern segregationists (though Rehnquist, as we have seen, faced intense scrutiny for his views of *Brown v. Board of Education* and related issues). That version of states' rights did not want the federal government telling them to integrate public schools and other public facilities. Rehnquist was not of that cloth. Those close to him to a person say he harbored no prejudices. Rehnquist simply believed that the Framers' true vision of the federal government was one of shared powers, where many, if not most, issues should remain under the control of state and local officials.

He believed to a certain extent that the Warren Court had ignored these federalism principles in favor of solving societal problems. However well intentioned the course of action, the federal government for far too long passed laws that invaded the province of the states. William Rehnquist managed to articulate a vision—or at least a set of principles—that would change the Supreme Court's jurisprudence. During his tenure the Court breathed new life into the Tenth Amendment, which reserves powers not given to the federal government to the states, and into the Eleventh Amendment, which provides a degree of sovereign immunity. The Rehnquist Court limited—but did not eliminate—the Court's enforcement powers under section 5 of the Fourteenth Amendment. His Court created what some scholars have termed "new federalism."[2]

In a familiar pattern Rehnquist first articulated his vision in dissenting opinions while an associate justice on the Burger Court. He could not win the votes of a majority of his colleagues, but he had mapped a course for the future. In 1970, the U.S. Congress passed the Economic Stabilization Act in part to check the problems of rising inflation in the country. The law empowered the president to issue orders that would stabilize wages, which he did by creating a Pay Board that imposed wage controls. These controls applied to state and local government employees in addition to federal employees.

The state of Ohio then passed legislation that provided for a wage increase of more than 10 percent—higher than the Pay Board would authorize. Two state employees, Ernest Fry and Thelma Boehm, sought a writ of mandamus in state court that would order their raises to be paid. The Ohio Supreme Court ruled in favor of the two employees and approved the legislation.

The federal government responded by filing an action in federal district court to stop the payment of these wage increases. The district court certified the issue to an appeals court, which upheld the constitutionality of the Economic Stabilization Act and ruled against the state employees. The appeals court reasoned that the U.S. Supreme Court decision in *Maryland v. Wirtz* controlled the present case.[3] In *Wirtz* the Court ruled that the Fair Labor Standards Act could apply to state-run schools and hospitals.

Seven members of the Supreme Court ruled that the Economic Stabilization Act could be applied to limit state and local employee wage increases. Justice William Douglas, who had dissented in *Wirtz,* determined that the writ should be dismissed as improvidently granted because the Economic Stabilization Act had expired in 1974. Rehnquist dissented, outlining basic themes of his principles of the basic power structure and relationship between federal and state governments. To Rehnquist, the federal legislation invaded the sovereign territory of the states and their "inherent affirmative constitutional limitation on congressional power."[4] He reasoned that the U.S. Congress had broad powers under the commerce clause but that "an activity sufficiently closely allied with traditional state functions" like wages paid to state employees "should be beyond Congress' commerce authority."[5]

In the opinion Rehnquist also tipped his hand as to his constitutional future as chief justice when he wrote that "important decisions of constitutional law are not subject to the same command of stare decisis as are decisions of statutory questions."[6] He believed that the Supreme Court erred in the *Wirtz* decision by invading the sovereign authority of the states.

Even as an associate justice, Rehnquist managed to make headway on his vision of federalism. He managed to strike a major blow toward his constitutional vision in *National League of Cities v. Usery.*[7] The case concerned the constitutionality of amendments to the Fair Labor Standards Act that extended minimum wage and maximum hour provisions to most state and local government officials. Several cities and states challenged the provisions as invading their rights under the Tenth Amendment, which provides that powers not granted to the federal government are reserved to the states. In essence, the objecting cities and states were arguing that the extension of the federal law invaded their sovereign power to conduct their traditional activities as they saw fit.

Rehnquist managed to convince a bare majority of the Court—five members—to accept this argument. He wrote that the Fair Labor Standards Act amendments exceeded Congress's powers under the commerce clause because they operated "to directly displace the States' freedom to structure integral operations in areas of traditional governmental functions."[8] Rehnquist's opinion resurrected the Tenth Amendment as an important constitutional limitation on the power of the federal government: "States as States stand on a quite different footing from an individual or a corporation when challenging the exercise of Congress' power to regulate commerce."[9] The Court overturned the 1968 *Maryland v. Wirtz* provision in the process, much as Rehnquist had asked for in his dissenting opinion a year earlier.

Rehnquist's victory did not last in the Burger Court years because he lost the vote of Justice Harry Blackmun, who switched sides. In *Garcia v. San Antonio Metropolitan Transit Authority* Blackmun wrote the Court's opinion and in the process overruled *National League of Cities.* The case involved the mass transit system of San Antonio, whose officials asserted they were immune from the requirements of the Fair Labor Standards

Act.[10] Blackmun wrote that the years since *National League of Cities* had shown that Rehnquist's standard of "traditional functions" was unworkable and "inconsistent with established principles of federalism."[11]

Justice Powell authored the primary dissenting opinion, though Rehnquist added his own short opinion in oft-cited language. He wrote that "I do not think it incumbent on those of us in dissent to spell out further the fine points of a principle that will, I am confident, in time again command the support of a majority of this Court."[12]

The tea leaves did not portend favorably for Rehnquist in the Burger Court years after *Garcia.* In 1982, the Court upheld key provisions of a federal public utility law in *FERC v. Mississippi* over a state's constitutional objections.[13] In dissent Rehnquist argued that the federal law that imposed regulatory guidelines over state public utility commissions violated the Tenth Amendment. While he lost the vote, Rehnquist picked up a new ally in the form of his former Stanford Law School classmate and former Arizona legislator Sandra Day O'Connor—the Court's newest member. O'Connor wrote, "State legislative and administrative bodies are not field offices of the national bureaucracy. Nor are they think tanks to which Congress may assign problems for extended study. Instead, each State is sovereign within its own domain, governing its citizens and providing for their general welfare."[14] Rehnquist was on his way to obtaining the votes of enough colleagues to force change.

THE ERA OF THE FEDERALISM FIVE AND CHANGE OF COURSE ON THE COMMERCE CLAUSE

Eventually, Rehnquist's faith in the future of the primacy of his views on federalism proved prescient as he managed to change the direction of the Court on this issue. While he never managed to overrule *Garcia,* he revived federalism, redirected attention to the Tenth Amendment, and enlarged the reach of the Eleventh Amendment and its grant of sovereign immunity. The key to his success was the appointment of new justices Antonin Scalia, Anthony Kennedy, and Clarence Thomas. Rehnquist, Scalia, Thomas, Kennedy, and O'Connor became known as "the Federalism Five" for a series of rulings that ushered in significant, some would say even revolutionary, change. For instance, the Court, for the first time in nearly 60 years, invalidated a law that Congress justified under its commerce clause powers. The case arose after authorities arrested a 12th-grade high school student in San Antonio, named Alfonzo Lopez, Jr., for carrying a weapon on school grounds. Federal agents soon charged Lopez with violating the Gun-Free School Zones Act of 1990, which prohibits the knowing possession of firearms in school zones.

A federal jury convicted Lopez and sentenced him to six months supervisory probation and two years supervised release. On appeal a federal appeals court reversed Lopez's conviction, finding that the law was beyond Congress's commerce clause powers. The government appealed to the U.S. Supreme Court. In a 5–4 decision the Supreme Court also reasoned that the law exceeded Congress's commerce clause powers. "We start with first principles," Chief Justice Rehnquist wrote. "The Constitution creates a Federal Government of enumerated powers."[15]

Rehnquist discussed the history of Congress's commerce clause powers, expanded during the time of President Franklin Delano Roosevelt in the 1930s. In 1937, the Supreme Court upheld the National Labor Relations Act after Justice Owen Roberts switched sides in the famous "switch in time that saved nine." President Roosevelt, upset over many Court rulings striking down his New Deal legislation, had proposed a court-packing plan by which he could add new justices more in tune with progressive economic reforms. While scholarship suggests Roberts had already voted to uphold federal legislation, speculation abounded that his change in sentiment was due, at least in part, to presidential pressure. Whatever the reason, the U.S. Supreme Court changed its constitutional jurisprudence by giving Congress a broad degree of deference in economic matters. Federal laws dealing with economic issues had only to pass the lenient rational basis test, and the Court broadened Congress's commerce clause powers.

In *NLRB v. Jones & Laughlin Steel Corp.* the Supreme Court abandoned the distinction between "direct" and "indirect" effects on Congress. According to the Court, Congress had the power to regulate matters that had a direct or indirect effect on interstate commerce, even if the matters appeared to be intrastate. Intrastate activities that "have such a close and substantial relation to interstate commerce" were enough to justify the legislation under the commerce clause.[16]

The broadest display of Congress's commerce clause power came in 1942 in *Wickard v. Filburn.* In that decision the Court ruled that Congress could impose penalties on farmers such as Roscoe Filburn, who exceeded the national quotas on wheat production. Though Filburn's activities were intrastate, local, and involved only the consumption of wheat, the Court still ruled that such local consumption had an effect on interstate commerce. The fact that "commerce among the states in wheat is large and important" was enough for the Court to uphold the legislation and fine placed on farmer Filburn.[17]

Rehnquist cited these cases and others in *Lopez,* noting that they "ushered in an era of Commerce Clause jurisprudence that greatly expanded the previously defined authority of Congress under that Clause."[18] Despite these precedents, Rehnquist emphasized that Congress's commerce clause powers were not boundless. He summarized that Congress could regulate commerce under "three broad categories": (1) the channels of interstate commerce; (2) the intrumentalities of interstate commerce; and (3) "activities having a substantial relation to interstate commerce."[19]

The question was whether a high school student's possession of a gun on school property had a substantial relation to interstate commerce. To the Federalism Five, it did not. "Even Wickard, which is perhaps the most far reaching example of Commerce Clause authority over instrastate activity, involved economic activity in a way that the possession of a gun in a school zone does not," Rehnquist wrote.[20] "The possession of a gun in a local school zone is in no sense an economic activity that might, through repetition elsewhere, substantially affect any sort of interstate commerce."[21] The criminal gun possession law was simply not an economic measure implicating Congress's commerce clause power. The matter was for the state and local governments to regulate under their general police powers. Justice Kennedy, joined by O'Connor, noted in his concurring opinion that over 40 states already had similar gun-free school zone laws.[22]

The most interesting concurring opinion came from Justice Thomas, who again showed his unique, independent streak. Thomas called on the Court to reevaluate its basic "substantial effects" commerce clause test and return to the Founders' original understanding of the clause. He urged his colleagues to construct "a standard that reflects the text and history of the Commerce Clause without totally rejecting our more recent Commerce Clause jurisprudence."[23]

The liberal wing of the Court—Stevens, Souter, Breyer, and Ginsburg—dissented with all except Ginsburg, writing separate opinions. Stevens noted the "radical character of the Court's holding."[24] Souter said Rehnquist's opinion had "tug[ged] the Court off course" and returned it to "the untenable jurisprudence … of almost 60 years ago."[25] Breyer said Rehnquist's opinion creates "serious legal problems," including conflict with decades of prior precedents and the creation an unworkable distinction between commercial and noncommercial activities.[26] Breyer reasoned that gun violence near schools did not have a negative economic impact by hindering education.

The *Lopez* decision was a watershed as it was the first time in more than 60 years that the Court had invalidated a federal law as exceeding Congress's commerce clause powers. The decision ushered in a new era in which federal statutes fell at an amazing rate.

One of the more high-profile decisions involved the alleged rape of a female student by two football players from Virginia Tech. Christy Brzonkala sued Antonio Morrison and James Crawford under the civil remedy provision of the Violence against Women Act of 1994. The provision enabled victims of gender-motivated violence to sue their perpetrators in federal court for compensatory and punitive damages. The players contended that like the gun law struck down in *Lopez,* the civil remedy provision of the gender violence law exceeded Congress's authority.

The Rehnquist Court voted 5–4 in *U.S. v. Morrison* against the constitutionality of the provision.[27] The alignment mirrored that of the *Lopez* decision, with the Federalism Five in the majority. Justice Scalia wrote the majority opinion, emphasizing that *Lopez* revolved around the "noneconomic, criminal nature of the conduct." Scalia wrote that "gender-motivated crimes of violence are not, in any sense of the phrase, economic activity."[28] He explained that "the regulation and punishment of intrastate violence that is not directed at the instrumentalities, channels, or goods involved in interstate commerce has always been the province of the States."[29]

However, unlike the *Lopez* case, the Federalism Five had to address another argument supporting congressional power. Brzonkala and the federal government argued that Congress acted within its remedial power under section 5 of the Fourteenth Amendment. Section 5 provides that Congress can "enforce" by "appropriate legislation" the guarantees of the Fourteenth Amendment's due process and equal protection clauses. They argued that the Violence against Women Act was an "appropriate" way to "enforce" women's right to equal protection. They said that the criminal justice system was infected with a pervasive bias against victims of gender-motivated violence. This law was a means to correct this serious problem.

However, Justice Scalia rejected these arguments. He reasoned that the law was not designed to address discrimination by state officials but wrongs committed by private individuals. He cited long-standing cases that the Fourteenth Amendment only prohibits discriminatory conduct by state officials. He wrote that the "law is not aimed at proscribing discrimination by officials which the Fourteenth Amendment might not itself proscribe; it is directed not at any State or state actor, but at individuals who have committed criminal acts motivated by gender bias."[30]

Justice Souter again criticized the Federalism Five, questioning the foundation of its *Lopez* decision and its result in *Morrison.* "Why is the majority tempted to reject the lesson so painfully learned in 1937?" he queried, referring to what Souter termed the New Deal Court's abandonment of a distinction between commercial and noncommercial conduct. He criticized the Federalism Five's creation of a "new federalism" that ignores "the facts of an integrated national commerce."[31] Once again, Breyer authored a dissenting opinion in which he criticized the majority's economic/noneconomic distinction as unworkable.

The *Lopez* and *Morrison* precedents changed the legal landscape, though the question remains how far they will reach into the future. The Rehnquist Court may have limited their reach in its 2005 decision *Gonzales v. Raich,* which examined whether California's medical marijuana law (the California Compassionate Use Act) prevented the federal government from enforcing its controlled substances law criminalizing marijuana.[32] Angel Raich and Diane Morrison cultivated and used marijuana for medicinal purposes in compliance with the California law. However, their activities violated federal drug laws. They contended that the application of the federal Controlled Substances Act to the intrastate cultivation and use of marijuana exceeded Congress's power to regulate interstate commerce.

The U.S. Supreme Court ruled 6–3 that Congress could criminalize the growth and use of marijuana even in a state like California that provides for use of the drug for certain medicinal purposes. The four liberal justices—Stevens, Souter, Ginsburg, and Breyer—obtained the votes of two members of the Federalism Five: Kennedy and Scalia. The federal drug law is a "valid exercise of federal power, even as applied to the troubling facts of this case," wrote Justice Stevens. "Unlike those at issue in *Lopez* and *Morrison,* the activities regulated by the CSA are quintessentially economic."

Chief Justice Rehnquist compiled a long pro-law enforcement record, but he remained faithful to his federalism principles. He and Justice Thomas joined an opinion penned by Justice Sandra Day O'Connor that found the case "materially indistinguishable" from *Lopez* and *Morrison.* She wrote that if she were a California legislator, she would not have voted for the act, but she concluded that "the federalism principles that have driven our Commerce Clause cases require that room for experiment be protected in this case."

ANTICOMMANDEERING PRINCIPLE

The Rehnquist Court decided another line of federalism cases that breathed life into the Tenth Amendment. It involved federal programs that force or commandeer state officials to implement a federal law. In *New York v. United States* the U.S. Supreme Court invalidated a key provision in the Low-Level Radioactive Waste Policy Amendments Act of 1985. The so-called take-title provisions required states to pass laws providing for the disposal of radioactive waste generated in their borders or take title to the radioactive waste. Taking title to the waste means that the states become liable if they do not dispose of the waste properly.[33]

The Supreme Court upheld other portions of the federal law but invalidated the take-title provision on Tenth Amendment grounds. The Court deemed that the take-title provision was a classic example of the federal government commanding a state government to enforce a federal regulator program. "Because an instruction to state governments to take title to waste, standing alone, would be beyond the authority of Congress, and because a direct order to regulate, standing alone, would also be beyond the authority of Congress to regulate, it follows that Congress lacks the power to offer the States a choice between the two," Justice O'Connor wrote for the Court.[34]

The Court applied this "anticommandeering principle" to invalidate another federal law on Tenth Amendment grounds in the Brady Bill case. The Brady Bill was named after former White House press secretary James Brady, who was gunned down by John Hinckley, Jr. when he attempted to assassinate President Ronald Reagan. One provision of the law required chief law enforcement officers (CLEOS) to conduct background checks on would-be handgun purchasers. In *Printz v. United States* the U.S. Supreme Court invalidated this provision under the authority of the radioactive waste decision.[35] Justice Scalia cited the general rule articulated in New York that the federal government cannot compel the states to enact a federal regulatory program. "The mandatory obligation imposed on CLEOs to perform background checks on prospective handgun purchasers plainly runs afoul of that rule," he wrote.[36]

Once again, the Stevens, Souter, Ginsburg, and Breyer bloc dissented. "There is not a clause, sentence, or paragraph in the entire text of the Constitution of the United States that supports the proposition that a local police officer can ignore a command contained in a statute enacted by Congress pursuant to an express delegation of power enumerated in Article I," Stevens wrote.[37]

STATE IMMUNITY AND CIVIL RIGHTS LAWS

Another line of the Rehnquist Court's federalism cases emerged with the revival of the Eleventh Amendment, which provides that citizens of one state cannot sue another state in court. The amendment was drafted in direct response to the Supreme Court's 1792 decision *Chisholm v. Georgia,* which allowed a South Carolina citizen to sue the state of Georgia over clothing manufactured and supplied for the Revolutionary War. The Eleventh Amendment was the first of only four times—including also the Fourteenth, Sixteenth, and Twenty-Sixth Amendments—in American legal history when Congress proposed and the states ratified a constitutional amendment to override a U.S. Supreme Court decision.

The Federalism Five of the Rehnquist Court breathed new life into the Eleventh Amendment by interpreting it as a very broad grant of state sovereign immunity. These cases are often called the sovereign immunity cases. The Court flexed its muscles in *Seminole Tribe of Florida v. Florida,* a dispute over Native Americans' operation of casinos. The Seminole Tribe sued Florida because the state's then governor Lawton Chiles, an opponent of gambling, refused to negotiate in good faith with the tribe in violation of the federal Indian Gaming Act.[38]

Writing for the Federalism Five, Chief Justice Rehnquist reasoned that the Eleventh Amendment's broad grant of state sovereign immunity meant that the Seminole Tribe could not sue the state of Florida in federal court. "Even when the Constitution vests in Congress complete law-making authority over a particular area, the Eleventh Amendment prevents congressional authorization of suits by private parties against unconsenting States," he wrote. Rehnquist also reasoned that Congress could not get around the commands of the Eleventh Amendment by asserting its commerce clause powers in Article I. In other words the Eleventh Amendment impacted the judiciary's constitutional authority in Article III, which could not be circumvented by Congress's constitutional powers in Article I of the Constitution.

The decision prompted impassioned dissents. Justice Stevens called the majority's opinion "profoundly misguided," while Justice Souter emphasized the radical nature of the majority opinion. He wrote that "the Court today holds for the first time since the founding of the Republic that Congress has no authority to subject a State to the jurisdiction of a federal court at the behest of an individual asserting a federal right."[39]

Seminole Tribe led to other sovereign immunity decisions, many involving whether states could be sued for money damages under various federal civil rights laws. Congress can abrogate or dismiss state's Eleventh Amendment immunity under its powers under section 5 of the Fourteenth Amendment. Section 5 of the Fourteenth Amendment gives Congress the power to enforce the guarantees of the Fourteenth Amendment. Congress can do this if it clearly states its intention to waive state immunity and if it enacts a law that is congruent and proportional to the perceived problem.

In 1997, the Supreme Court ruled in *City of Boerne v. Flores* that Congress exceeded its section 5 power when it passed a religious liberty law that reinterpreted the free exercise clause of the First Amendment. In other words, Congress had sought to modify the Court's interpretation of the Constitution. The Court ruled that this new religious liberty law was not congruent and proportional to the perceived problem; rather, it was an unconstitutional grab of power by Congress to interpret the Constitution.

In *Kimel v. Florida Bar of Regents*[40] the Court had to apply the principles of sovereign immunity from *Florida Seminole* and the principles of Congress's section 5 enforcement powers from *City of Boerne.* The issue was whether a state could be sued in federal court for violating a federal age discrimination law. The state contended that it had Eleventh Amendment immunity. The state employee who alleged age discrimination contended that Congress was merely exercising its proper powers under section 5 of the Fourteenth Amendment. The Court ruled 5–4 in *Kimel* that Congress could not validly waive state immunity from age discrimination suits. "In light of the indiscriminate scope of the Act's substantive requirements, and the lack of evidence of widespread and unconstitutional age discrimination by the States, we hold that the ADEA is not a valid exercise of Congress' power under §5 of the Fourteenth Amendment," Justice O'Connor wrote for the Court.[41]

The next year, the Court ruled in *Board of Trustees of the University of Alabama v. Garrett* that the state of Alabama could not be sued in federal court for alleged violations of a federal disability discrimination law.[42] Once again, this time in an opinion by Chief Justice Rehnquist, the Federalism Five ruled that Congress did not have a constitutional basis for waiving state immunity under its section 5 powers.

The decisions limiting the reach of federal age and disability discrimination laws to state employers outraged many of those concerned with eradicating discrimination in the workplace. Martin Garbus blasted the Court's decisions in his book *Courting Disaster:* "As a consequence of the *Garrett* and *Kimel* cases, much of the federal statutes protecting the aged and disabled against discrimination have been thrown into the wastebasket."[43] Would these federalism-based decisions lead to the invalidation of virtually the entire gamut of civil rights legislation? In 1964, Congress had seemingly removed state sovereign immunity when it passed Title VII of the Civil Rights Act, the major federal antidiscrimination employment law. The Burger Court had confronted the collision of states' Eleventh Amendment immunity and Congress's Fourteenth Amendment enforcement power. In a unanimous opinion written by none other than Associate Justice Rehnquist, the Court had ruled that "Congress may, in determining what is 'appropriate legislation' for the purpose of enforcing the provisions of the Fourteenth Amendment, provide for private suits against States or state officials which are constitutionally impermissible in other contexts."[44]

To the surprise of many, the Rehnquist Court retreated somewhat in an opinion by the chief justice. In *Nevada Department of Human Resources v. Hibbs* the Court ruled 6–3 that Congress could waive state sovereign immunity when it passed the Family Medical Leave Act of 1993 (FMLA).[45] This law enables covered employees to take up to 12 weeks of leave (paid or unpaid at the employer's discretion) for the serious health condition of a family member, the birth of a child, and similar serious familial issues.

The question was how could the Court reconcile *Hibbs* with the earlier decisions in *Kimel* and *Garrett.* If Congress exceeded its power in waiving state immunity with respect to federal age and disability discrimination suits for money damages, how could it not do the same with respect to the Family and Medical Leave Act? In fact, seven of the nine justices were consistent in their votes from *Kimel* to *Hibbs.* The four liberal justices—Stevens, Souter, Ginsburg, and Breyer—voted to uphold Congress's abrogation of state immunity in all three cases. Likewise, Justices Scalia, Thomas, and Kennedy would have voted to deny Congress's abrogation of state immunity in all three cases. The two justices who changed their positions were Chief Justice Rehnquist and Justice O'Connor.

Rehnquist distinguished *Hibbs* based on the fact that the FMLA addressed problems of gender discrimination and stereotyping as opposed to age and disability. The difference is one of constitutional magnitude under Fourteenth Amendment equal protection jurisprudence. Age and disability are not suspect classes, but distinctions based on gender are a quasi-suspect class subject to greater judicial scrutiny. Rehnquist also noted that "the FMLA is narrowly targeted at the faultline between work and family—precisely where sex-based overgeneralization has been and remains strongest—and affects only one aspect of the employment relationship."[46] Furthermore, Congress was able to show more of a widespread pattern of gender discrimination than disability and age discrimination.

The Court also upheld the application of Title II of the Americans with Disabilities Act (ADA) to courthouses in *Tennessee v. Lane.*[47] The case involved a paraplegic criminal defendant named George Lane, who literally had to crawl up flights of stairs to reach the courtroom of his destination. Recall that in the *Garrett* case the Rehnquist Court ruled that states could not sued for monetary damages for alleged violations of Title I of the ADA. Title I deals with disability discrimination in employment. Title II of the ADA deals with disability in the provision of public services. The difference was significant to Justice O'Connor, who left the Federalism Five to join the familiar bloc of Stevens, Souter, Ginsburg, and Breyer to form a new majority that ruled that at least in cases "implicating the fundamental right of access to the courts," Title II can be enforced on state governments. The key to the case was that the fundamental right of access to the courts triggered serious due process concerns.

CONCLUSION

When Supreme Court watchers and legal experts discuss the impact of the Rehnquist Court, federalism comes to the forefront. Law professor Ilya Somin was on target when discussing Rehnquist: "Perhaps his most important departure from previous Court practice was his revival of the principle that the Constitution limits federal government power in order to protect federalism."[48] Many experts across ideological lines mention federalism as one of the key hallmarks of the Rehnquist Court. Disagreement surfaces over the merits and the reach of the Court's decisions.

As in most areas of constitutional law, the Rehnquist Court's jurisprudence on federalism has received mixed reviews. Law professor Mark Tushnet writes that the chief justice's "federalism was less than a constitutional doctrine or even, I think, a vision; it was instead an intuition that led him to particular results for which his opinions did not provide elaborated defenses."[49] Tushnet and others criticize the Court's federalism jurisprudence as unwarranted and even radical.

Other scholars view the Court's federalism decisions in a more positive light. Law professor Marci Hamilton criticizes those who characterized the Court's federalism decisions with a "sky is falling" argument. She writes that the Court's federalism decisions were moderate as a whole. "These cases show the Court never wanted to start a federalism revolution in the first place. It only wanted, quite properly, to be careful to honor the entirety of the constitutional scheme—which does allow a place for state power."[50]

Whether radical or more moderate, the Rehnquist Court certainly made an impact in the area of federalism. In so doing, it breathed new life into the Tenth and Eleventh Amendments and reinvigorated the notion that state autonomy is an important concept in the constitutional structure of the United States of America.

Chapter 6

FREEDOM OF RELIGION

> The Establishment Clause presents especially difficult questions of interpretation and application.
>
> —William Rehnquist (1983)[1]

> The free exercise of religion means, first and foremost, the right to believe and profess whatever religious doctrine one desires.
>
> —Antonin Scalia (1990)[2]

"Congress shall make no law respecting an establishment of religion or prohibiting the free exercise thereof." These 16 words contain the two religion clauses of the First Amendment. The first clause—"Congress shall make no law respecting an establishment of religion"—is called the establishment clause. The second—"or prohibiting the free exercise thereof"—is the free exercise clause.

The establishment clause prohibits an official governmental church and provides a degree of separation between church and state, though how much separation remains a source of great controversy. The free exercise clause generally ensures that individuals can practice their religious faith—or lack thereof—without governmental intervention.

Sometimes the two clauses conflict or act in tension with each other. What, for example, would happen if a public school student desired to deliver a religious speech at her graduation? School officials may attempt to limit such a speech or distance themselves from it because of the establishment clause. They would not want outside observers believing that the school was endorsing the student's religious beliefs. However, if school officials censored the student's speech, the student may claim that her free exercise rights had been violated. She would not have been allowed freely to exercise her religious beliefs. School officials may decide to accommodate the student's desires to deliver the speech with religious messages. But will the school district, by accommodating the student's preferences, have crossed the line and impermissibly advanced or endorsed religion?

Ideally, the two clauses complement each other and support the vision of governmental neutrality toward religion. Chief Justice Rehnquist and others on the Court also worked hard for judicial recognition that there is some "play in the joints" for laws that are not compelled by the free exercise clause or forbidden by the establishment clause.[3]

But many times over the course of nearly 20 years, the Rehnquist Court did not articulate a coherent vision of the religion clauses of the First Amendment. For much of the Rehnquist Court's tenure the justices disagreed mightily over calibrating the proper balance between the two clauses and the meaning of them both.

ESTABLISHMENT CLAUSE

General Vision and Meaning

The establishment clause is one of the most divisive provisions in the Bill of Rights. Scholars, historians, and members of the U.S. Supreme Court vigorously disagree over the meaning of the establishment clause, which ensures a degree of separation between church and state. The question is just how much separation there should be.

In 1947, the U.S. Supreme Court explained the meaning of the establishment clause while extending its application to the states in *Everson v. Board of Education.* The case concerned New Jersey policy paying for the bus transportation costs of students attending parochial schools. A narrowly divided Court ruled 5–4 that the practice comported with the Constitution. However, Justice Hugo Black's majority opinion laid the foundation for the future:

> The "establishment of religion" clause of the First Amendment means at least this: Neither a state nor the Federal Government can set up a church. Neither can pass laws which aid one religion, aid all religions, or prefer one religion over another.... In the words of Jefferson, the clause against establishment of religion by law was intended to erect "a wall of separation between church and State."[4]

Black invoked President Thomas Jefferson's 1802 letter to the Danbury Baptists and his famous "wall of separation" metaphor. *Everson* set the stage for the controversial Warren Court decisions of the 1960s that struck prayer in public schools, leading to bumper stickers that asked, "Why Should God Bless Us When We've Kicked Him Out of Our Public Schools." For example, in its 1962 decision *Engel v. Vitale* the Warren Court invalidated the New Board of Regents' authorized 22-word prayer for its public school students. "We think that by using its public school system to encourage recitation of the Regents' prayer, the State of New York has adopted a practice wholly inconsistent with the Establishment Clause," Justice Black wrote for the Court.[5] Black's opinion focused on the history of religious intolerance in England that caused the future colonists to flee their home country to America. Interestingly, Black did not cite a single case in his opinion. The next year, the Court again struck down school-sponsored prayer in public schools in companion cases out of the states of Pennsylvania and Maryland. The Warren Court had created a fairly high wall between church and state, a wall that Associate Justice William Rehnquist sought to lower on his ascension to the high court.

Rehnquist vehemently disagreed with the Court's establishment clause doctrine and the separationist decisions of the Warren Court. Rehnquist took a much narrower view of the establishment clause and sought to knock down the high and impregnable "wall of separation" between church and state. Rehnquist saw the establishment clause as preventing the establishment of a national religion, such as the Anglican Church in England centuries ago, or the government preferring one religious sect over others. He did not see the establishment clause as mandating that the government treat religion on the same level as nonreligion.

In 1985, the Burger Court struck down an Alabama moment-of-silence law in *Wallace v. Jaffree,* finding that the legislation was a patent attempt to return prayer to public school. Chief Justice Warren Burger, Justice Byron White, and William Rehnquist dissented. Rehnquist took no prisoners in his dissent, taking aim at the view of the establishment clause that Justice Black had advocated in numerous cases during the Warren Court era: "It is impossible to build sound constitutional doctrine upon a mistaken understanding of constitutional history, but unfortunately the Establishment Clause has been expressly freighted with Jefferson's misleading metaphor for nearly 40 years."[6] According to Rehnquist, this metaphor was one "based on bad history" and "should be frankly and explicitly abandoned."[7]

Rehnquist believed that the Founders created the establishment clause to prevent the establishment of a national religion and perhaps to prevent governmental preference of religious sects. The Founders did not intend to elevate atheism to the level of religious faith and certainly did not intend to cleanse religion from the public square. The proper view of the establishment clause focused on history, the history of the influence and visibility of religion in public life, he said.

Many contend that Rehnquist selectively culled from the historical record to supplement his vision of the establishment clause. Religious liberty expert Douglas Laycock contends that the Founders did not intend for the government to use the establishment clause to permit government to treat religion across the board better than nonreligion. "His [Rehnquist's] claim that the Founders meant to forbid preference among religious sects but meant to permit nonpreferential aid to religion over nonreligion is almost certainly wrong," Laycock says. "It certainly is true that the Founders permitted forms of government speech endorsing religion that we wouldn't permit today, but that doesn't mean the Founders permitted nonpreferential treatment of religion in general in terms of financial support and other kinds of support. There were many proposals in the 1780s, including in the drafting of the First Amendment, that permitted nonpreferential support for religion, and they were all rejected."[8] He adds, "In general, Rehnquist picked and chose quite selectively from the historical record in his dissent, though the other side was just as guilty."[9]

For his entire career as an associate and chief justice William Rehnquist laboriously campaigned for his historical understanding of the establishment clause. At times he succeeded, particularly during the last few years of his tenure, but in many decisions he found himself on the losing side.

On the opposite side of the establishment clause from Rehnquist were Justices William Brennan and John Paul Stevens. Brennan, the architect of many Warren Court constitutional law decisions, fervently believed in a strong separation between church and state. Stevens is harder to qualify, but he consistently invalidated many programs as violative of the establishment clause. For instance, in 1990, the U.S. Supreme Court ruled in *Westside Community Board of Education v. Mergens* that the Equal Access Act, a federal law that prohibited school officials from discriminating against student clubs based on religious or philosophical viewpoint, did not violate the establishment clause.[10] The lone dissenter was Stevens.

The most interesting or unusual view of the establishment clause on the Rehnquist Court comes not from Stevens, but from the pen of Justice Clarence Thomas. In the controversial case involving atheist Michael Newdow's challenge to the Pledge of Allegiance (for Congress's addition of the words *under God* in 1954), Thomas called for a "rethinking of the Establishment Clause."[11] He referred to the clause as a "federalism" provision and would not extend it to the states via the Fourteenth Amendment. This means that Thomas does not view the establishment clause as creating an individual right. "On the Court he is way out in right field on this issue," says Texas law school professor Douglas Laycock. "The heart of Thomas' argument is that the Establishment Clause doesn't create an individual right and I think this misunderstands the Establishment Clause." Thomas's view, however, does confirm the thinking of scholars on both the right and the left that Thomas may be the Court's most original constitutional thinker.

A Much Maligned Test and Alternatives

Rehnquist attacked not only Black's establishment clause ruling in *Everson* but also Chief Justice Burger's three-part test from *Lemon v. Kurtzman.*[12] The so-called *Lemon* test contained three prongs: whether the regulation had a secular purpose; whether it had a primary effect that advanced or inhibited religion; and whether it caused an excessive entanglement between church and state. According to Rehnquist, the *Lemon* test failed to produce consistent results and "has no more grounding in the history of the First Amendment than does the wall theory upon which it rests."[13]

Other justices attacked the *Lemon* test, most notably Justice Antonin Scalia, who offered the following oft-quoted purple prose about the test: "Like some ghoul in a late-night horror movie that repeatedly sits up in its grave and shuffles abroad, after being repeatedly killed and buried, Lemon stalks our Establishment Clause jurisprudence once again."[14]

Two other justices—Sandra Day O'Connor and Anthony Kennedy—have put forth their own vision of the establishment clause. In a 1984 concurring opinion O'Connor proposed her endorsement test, which asks whether a reasonable observer would view the challenged religious practice as a governmental endorsement of religion.[15] She proposed the test as a "clarification" of the Court's establishment clause jurisprudence. Over the years, the test has become more, sometimes becoming the primary mode of analysis. The Court has used this test frequently in religious display cases. "O'Connor's endorsement analysis was very significant," Laycock says. "It certainly is a legacy of the Rehnquist Court, though not of Chief Justice Rehnquist, who never supported it."[16]

In a 1989 dissenting opinion Justice Anthony Kennedy offered his "coercion" test—that the government "may not coerce anyone to support or participate in any religion or its exercise."[17] Kennedy used his coercion analysis then to vote to uphold religious displays but used the same analysis in a majority opinion in 1992 to strike down school prayer.[18] He wrote that "prayer exercises in public schools carry a particular risk of indirect coercion.... What to most believers may seem nothing more than a reasonable request that the nonbeliever respect their religious practices, in a school context may appear to the nonbeliever or dissenter to be an attempt to employ the machinery of the State to enforce a religious orthodoxy."[19]

Much to the chagrin of many of the justices, the Rehnquist Court largely used the *Lemon* test. "They don't feel bound by the Lemon test but use it when convenient. The problem is that they can't agree on what to replace it with and that's why there are so many tests," Laycock says. The Court has alternatively employed Rehnquist's historical interpretation, O'Connor's endorsement, and Kennedy's coercion test. With no clear guidepost it is easy to see how the Court failed to produce consistent results in this arena.

School Prayer

Chief Justice Rehnquist found himself consistently in the minority in school prayer cases both as an associate and chief justice. In 1992, the Court continued in the tradition of the Warren Court by ruling 5–4 in *Lee v. Weisman* that a Rhode Island middle school violated the establishment clause by having a rabbi deliver a nonsectarian prayer at graduation.[20]

Justice Kennedy employed his aforementioned coercion analysis to conclude that the graduation prayer amounted to a form of psychological coercion on the non-Christian students in the audience. He explained, "The undeniable fact is that the school district's supervision and control of a high school graduation ceremony places public pressure, as well as peer pressure, on attending students to stand as a group or, at least, maintain respectful silence during the invocation and benediction. This pressure, though subtle and indirect, can be as real as any overt compulsion."[21]

Justice Antonin Scalia characteristically responded with a biting dissent, calling Kennedy's opinion "bereft of any reference to history"[22] and his new theory as "psycho-coercion."[23] Scalia's opinion looked much like Rehnquist's dissent in the Alabama moment-of-silence decision, referring to the religious language in the Declaration of Independence and the practices of early presidents to call for a national thanksgiving day of prayer.

Scalia criticized Kennedy's coercion analysis, pointing out (with prescience) that the same logic could be applied to invalidate the recitation of the Pledge of Allegiance in public schools. Unlike Kennedy, who saw subtle coercive pressure on religious minorities, Scalia saw only "minimal inconvenience."[24]

In 2000, the Court returned to the school prayer issue, ruling 6–3 that a Texas school district practice of having prayer over the loudspeakers at high school football games violated the establishment clause.[25] Finding himself the senior justice in the majority, Justice Stevens kept the case for himself. He concluded that the practice amounted to governmental sponsorship and endorsement of religion that did not comport with the Court's precedents.

It mattered little to Justice Stevens that the students apparently voted on the messages to be broadcast over the loudspeakers. "The policy is invalid on its face because it establishes an improper majoritarian election on religion, and unquestionably has the purpose and creates the perception of encouraging the delivery of prayer at a series of important school events," he wrote.[26] Rehnquist, Scalia, and Thomas dissented, with the chief justice accusing Stevens's opinion of "bristl[ing] with hostility to all things religious in public life."[27]

Religious Displays

Whatever the merits of its decisions, the Rehnquist Court at least acted consistently in the area of school-sponsored prayer in public schools. The same could not be said of the Court in the religious display arena. In 1989, the Court had to determine whether two religious displays in downtown Pittsburgh violated the establishment clause.[28] The displays were a crèche depicting the Nativity placed in a courthouse and an 18-foot menorah placed outside a city building next to a 45-foot Christmas tree. The ACLU challenged both displays as violations of the establishment clause.

In a split decision, the Court rejected the Nativity in the courthouse 5–4 but upheld the menorah next to the Christmas tree by a vote of 6–3. Three justices—Brennan, Marshall, and Stevens—believed both displays violated the Constitution. Four justices—Rehnquist, White, Kennedy, and Scalia—believed both displays were constitutional. That left Justices Harry Blackmun and Sandra Day O'Connor as the only justices who voted to uphold one display but strike down the other. Blackmun reasoned that the crèche was impermissible because it stood alone on government property, while the menorah's "particular physical setting" (being placed next to the secular Christmas tree and a sign) was permissible. The closely divided nature of the Court's decision in *Allegheny County v. ACLU* was not surprising as the Burger Court in 1984 had upheld a crèche display in Pawtuckett, Rhode Island, by a narrow 5–4 vote.[29]

The waning days of the Rehnquist Court saw the Court finally tackle an issue that had been exploding in the lower courts for many years—the constitutionality of Ten Commandments plaques and monuments. The Burger Court had issued a 5–4 per curiam decision in *Stone v. Graham,* striking down a Kentucky law requiring the posting of the 10 Commandments in public schools.[30] However, *Stone v. Graham* could be read narrowly in the school context, where the Court is most concerned about subtle, coercive pressure on students. Some contended that the *Stone* case was not persuasive in the case of a Ten Commandments monument in a public park.

In June 2005, the Rehnquist Court issued two split 5–4 decisions in Ten Commandments display cases that arose out of Texas and Kentucky. The Texas case—*Van Orden v. Perry*[31]—involved a Ten Commandments monument in a public park. The Kentucky case—*McCreary County v. ACLU*[32]—involved Ten Commandments plaques in two courthouses. The Court upheld the Texas monument, which had stood in the park for more than 40 years, but rejected the Kentucky courthouse plaques.

The chief justice finally managed to find himself on the winning side of a religious display case. He declined to apply the *Lemon* test, finding it "not useful in dealing with the sort of passive monument that Texas has erected on its Capitol grounds." Rehnquist noted that the Ten Commandments appears on many government monuments, including the Supreme Court building. The Court's room contains a frieze up above that includes a picture of Moses holding a stone tablet. "Our opinions, like our buildings, have recognized the role the Decalogue plays in America's heritage," he wrote.[33]

The outcome determinative factor was the vote of Justice Stephen Breyer, who switched sides and became the deciding vote in each case. Context again became crucial, particularly for Breyer, who stressed the fact that the monument had stood for such a long time without complaint. "Those 40 years suggest that the public visiting the capitol grounds has considered the religious aspect of the tablets' message as part of what is a broader moral and historical message reflective of a cultural heritage."[34]

To be fair, the context in each case was quite different. The Ten Commandments monument had been placed there in the 1950s, while the displays in the Kentucky courthouses were placed there in 1999. The monument in the Texas case was surrounded by other historical and non-religious-based displays, while the Kentucky displays stood alone.

However, the justices who remain from the Rehnquist Court on the Roberts Court continue to be deeply divided as two groups of four justices would have voted to uphold or deny the displays in both cases. Only Justice Breyer switched sides to provide the different outcomes.

Public Funding Cases

The one area in which Chief Justice Rehnquist managed to win support for his views in the establishment clause area concerned public funding for schools and other organizations. In *Mueller v. Allen,* then associate justice Rehnquist wrote the opinion for a five-member majority rejecting an establishment clause challenge to a Minnesota law that allowed parents, including those parents who send their children to private religious schools, to deduct for various school expenses. "Most importantly, the deduction is available for educational expenses incurred by all parents, including those whose children attend public schools and those whose children attend nonsectarian private schools or sectarian private schools," Rehnquist wrote.[35]

In 1989, the Court unanimously ruled in *Witters v. Washington Dept. of Servs. for Blind* that a state could provide tuition aid, as part of a general vocational scholarship program, to a blind student studying at a religious college to become a pastor.[36] Then, in 1993, the Court narrowly ruled 5–4 in *Zobrest v. Catalina Foothills School District* that a federal program allowing sign language interpreters to be funded for deaf students in private religious schools as well as students in public schools did not violate the establishment clause.[37]

These decisions culminated in the Court's 5–4 2002 decision in *Zelman v. Simmons-Harris,* where the Court upheld a school voucher program. The state of Ohio established a voucher program called the Pilot Project Scholarship Program in the city of Cleveland to help address the poor state of education in the city's schools. A federal court had called the city's schooling a "crisis of magnitude."[38]

Under the program, the state provides tuition aid to low-income parents and then allows these parents to use that money to send their children to other schools, including private, religious schools that participate in the program. The vast majority of participating families sent their children to private Catholic schools. Forty-six of the 56 schools that participated were Catholic schools. Other taxpayers challenged the program on establishment clause grounds, arguing that it amounted to state support of Catholic schools.

Chief Justice Rehnquist ruled that the voucher program was constitutional. He emphasized that it was "a program of true private choice" that was "neutral" toward religion. He explained,

> Mueller, Witters and Zobrest thus make clear that where a government aid program is neutral with respect to religion, and provides assistance directly to a broad class of citizens who, in turn, direct government aid to religious schools wholly as a result of their own genuine and independent private choice, the program is not readily subject to challenge under the Establishment Clause.[39]

Rehnquist concluded that the Ohio program was "entirely neutral with respect to religion" and "a program of true private choice."[40]

Religious liberty expert Douglas Laycock says the Rehnquist Court guided by the chief justice reached the right result in the voucher case: "The Court realized that if you offer to fund all kinds of schools—public, private, secular, religious, charter, and magnet—then you are not really supporting any ideology. Rather, you are supporting education. That is an enormously controversial position but I think a correct one. Chief Justice Rehnquist deserves a lot of credit for that. It was a position that he took from the beginning as an associate justice in dissenting opinions in the early 1970s."[41]

Free Exercise Clause

The complement—or counter—to the establishment clause is the free exercise clause. The Warren Court had created strong protections for free exercise of religion, providing that the government could not infringe on a person's religious rights, unless such infringements passed strict scrutiny. In 1963, the Warren Court ruled in *Sherbert v. Verner* that the state of South Carolina could not deny unemployment compensation benefits to Seventh-day Adventist Adele Sherbert, who was fired from her job for refusing to work on Saturdays, the Sabbath day of her faith.[42] Justice Brennan reasoned for a unanimous Court that the state had engaged in "religious discrimination" by specifically prohibiting employers from making employees work on Sundays, while denying benefits to claimants like Adele Sherbert.

The Burger Court continued this highly protective standard in *Wisconsin v. Yoder,* a 1972 decision determining that the state of Wisconsin violated the free exercise rights of Amish parents by forcing them to adhere to the state's compulsory educational laws.[43] The state had attempted to force the Amish to have their children attend high school until age 16, which conflicted with the group's religious traditions.

The Rehnquist Court dramatically curtailed the scope of free exercise protection in its 1990 decision *Employment Division v. Smith.*[44] The case involved two Native American drug rehabilitation counselors in Oregon who were terminated from their jobs for injesting peyote—a hallucinogenic drug—for religious reasons. The two sought unemployment benefits just like Adele Sherbert did years ago.

The U.S. Supreme Court rejected their claims, distinguishing *Sherbert* on the fact that the two counselors—Galen Black and Alfred Smith—had violated state criminal laws against illegal drug use. But the majority of the Court went much further than distinguishing the *Smith* case as a criminal case from the *Sherbert,* case which involved civil law. Justice Scalia ruled that the *Sherbert* test should not apply to generally applicable laws that do not specifically target religious practices.

Scalia reasoned that the *Sherbert* test and its requirement of a compelling governmental interest could create a "private right to ignore generally applicable laws."[45] Four justices—O'Connor, Brennan, Marshall, and Blackmun—disagreed with Scalia's analysis. O'Connor concurred in the decision because she believed that even under the *Sherbert* compelling interest test, Black and Smith would lose because the state had a compelling interest in enforcing its drug laws. The other three justices dissented from the analysis and the final holding. O'Connor wrote that Scalia's ruling "dramatically departs from well-settled First Amendment jurisprudence, appears unnecessary to resolve the question presented, and is incompatible with our Nation's fundamental commitment to individual religious liberty."[46]

The *Smith* decision changed the landscape of the free exercise clause. "Before *Smith,* the Court often ruled that the First Amendment required government to demonstrate a compelling state interest before denying a religious exemption to a law or regulation," explained religious liberty expert Charles Haynes. "After *Smith,* the government no longer had to worry about accommodating religious practices that are in conflict with general laws."[47]

The *Smith* decision sparked outrage within the religious liberty community. A coalition of groups—including the National Association of Evangelicals, the Southern Baptist Convention, the Mormon Church, the Traditional Values Coalition, and the ACLU—joined forces to urge Congress to take action. Congress responded by passing a law designed to restore religious freedom to America. Entitled the Religious Freedom Restoration Act (RFRA), the 1993 law legislatively overturned the *Smith* decision. The preamble of the law criticized the Court's decision, providing that "the Supreme Court virtually eliminated the requirement that the government justify burdens on religious exercise imposed by laws neutral toward religion."

RFRA required the government to show that any regulation substantially burdening the free exercise of religion advanced a compelling government interest in the least restrictive way possible. RFRA restored—and some said expanded—the compelling interest test articulated in the *Sherbert* and *Yoder* decisions.

The *Smith* decision caused not only outrage, but also a power struggle between Congress and the Supreme Court. In 1997, the U.S. Supreme Court resolved the debate through a case in Texas involving a church zoning dispute. The Court ruled 6–3 in *City of Boerne v. Flores* that Congress exceeded its constitutional authority in defining the level of religious liberty in the country.[48]

Congress had justified its authority to pass RFRA by invoking section 5 of the Fourteenth Amendment, which provides that Congress has the power "to enforce, by appropriate legislation" the provisions of the Fourteenth Amendment. Congress thought it had the power to pass RFRA based on prior Supreme Court precedent. In 1965, Congress passed the Voting Rights Act, a provision of which banned literary tests as a prerequisite for voting. Congress passed the law partially in response to a 1959 Supreme Court decision upholding literary tests.[49] A year after the passage of the Voting Rights Act, the Court upheld the statute.[50]

A majority of the Supreme Court did not find a parallel to the Voting Rights Act case. The Court noted the disparities in the legislative records of the two laws, noting that Congress had much more evidence of discrimination and harm in the voting rights context in the 1960s. In *Boerne* the Court did not see Congress enforcing the free exercise of religious right; they saw Congress as substantively changing the meaning of the free exercise clause. "Legislation which alters the meaning of the Free Exercise Clause cannot be said to be enforcing the Clause," Kennedy wrote. "Congress does not enforce a constitutional right by changing what the right is."[51]

The majority saw Congress as invading its turf as the final interpreter of the Constitution. "The power to interpret the Constitution in a case or controversy remains in the judiciary," Kennedy wrote.[52] The majority invalidated RFRA as applied to state and local governments, provoking an impassioned dissent from O'Connor, who reiterated her distaste for the Court's decision in *Smith.*

"I was surprised by the Boerne decision though it is easy to understand politically," said Laycock, who argued the case on behalf of the church and in defense of the statute before the high court. "Boerne changed the law on the scope of Congressional power to enforce the Fourteenth Amendment."

"I think the decision can be understood in part because the Court was just angry at Congress, who had been in their face about the issue," he explained. "There was that awful preamble in RFRA that talked about how wrong the Court had been in *Smith.* Plainly, there was a little bit of 'who is king of the hill' going on between the Court and Congress."[53]

The tug of war between Congress and the Court may continue, though it will be up to the Roberts Court. In 2000, Congress responded to the *Boerne* decision by passing a narrower religious liberty law called the Religious Land Use and Institutionalized Persons Act (RLUIPA). This law employs the *Sherbert* compelling interest standard but is tied to Congress's spending and commerce clause powers rather than Congress's powers under section 5 of the Fourteenth Amendment.

The Rehnquist Court never had the opportunity to fully address the constitutional issues surrounding RLUIPA, though in its last term the Rehnquist Court did rule that the part of RLUIPA dealing with the religious liberty rights of institutionalized persons did not violate the establishment clause.[54]

CONCLUSION

Justice Thomas may be considered an outlier for his position on the establishment clause, but he is correct when he opined that the Court's decisions in this area "render the Establishment Clause impenetrable and incapable of consistent application."[55] The highly fractured decisions in the 10 Commandments cases show there was a deep divide even at the end of the Rehnquist Court on church-state separation issues.

The Court perhaps wisely avoided the most controversial decision in the establishment clause arena since the 1960s when it avoided deciding whether the inclusion of the words *under God* in the Pledge of Allegiance violated the establishment clause. The Court decided the case of *Elk Grove Unified School District v. Newdow* on standing grounds.[56]

Disputes will always remain over the establishment clause, though the Roberts Court could provide more clarity in its views than the Rehnquist Court. Many believe that Chief Justice John G. Roberts, a former Rehnquist clerk, and Justice Samuel Alito will subscribe to the Rehnquist vision of the establishment clause. If so, there could be a fundamental change in this area of constitutional law. Perhaps Chief Justice Rehnquist will achieve his vision postmortem.

On the free exercise front, the Rehnquist Court will always be remembered for the ongoing exchange it had with Congress after its controversial *Smith* decision. The larger question remains what the future will hold for *Smith* and the level of religious liberty protection in general. The lower courts have not agreed on how to interpret *Smith* and what constitutes a generally applicable law. It would not be surprising if the Roberts Court confronts these issues and decides the level of free exercise protection in the near future.

Chapter 7

FREEDOM OF EXPRESSION

> The First Amendment protects expression, be it of the popular variety or not. And the fact that an idea may be embraced and advocated by increasing numbers of people is all the more reason to protect the First Amendment rights of those who wish to voice a different view.
>
> —Chief Justice William Rehnquist (2000)[1]

First Amendment free expression jurisprudence has been described as labyrinthine, complex, confusing, and confounding. In the words of one scholar the Court "has developed a dense mass of overlapping doctrines."[2] The Court has employed numerous methodological tools that increase the chances for unpredictability and even inconsistency. Two primary tools include categorization—identifying speech as falling into either a protected or an unprotected category—and content discrimination—determining whether a governmental policy regulates speech based on content.

Under the categorical model, the Court determines whether certain speech fits into one of several narrow categories of unprotected speech such as obscenity, fighting words, child pornography, incitement to imminent lawless action, and true threats. If speech qualifies as one of these categories, then it receives no First Amendment protection. The Court has developed elaborate tests over the years to define whether speech falls into these groups of expression. The Warren Court, for instance, struggled mightily in the 1950s and 1960s to define obscenity, a category of hard-core sexual expression with no societal value. Justice Potter Stewart once famously opined in a 1964 obscenity opinion that he might never be able to come up with a coherent definition but that "I know it when I see it."[3]

The most common methodological tool that the Court has used is the content discrimination model, which asks whether the speech discriminates against speech based on content or whether the law applies across the board to all expression without regard to content. The determination is often outcome determinative as content-based laws are subject to strict scrutiny, while content-neutral laws are subject only to intermediate scrutiny. As Justice Souter once wrote, "Strict scrutiny leaves few survivors."[4]

To complicate matters, the Court also often relies on other doctrines, such as determining whether the law sweeps too broadly and prohibits unprotected speech as well as protected speech. This is called the overbreadth doctrine. Still, other times, the Court seeks to determine whether a law is clear and not vague, whether the law properly defines what is acceptable conduct and what is proscribable. In addition, the Court has created separate bodies of First Amendment law depending on the speaker's relationship to the government. For instance, the Court has created different tests for the free speech rights of public school students, prisoners, and public employees.

UNPREDICTABILITY OF THE COURT'S FIRST AMENDMENT JURISPRUDENCE

The Rehnquist Court's record on the First Amendment defies easy characterization other than its unpredictability. The unpredictable nature surfaced early in the Rehnquist Court in the celebrated case involving televangelist Jerry Falwell, the head of the Moral Majority, and pornographer extraordinaire Larry Flynt. The dispute arose after Flynt lampooned Falwell in his *Hustler Magazine.* Flynt produced a parody of the Campari liqueur ads on television, which featured celebrities talking about their first time—their first time tasting the liqueurs. The ads played on the double sexual entendre. Flynt produced a parody entitled "Jerry Falwell Talks about His First Time." The parody had Falwell saying his first sexual experience was with his mother in an outhouse.

The outraged Falwell sued Flynt in federal court for invasion of privacy, libel, and intentional infliction of emotional distress. Falwell lost on the privacy and libel claims but received a $200,000 verdict from the jury for intentional infliction of emotional distress. On appeal Flynt contended that the parody was protected expression under the First Amendment.

The decision concerned many First Amendment advocates because it is far easier for a public figure like Jerry Falwell to recover damages for intentional infliction of emotional distress than it is for libel, where the public figure has to show evidence of actual malice defined as knowing falsity or reckless disregard for the truth.

Many feared that the U.S. Supreme Court would diminish First Amendment freedoms by ruling against the despicable Flynt. Even the audacious porn magnate was nervous about the Court's decision. "I regret I have brought this issue before the Court and that the national press could be affected by this decision," Flynt said on the day of oral argument before the high court. "It makes me feel very badly."[5] Media lawyers feared the decision could weaken the lofty protections for the free press by enabling those whose feelings were hurt by unflattering news portrayals to file similar emotional distress claims.

To the surprise of many, the U.S. Supreme Court unanimously ruled in favor of Larry Flynt by 8–0 (the recently confirmed Justice Kennedy did not participate). Of even greater surprise was that the new chief justice, William H. Rehnquist, offered an opinion so protective of the press and the First Amendment. He wrote that "in the world of debate about public affairs, many things done with motives that are less than admirable are protected by the First Amendment." He reasoned that if strong protections were not in place for satire and parody, then "there can be little doubt that political cartoonists and satirists would be subjected to damages awards without any showing that their work falsely defamed its subject."[6]

Rehnquist rejected the idea that intentional infliction of emotional distress claims could be governed by an "outrageousness" standard without harming First Amendment freedoms: "'Outrageousness' in the area of political and social discourse has an inherent subjectiveness about it which would allow a jury to impose liability on the basis of the jurors' tastes or views, or perhaps on the basis of their dislike of a particular expression. An 'outrageousness' standard thus runs afoul of our longstanding refusal to allow damages to be awarded because the speech in question may have an adverse emotional impact on the audience."[7]

Free speech expert Robert O'Neil, founder of the Thomas Jefferson Center for the Protection of Free Expression, recalls his surprise at the Court's unanimous decision authored by the new chief justice: "I am still baffled that it came out that way, including some of the broad language that Rehnquist used in talking about protecting political cartoons."[8] Jane Kirtley, who filed an amicus brief for the Reporters Committee for Freedom of the Press in support of Flynt, also was surprised: "I'm not sure anyone would have expected Rehnquist to write the opinion, or, if we'd been told he was writing it, would have expected a victory, especially one that was unanimous. But the scuttlebutt was that Rehnquist was persuaded by the wonderful cartoonists' amicus brief (with that appendix of historical political cartoons), which proves that a picture really is worth 1,000 words."[9]

The *Guardian* in London wrote that "the U.S. Supreme Court has demonstrated its capacity to spring legal surprises."[10] The *Chicago Tribune* raved in an editorial, "All eight justices who heard the case, including those alleged enemies of the press William H. Rehnquist and Antonin Scalia, deserve a standing ovation."[11] Even the *New York Times* praised the new chief justice and his decision, writing that "the Rehnquist Court has fashioned a sparkling vindication of free speech."[12]

The unpredictability of the Rehnquist Court carried over into later years, even when the Court had the same membership for more than a decade. The Court's First Amendment record can rarely be explained by any sort of rough liberal-conservative calculus. Many experts characterize the Rehnquist Court into a group of three conservatives (Rehnquist, Scalia, and Thomas), three moderates (Kennedy, O'Connor, and Breyer), and three liberals (Souter, Stevens, and Ginsburg). For example, in many federalism cases O'Connor and Kennedy joined the three conservatives to form the "Federalism Five" against the four more liberal justices.

Such alliances often simply do not work when analyzing the free expression jurisprudence of the Rehnquist Court. The classic example is the early Rehnquist Court's 5–4 decision in the controversial flag-burning case of Gregory Lee Johnson. The defendant burned an American flag outside the Republican National Convention in Dallas, Texas, in 1994, yelling, "America, the Red, White and Blue, we spit on you."

Charged under a Texas flag desecration law, Johnson asserted that he was being punished for his political speech. The state of Texas countered that it had a compelling interest in protecting the flag as a symbol of national unity and nationhood. Justice William Brennan, long a defender of First Amendment freedoms, wrote the majority opinion: "If there is a bedrock principle underlying the First Amendment, it is that the government may not prohibit the expression of an idea simply because it finds the idea itself offensive or disagreeable."[13] He pointed out that many of our Founding Fathers "were not known for their reverence for the Union Jack," the flag of England. To Brennan, the state sought to impose its own political orthodoxy on a protestor, a result anathema to his broad conception of free expression. Brennan predictably received the votes of his fellow liberals Thurgood Marshall and Harry Blackmun. However, it was two recent Reagan appointees who carried the day for the majority—Anthony Kennedy and Antonin Scalia. Kennedy wrote a concurrence, explaining that "sometimes we must make decisions we do not like."[14]

Chief Justice Rehnquist wrote a dissent joined by Justices White and O'Connor that emphasized the unique history of the flag as a symbol of national importance. "It was Johnson's use of this particular symbol, and not the idea that he sought to convey by it or by his many other expressions, for which he was punished."[15] Justice John Paul Stevens, normally a staunch defender of First Amendment values and, in the later days of the Rehnquist Court, the most ardent liberal, filed a separate dissenting opinion that made a similar point. Stevens, a former World War II navy veteran, wrote that Johnson "was prosecuted because of the method he chose to express his dissatisfaction with those polices," not because of his political dissent.[16]

Still another example of strange alignments occurred in *United States v. Playboy Entertainment Group, Inc.*[17] The case involved the constitutionality of a federal law requiring cable operators either to scramble sexually explicit channels in full or limit such programming to certain late-night hours. Congress passed the law in 1996 in order to deal with the problem of signal bleed, a phenomenon by which some visual and audio portions of the sexually explicit channels may be available to nonsubscribers. Congress insisted that the measure was necessary to protect minors from harmful materials on cable television. Playboy Entertainment Group countered that there was a less speech-restrictive alternative provided for in the congressional statutory scheme—the use of lock boxes that could be made operational on subscriber request. Thus parents could prevent the problem simply by contacting their cable company.

The Rehnquist Court ruled 5–4 to strike the law down on First Amendment grounds. Justice Kennedy's opinion read like a *paean* to free speech: "The history of the law of free expression is one of vindication in cases involving speech that many citizens may find shabby, offensive, or even ugly."[18] Joining the First Amendment–friendly Kennedy in the majority were Justices John Paul Stevens, David Souter, Ruth Bader Ginsburg, and, to the surprise of some, Clarence Thomas. In his separate concurrence Thomas wrote that he was "unwilling to corrupt the First Amendment" to adopt the government's position.[19]

This is not to suggest that the traditional conservative-liberal dichotomy never exists in the jurisprudence of the Rehnquist Court. Sometimes it does, as reflected in the hotly contested case involving gay assistant scoutmaster James Dale excluded from the Boy Scouts. Dale sued under New Jersey state antidiscrimination laws.

Chief Justice Rehnquist wrote that the forced inclusion of the gay scoutmaster into the scout group infringed on the group's right to freedom of expressive association. While not textually based in the First Amendment, the Court had recognized such a constitutional right since 1958, when the state of Alabama had tried to obtain the membership list of the NAACP. Rehnquist reasoned that "a state requirement that the Boy Scouts retain Dale as an assistant scoutmaster would significantly burden the organization's right to oppose or disfavor homosexual conduct."[20]

Justice Stevens, writing for himself, Souter, Breyer, and Ginsburg, questioned the majority's expressive association analysis. He contended that the case did not comport with the Burger Court's precedents in cases involving the exclusion of women from all-male clubs and organizations. "We have squarely held that a State's antidiscrimination law does not violate a group's right to associate simply because the law conflicts with that group's exclusionary membership policy," he wrote.[21]

Similarly, in *Republican Party of Minnesota v. White* the Court ruled 5–4 that the state of Minnesota could not prohibit judicial candidates from announcing their views on disputed legal or political issues.[22] The familiar five of Scalia, Kennedy, Thomas, Rehnquist, and O'Connor invalidated the restriction, while the four more "liberal" justices voted to uphold the speech-restrictive measure.

The *Dale* and *White* decisions show that the labels of conservative and liberal have limited, if any, utility in the free expression context. Many times, the more conservative justices on the Court protect expression more expansively than the more liberal justices. Scholar Ronald Collins has written that "there was a time when one could gauge the 'liberality' of the Court by its First Amendment voting record.... But times and circumstances have changed that. Labels can be misleading."[23] Many times, the most ardent defender of the First Amendment is a Republican nominee.

University of California, Los Angeles law professor Eugene Volokh has analyzed the voting records of the justices in free speech cases from 1994 to 2002 and produced some surprising results. Justice Kennedy, a Reagan appointee, ranked by far the most First Amendment friendly. The most surprising result may be that Justice Clarence Thomas, considered a reactionary conservative by some, ranked second, just ahead of the more liberal David Souter. Volokh's rankings were (1) Kennedy, (2) Thomas, (3) Souter, (4) Stevens, (5) Ginsburg, (6) Scalia, (7) O'Connor, (8) Rehnquist, and (9) Breyer.[24]

Thomas, for instance, has proven to be the Court's most consistent defender of free speech in the areas of commercial speech and campaign finance.[25] In 1996, Thomas wrote a concurring opinion in a case involving the restriction of liquor price advertising in Rhode Island: "I do not see a philosophical or historical basis for asserting that 'commercial' speech is of 'lower value' than 'noncommercial' speech." Similarly, when the Court upheld the vast majority of the Bipartisan Campaign Reform Act of 2002, a massive campaign finance law, Thomas vigorously dissented, writing,

> The First Amendment provides that "Congress shall make no law ... abridging the freedom of speech." Nevertheless, the Court today upholds what can only be described as the most significant abridgment of the freedoms of speech and association since the Civil War. With breathtaking scope, the Bipartisan Campaign Reform Act of 2002 ... directly targets and constricts core political speech, the "primary object of First Amendment protection."[26]

DEVELOPMENT OF POSITIVE AND NEGATIVE DOCTRINES FOR EXPRESSION

Viewpoint Discrimination

The Rehnquist Court advanced a number of First Amendment doctrines that both advanced and inhibited the development of free expression. For instance, the Rehnquist Court expounded on the central principle that viewpoint discrimination, a subset of content discrimination, was anathema to the First Amendment. Earlier courts had hinted at the principle in cases involving student speech and military uniforms, but the Rehnquist Court made the principle a clarion call.

Justice Antonin Scalia went so far as to write in *R.A.V. v. City of St. Paul* that a city could not selectively ban certain fighting words when writing to invalidate a city cross-burning ordinance.[27] While other justices, such as Stevens, preferred a traditional overbreadth analysis, Scalia insisted that the state could not limit its prohibition of bias-motivated expressive conduct to those based on race, color, creed, and gender. "Those who wish to use 'fighting words' in connection with other ideas—to express hostility, for example, on the basis of political affiliation, union membership, or homosexuality—are not covered," he wrote. "The First Amendment does not permit St. Paul to impose special prohibitions on those speakers who express views on disfavored subjects."[28]

The Court used the viewpoint discrimination doctrine to prohibit a public university from denying funding to a student Christian publication[29] and to strike down a federal regulation limiting legal services lawyers receiving federal funds from challenging the constitutionality of existing welfare laws.[30] Justice Kennedy explained that viewpoint discrimination is an egregious form of content discrimination.

Secondary Effects

The Rehnquist Court expanded the Burger Court's development of the secondary effects doctrine, a doctrine that contorts the content discrimination principle to allow municipalities to regulate adult entertainment. In

1976, the Burger Court upheld a Detroit "anti-skid-row ordinance" that zoned adult businesses. Even though adult businesses were singled out in the ordinance, the Court treated the zoning regulation as content-neutral. In a footnote Justice John Paul Stevens explained that the zoning ordinance was designed to address the harmful, secondary effects associated with adult businesses—decreased property values and increased crime—as opposed to the "dissemination of 'offensive' speech."[31] Ten years later, the Burger Court upheld another adult business zoning law in Renton, Washington, allowing city officials to rely on studies of the harmful secondary effects allegedly caused by adult businesses in nearby Seattle. The Court explained that a seemingly content-based law should be treated as content-neutral if its purpose is to address the harmful secondary effects of adult businesses.[32]

The Rehnquist Court extended the secondary effects doctrine from the zoning context to direct restrictions on the content of expression. In *Barnes v. Glen Theatre* Justice David Souter, in his concurring opinion, ruled that an Indiana public indecency law was a constitutional way to address the harmful secondary effects associated with nude performance dancing. The law was used to prohibit dancers in adult businesses from dancing completely nude. Souter reasoned that the general public nudity law was not related to the suppression of free expression but to the harmful effects of adult businesses. In the words of adult entertainment lawyer John Weston, "Souter basically extended a time, place and manner concept into a direct attack on free expression."[33]

The Rehnquist Court used the secondary effects doctrine to uphold a similar Pennsylvania city ordinance designed to prohibit nude performance dancing. In *City of Erie v Pap's A.M.* the Court upheld the law by a 6–3 vote, saying that it was virtually "identical" to the Indiana public indecency law in *Barnes*.[34]

Ironically, Justice John Paul Stevens, who first introduced the concept of secondary effects, and Justice David Souter, who first extended the secondary effects rationale from the zoning context to direct regulation on the content of adult expression, both dissented in *Pap's*. Souter went so far as to admit that he erred in extending the secondary effects doctrine to the direct regulation of expression: "I have come to believe that a government must toe the mark more carefully than I first insisted."[35]

The Rehnquist Court attempted to limit the secondary effects doctrine early on in the 1988 decision *Boos v. Barry*. There the Court struck down the part of a law that prohibited protestors from displaying signs within 500 feet of foreign embassies that placed the foreign government in "public odium" or "public disrepute." The Court rejected the government's argument that the ordinance furthered the secondary effect of shielding international diplomats from harm. The Court reasoned that "listeners' reaction to speech" is not a valid secondary effect.[36]

Despite this limitation, lower courts have used the secondary effects doctrine in a variety of contexts far removed from adult business land use cases. One court even used the doctrine to uphold a restrictive student dress code. These developments show that Justice William Brennan may have been prescient when he warned that the secondary effects doctrine would lead to an "evisceration of First Amendment freedoms."[37]

Government Speech

Another instance of the Rehnquist Court advancing a doctrine to limit free expression challenges is the government speech doctrine, which essentially means that the government has the right to engage in certain expression without infringing on the free speech rights of others. Chief Justice Rehnquist developed the doctrine in *Rust v. Sullivan,* which involved a First Amendment challenge to federal regulations that prohibited recipients of federal funding of public health services to counsel patients about abortion. The challengers asserted that the regulations amounted to an unconstitutional gag order on expression. They contended that the regulations imposed a viewpoint discriminatory condition on government subsidies. The government countered that it could set limits on the programs it chose to fund. Rehnquist sided with the government, writing, "The Government can, without violating the Constitution, selectively fund a program to encourage certain activities it believes to be in the public interest, without at the same time funding an alternative program which seeks to deal with the problem in another way."[38]

The contours of the government speech doctrine have not been fully delineated, but it could be far reaching. The Rehnquist Court has used the government speech doctrine to thwart challenges to a beef-checkoff program, which required beef producers to contribute money for generic beef advertising. "The message set out in the beef promotions is from beginning to end the message established by the Federal Government," Justice Antonin Scalia wrote for the majority in *Johanns v. Livestock Marketing Association.*[39]

An interesting issue percolating in the lower courts concerns whether specialty license plates issued by the government are the government's own speech subject to the government speech doctrine or are considered a mixed form of private and government speech. The Roberts Court will likely explain the contours of the government speech doctrine as John Roberts was the government's attorney who successfully defended the funding program in *Rust v. Sullivan* before the U.S. Supreme Court.

AREAS OF FIRST AMENDMENT EXPANSION

In certain areas the Rehnquist Court showed a willingness to expand First Amendment protections. For example, the Court struck down Congress's first attempt to limit speech on the Internet in *Reno v. ACLU.*[40] In that decision the Court invalidated provisions of the Communications Decency Act that limited the transmission of "patently offensive" and "indecent" online communications. The government had argued that the measures were necessary to protect minors, but the Court rebuffed the measure as an overly vague measure that would infringe on the free speech rights of adults. As the late First Amendment attorney Bruce Ennis said, the Court's decision gave the Internet its "legal birth certificate."[41] The Court also refused to allow the government to enforce Congress's second broad Internet speech restriction, the so-called Child Online Protection Act.[42]

The Rehnquist Court's protection of expression perhaps can be most clearly demonstrated in the area of commercial speech, once defined as speech that does no more than propose a commercial transaction. "This is the area of speech where the Court has clearly advanced First Amendment protection," says O'Neil.

For years, commercial advertising received no First Amendment protection at all. In 1942, the U.S. Supreme Court ruled that entrepreneur F. J. Chrestensen could not print handbills advertising tours of his submarine in New York City. The Court wrote that "the Constitution imposes no such restraint on government as respects purely commercial advertising."[43]

The Court did not grant any First Amendment protection to commercial speech until the mid 1970s, most explicitly in a 1976 case involving the regulation of pharmacy advertising.[44] There the Court realized that consumers' interests in price advertising may be more advanced than political issues. The state had argued that consumers could be harmed by the advertising. The Court responded,

> There is, of course, an alternative to this highly paternalistic approach. That alternative is to assume that this information is not in itself harmful, that people will perceive their own best interests if only they are well enough informed, and that the best means to that end is to open the channels of communication rather than to close them.[45]

The very next year, the Court ruled 5–4 in 1977 that the First Amendment protected two Arizona lawyers' efforts to advertise their prices for low-cost legal services in a newspaper.[46] Justice Rehnquist dissented, as he often did in the early commercial speech cases.

In 1980, the Burger Court reined in the expansion of commercial speech somewhat by establishing a test that subjected regulations of commercial speech to intermediate scrutiny.[47] This meant that commercial speech receives First Amendment protection but that protection is limited. As the Court wrote in an earlier case, commercial speech was relegated to a "subordinate position in the scale of First Amendment values."[48] The so-called *Central Hudson* test established that government officials could freely regulate commercial speech that was false or misleading. If the commercial speech was truthful and nonmisleading, then the government had to show that its regulation directly advanced a substantial government interest in a narrowly tailored way. The net result was that the lower courts upheld many restrictions on commercial speech.

In 1996, the U.S. Supreme Court strengthened protections for commercial speech by adding more bite to the *Central Hudson* test. The Court ruled in *44 Liquormart, Inc. v. Rhode Island* that complete bans on truthful, nonmisleading advertising will seldom pass constitutional muster. "The First Amendment directs us to be especially skeptical of regulations that seek to keep people in the dark for what the government perceives to be their own good," Justice Stevens wrote for a unanimous Court. "That teaching applies equally to state attempts to deprive consumers of accurate information about their chosen products."[49] Ever since *44 Liquormart,* the Court has viewed commercial speech restrictions with greater scrutiny. Relying on this precedent, the Court has invalidated restrictions on gambling advertising,[50] tobacco advertising,[51] and drug compounding advertisements.[52]

AREAS OF REDUCED FIRST AMENDMENT EXPRESSION

In other areas the Rehnquist Court has not proven sensitive to, and has largely avoided, First Amendment claims. A prime example concerns student free expression claims. The Court has agreed to review only one pure public school student free expression case at the secondary level, *Hazelwood School District v. Kuhlmeier.*[53] The case involved a student newspaper produced by the students as part of their journalism class. The students produced two articles that the school principal found objectionable. They dealt with the subjects of teen pregnancy and the impact of divorce on teens. The principal ordered the articles excised from the newspaper, an act that several students found arbitrary and censorial enough that they filed a lawsuit.

The students contended that the principal violated their First Amendment rights under the Warren Court's classic student speech case, *Tinker v. Des Moines Independent Community School District.*[54] In *Tinker,* several Iowa students—including John Tinker, Mary Beth Tinker, and Christopher

Eckhardt—wore black armbands to school to protest U.S. involvement in Vietnam. School officials learned of the impending protest and quickly passed a no-armband rule, even though they allowed students to wear other symbols like Iron Crosses.

The students wore the armbands and were suspended. They took their case to the federal courts, and four years later, in 1969, the U.S. Supreme Court ruled 7–2 in their favor. The Court ruled that students do not shed their free speech rights at the schoolhouse gate and articulated the following standard: School officials may not censor student expression, unless they can reasonably forecast that the student expression will create a substantial disruption or material interference with school activities or an invasion of the rights of others.

The students at East Hazelwood High School had a strong argument under the *Tinker* standard. The school officials could not point to any facts that would show the articles would create any type of disruption. However, school officials prevailed before the Court by a 5–3 vote, with Justice Byron White writing the majority opinion.

White distinguished the students' curricular speech as school sponsored as opposed to the student-initiated speech of the students in *Tinker.* According to White, school officials have broader authority to regulate school-sponsored student expression. The new *Hazelwood* standard provided that "educators do not offend the First Amendment by exercising editorial control over the style and content of student speech in school-sponsored expressive activities so long as their actions are reasonably related to legitimate pedagogical concerns."[55] Such legitimate educational reasons to censor identified by the Court dealt with student speech that included poor grammar, inadequate research, vulgarity, or even student expression that associated the school with matters of political controversy. Three justices, led by Brennan, dissented bitterly. Brennan accused the majority of upholding "brutal censorship."

Brennan and the dissenters may have been right. The majority's *Hazelwood* standard—"reasonably related to legitimate pedagogical concerns"—is remarkably similar to the Rehnquist Court's standard for prison inmates. A year before, the Court, in *Turner v. Safley,* ruled that prison officials do not violate inmates' constitutional rights as long as their actions are "reasonably related to legitimate penological concerns."[56] The Court simply replaced "penological" with "pedagogical" and afforded students the same level of free expression protection as inmates. Student rights advocates deplore the reality that public school students—at least with respect to school-sponsored speech—possess the same level of First Amendment rights as prison inmates.

If any group has received worse treatment from the Rehnquist Court, it is inmates. Early on, Justice Sandra Day O'Connor proclaimed in the case of Missouri inmate Leonard Safley that "prison walls do not form a wall separating prison inmates from the protections of the Constitution."[57] The Court then watered down a standard developed by the Burger Court to the rational basis "reasonably related to a legitimate penological interest" standard. Supreme Court scholar Ronald Collins pointed out that "no one on the current Court seems to like free-speech claims raised by prisoners—they lose unanimously."[58]

PUBLIC EMPLOYEES

The Rehnquist Court continued to adhere to the basic test for public employee free expression claims articulated by the Warren and Burger Courts. In 1969, the Warren Court ruled in *Pickering v. Board of Education* that a public school teacher could not be fired for writing a letter to the editor of his local newspaper critical of school district decisions regarding the allocation of funds.[59] In 1983, the Burger Court ruled in *Connick v. Myers* that district attorney Harry Connick, Sr. (the father of the famous jazz musician) did not violate the First Amendment rights of assistant district attorney Sheila Myers when he terminated her for circulating a critical questionnaire in the office.[60]

The *Pickering-Connick* test provides that employees first must establish that their speech touches on matters of public concern—important political or social issues—as opposed to expression that amounts to more than just a personal grievance. If the employees passes this threshold requirement, the Court then balances the employee's free speech interests against the employer's efficiency interests.

The Rehnquist Court has applied the basic *Pickering-Connick* test in its decisions. For example, in 1987, the Court ruled in *Rankin v. McPherson* that a low-ranking clerical employee could not be dismissed, consistent with the First Amendment, for telling a fellow employee that she wished would-be assassin John Hinckley, Jr. had killed President Ronald Reagan when he shot him. The Court noted that the comment touched on a matter of public concern and was "unrelated to the functioning of the office."[61]

The Court issued an employer-friendly result in 1994 when it ruled in *Waters v. Churchill* that a public employer may fire an employee for speech that the employer reasonably believed was unprotected: "We think employer decisionmaking will not be unduly burdened by having courts look to the facts as the employer reasonably found them to be."[62]

The Court extended the protections of the *Pickering-Connick* test to independent contractors in the case of trash-hauler Keen Umbehr, who is now a practicing attorney in Kansas. The Court voted 7–2—with only Justices Scalia and Thomas dissenting—that the First Amendment limits the ability of government officials to retaliate against independent contractors for their political expression.[63] Umbehr had lost his contract with government officials because he had criticized council members on a variety of subjects. The officials contended that Umbehr had no First Amendment rights as an independent contractor, but the U.S. Supreme Court disagreed. Robert Van Kirk, Umbehr's brother-in-law, argued the case before the U.S. Supreme Court at the age of 30. He was surprised that Chief Justice Rehnquist voted in favor of Umbehr's First Amendment rights: "I had hoped he would be on our side, but certainly, if you were a betting man, you would think the chief would be on the other side, in favor of the government. I do recall, however, that at one point during oral argument the chief threw me a lifeline when I was under attack by Justice Scalia."[64]

CONCLUSION

First Amendment doctrine developed substantially during the nearly 20 years of the Rehnquist Court. The Court extended free speech protection to the Internet, increased protection for commercial speech, and even recognized that nude performance dancing fits within the "outer perimeters" of the First Amendment.

Burt Neuborne writes that "the Rehnquist Court has been among the strongest free speech courts in the nation's history."[65] Even critics of the Rehnquist Court acknowledge that the Court has developed certain First Amendment principles, such as the mantra against viewpoint discrimination. For example, First Amendment expert Jamin Raskin writes, "To give the devil its due … the Rehnquist Court has quite faithfully rejected frontal attacks on offensive speech in public places by way of the criminal and civil law."[66] Still, it maintained strong restrictions over other areas of free expression and developed doctrines, such as secondary effects and government speech, that threaten to curtail the vibrancy of free speech.

The Rehnquist Court's record on free expression remains hard to quantify. "There are a number of areas in which the Rehnquist Court had a mixed record," O'Neil explains. "In many areas of free expression, you don't find real movement in the speech and press areas, probably due to the complexity of the cases. It is very hard to find an outcome or endgame for this Court."

Chief Justice William Rehnquist. Photographed by Dane Penland, Smithsonian Institution. Collection, The Supreme Court Historical Society.

Associate Justice John Paul Stevens. Photographed by Joseph H. Bailey, National Geographic Society. Collection, The Supreme Court Historical Society.

Associate Justice Sandra Day O'Connor. Photographed by Richard Strauss, Smithsonian Institution. Collection, The Supreme Court Historical Society.

Associate Justice Antonin Scalia. Photographed by Joseph D. Lavenburg, National Geographic Society. Collection, The Supreme Court Historical Society.

Associate Justice Anthony Kennedy. Photographed by Robin Reid, Reid Photography. Collection, The Supreme Court Historical Society.

Associate Justice David Souter. Photographed by Joseph H. Bailey, National Geographic Society. Collection, The Supreme Court Historical Society.

Associate Justice Clarence Thomas. Photographed by Hugh Talman, Smithsonian Institution. Collection, The Supreme Court Historical Society.

Associate Justice Ruth Bader Ginsburg. Photographed by Steve Petteway, Supreme Court. Collection, The Supreme Court Historical Society.

Associate Justice Stephen Breyer. Photographed by Steve Petteway, Supreme Court. Collection, The Supreme Court Historical Society.

Chapter 8

CRIMINAL LAW I: HABEAS CORPUS AND CAPITAL PUNISHMENT

> Since 1976, hundreds of juries have sentenced hundreds of persons to death, presumably in the belief that the death penalty in those circumstances is warranted, yet virtually nothing happens except endlessly drawn out legal proceedings such as those adverted to above.... I do not think that this Court can continue to evade some responsibility for this mockery of our criminal justice system.
>
> —Associate Justice William Rehnquist (1981)[1]

> There is something to be said for popular abolition of the death penalty; there is nothing to be said for its incremental abolition by this Court.
>
> —Justice Antonin Scalia (2002)[2]

When William Rehnquist took the mantle of chief justice, many feared of the coming "Rehnquisition"—a dramatic curtailment of individual rights in the criminal justice arena. There was some evidence to support such fears. For years Rehnquist had railed against the excesses of the Warren Court. He criticized *Mapp v. Ohio*[3] when the Court extended the exclusionary rule to the states. He despised *Miranda v. Arizona*,[4] the decision that invalidated criminal confessions unless defendants were clearly informed of their rights. He was not particularly fond of *Gideon v. Wainwright*,[5] which had extended the right to counsel to all state criminal defendants facing felony charges.

President Richard Nixon appointed Rehnquist with the clear expectation that he would be an excellent "law and order" judge—a judge that would enable Nixon to fulfill a campaign promise to rein in the liberal Warren Court. Rehnquist's history must have given the president comfort, for Rehnquist had publicly criticized the Warren Court in print, campaigned for the conservative Barry Goldwater in the 1964 presidential campaign, and worked as an assistant attorney general in the Nixon administration from 1969 to 1971 before his nomination as an associate justice. To Nixon, Rehnquist could be trusted to be a perfect law and order justice to restore order to the Court. Professor Stephen Smith aptly wrote, "If there was a single issue that gave rise to the Rehnquist Court, it was criminal procedure."[6]

In many ways Rehnquist did not disappoint the pro-law-enforcement community for much of his career. Early in his tenure, he earned the moniker "the Lone Ranger" for his solo dissents, many of them in criminal cases. In *Green v. Georgia* the Court ruled 8–1 that capital defendant Roosevelt Green, Jr. was entitled to a new sentencing hearing because a trial judge excluded the testimony of a witness who said that Green's codefendant admitted committing the murder by himself.[7] The state charged Green and Carzell Moore with abducting, raping, and killing a store clerk. The state tried Moore first and offered the testimony of one of Moore's friends. This friend said that Moore admitted that he sent Green on an errand after the abduction and then proceeded to kill the store clerk by himself.

Green sought to introduce this testimony, but the trial judge disallowed it under a state evidence rule limiting hearsay. Eight members of the Court in a per curiam opinion wrote that the exclusion of this evidence violated due process. The Court reasoned that the state considered this testimony "sufficiently reliable" to use it against Moore, writing that "in these unique circumstances, the hearsay rule may not be applied mechanistically to defeat the ends of justice."[8]

Justice Rehnquist fired his angry solo dissent, accusing the Court of "embalming the law of evidence in the Due Process Clause of the Fourteenth Amendment to the United States Constitution." He wrote that the Constitution does not empower the Supreme Court to "supersede a State's code of evidence because its application in a particular situation would defeat what this Court conceives to be 'the ends of justice.'"[9]

Some observers interpreted Rehnquist's opinion as seeming not to care about the possibility that Roosevelt Green really did not fire a fatal shot at the store clerk. Instead, he focused on the Court not overstepping its constitutional bounds and invading the state's criminal law process.

In *Carter v. Kentucky* the U.S. Supreme Court ruled 8–1 that state trial court judges have a "constitutional obligation" to instruct juries that they must draw no adverse inferences when a defendant declines to testify on his own behalf.[10] The Fifth Amendment provides that no person be "compelled in any criminal case to be a witness against himself." The Warren Court extended this principle to the states in *Malloy v. Hogan* in 1964 and then ruled a year later in *Griffin v. California* that state juries cannot draw unreasonable inferences from a defendant's refusal to testify.[11]

The specific issue in the case of burglary defendant Lonnie Jo Carter was whether he had a constitutional right to have a trial judge issue a specific instruction to jurors that they cannot draw a negative inference from a defendant's refusal to testify. Carter decided not to testify because of his past felony convictions. His attorney had requested a "no adverse instruction" but was denied. Carter was convicted and later sentenced as a recidivist offender to 20 years.

The Court majority, in an opinion by Justice Potter Stewart, reversed Carter's conviction, holding that trial judges have a "constitutional obligation" to issue such instructions on the request of defense attorneys. Otherwise, according to the Court, many jurors will view the Fifth Amendment privilege as a "shelter for wrongdoers" and use it against defendants.

Justice Rehnquist dissented, saying that the Court had strayed far beyond the Warren Court decisions in *Malloy* and *Griffin.* He quoted approvingly from Justice Stewart's dissent in *Griffin* that "the formulation of procedural rules to govern the administration of criminal justice in the various States is properly a matter of local concern."[12]

In *Michigan v. Tyler* the U.S. Supreme Court ruled 8–1 that police officers can enter premises after a fire for a reasonable amount of time to determine the fire's cause. The Court also ruled that additional efforts to determine the cause of the fire at the location require the police to obtain a warrant based on probable cause.[13] Once again, Justice Rehnquist acted as "Lone Ranger," filing a solitary dissent. According to Rehnquist, the subsequent searches of the premises were reasonable within the meaning of the Fourth Amendment.

Sometimes Rehnquist's solitary dissents indicated a deep disgust with the state of the current law. His denial of certiorari in *Coleman v. Balkcom* is a good example. Wayne Carl Coleman had petitioned the U.S. Supreme Court to review his habeas corpus appeal of his capital crime allegedly committed years earlier. The Court denied review, but Rehnquist voted to hear the case. Rehnquist explained that he voted to hear the case not out of a concern for the constitutional rights of defendant Coleman but because of deep concerns he had about the misuse and length of habeas appeals. He wrote that "the case raises significant issues about the administration of capital punishment statutes in this country, and reflects the increasing tendency to postpone or delay the enforcement of those constitutionally valid statutes."[14]

Rehnquist questioned whether the existing criminal justice system was served by allowing capital defendants to engage in "protracted litigation" that thwarted the will of the people to enforce the death penalty in many states. He wrote,

> I do not think this Court can continue to evade some responsibility for his mockery of our criminal justice system. Perhaps out of a desire to avoid even the possibility of a "Bloody Assizes," this Court and the lower federal courts have converted the constitutional limits upon the imposition of the death penalty by the States and the Federal Government into arcane niceties which parallel the equity court practices described in Charles Dickens' "Bleak House." Even though we have upheld the constitutionality of capital punishment statutes, I fear that by our recent actions we have mistakenly sent a signal to the lower state and federal courts that the actual imposition of the death sentence is to be avoided at all costs.[15]

HABEAS CORPUS

Rehnquist managed to convince the majority of the Court to limit habeas corpus appeals. This probably amounted to the chief justice's greatest triumph in the criminal justice arena. In criminal cases, defendants first go through the standard trial and appeals process. This is known as the direct appeal phase. Once the direct appeal phase ends, defendants must resort to collateral attacks on their convictions, arguing that their constitutional rights were violated somewhere in the underlying trial process. This postconviction, or habeas, process relies on habeas corpus, the Latin term meaning "you have the body." In essence, habeas defendants allege that their confinement is unlawful because their convictions were tainted by unconstitutional processes or errors.

Over the years, Rehnquist moved the Court in his direction. Professor Joseph Hoffman writes that "federal habeas law today largely reflects the Rehnquistian vision of strictly limited federal court review of state criminal convictions."[16] Rehnquist made his presence felt when he wrote the Burger Court's opinion in *Wainwright v. Sykes.*[17] The decision dealt with whether convicted Florida inmate Larry Sykes was entitled to a new trial years later because his statements to police should have been inadmissible because he did not make them voluntarily. The problem was that Sykes's original trial counsel failed to object to the use of his inculpatory statements at trial or on direct appeal. Sykes first made this argument in state postconviction proceedings. After that failed, Sykes filed a federal habeas corpus action, seeking a new trial.

Rehnquist often viewed the habeas process as an unwarranted attack on the state court process. To Rehnquist, Sykes could not collaterally raise this claim because he and his counsel had defaulted on the issue by not raising an objection to the admissibility of this evidence at trial. Florida law had a "contemporaneous objection rule," which required defendants to make their objections in a timely fashion at trial.

To Rehnquist, this Florida law stood as an independent and adequate state procedural ground immune from collateral review by federal courts. A defendant could bypass this hurdle only be meeting a tough "cause and prejudice" standard. Under this test, a defendant must establish cause for failing to object in a timely manner at trial and then also show that this prejudiced his constitutional rights. Sykes lost his case because, in the words of Rehnquist, he "has advanced no explanation whatsoever for his failure to object at trial."[18]

The Rehnquist Court continued this trend of limiting habeas review in its decisions. In *Teague v. Lane* the Court rejected the habeas claims of an African American defendant who claimed that the prosecutor in his case used his peremptory challenges to dismiss prospective African American jurors.[19] First, the Court determined that the defendant was not entitled to the retroactive benefit of a more recent Supreme Court case that prohibited the racially discriminatory use of peremptory challenges in individual trials because this new case had been decided two and a half years after the defendant's trial.

The Court also denied his claims even under the U.S. Supreme Court's older "cause and prejudice" standard because he failed to meet it. Justice O'Connor wrote in her plurality opinion that "if a defendant fails to comply with state procedural rules and is barred from litigating a particular constitutional claim in state court, the claim can be considered on federal habeas only if the defendant shows cause for the default and actual prejudice resulting therefrom."[20] In her opinion she also announced a rule that would further limit the reach of federal habeas corpus claims: "New constitutional rules of criminal procedure will not be applicable to those cases which have become final before the new rules are announced."[21]

Rehnquist affected another major change in habeas law in the 1993 decision *Brecht v. Abrahamson.*[22] The case involved murder charges in Wisconsin against defendant Todd Brecht, convicted of shooting his brother-in-law. Brecht contended that the shooting was an accident, but he apparently did not offer this defense immediately after the shooting, but instead fled the scene. During the trial the prosecution repeatedly mentioned Brecht's silence concerning the "accidental shooting" defense. After losing his direct appeals, Brecht filed a habeas claim in federal court, contending that the reference to his silence after arrest violated his constitutional rights. He contended that this was not harmless error. He argued that the government had to prove that the error was harmless beyond a reasonable doubt, a very high burden of proof.

Writing for a five-member majority, Rehnquist reasoned that the "harmless error beyond a reasonable doubt" standard should not apply in habeas claims. To do so would undermine the state's interest in the finality of convictions. Instead, Rehnquist applied a different test—whether the error "had substantial and injurious effect or influence in determining the jury's verdict." Under this standard, the criminal defendant has the burden of proof to establish that any trial error caused actual prejudice.

Guided by the chief justice, the Supreme Court issued another habeas opinion in a death penalty case that attracted great controversy and commentary. It involved a Texas inmate, Leonel Herrera, who had confessed by writing to the murder of two police officers. However, years later, Herrera asserted that the actual culprit was his now-dead brother, not him. The testimony of several witnesses verified his claim.

However, the Court rejected his habeas claim by a 6–3 vote in *Herrera v. Collins.*[23] Chief Justice Rehnquist wrote that actual claims of innocence do not entitle a defendant to a new hearing unless he or she can show evidence of an "independent constitutional violation in the underlying state criminal proceeding."[24]

A frequent question that arises in habeas corpus cases concerns the adequacy of the underlying trial counsel. Many people end up on death row in part because they received poor legal representation. The complexity of habeas corpus law would seem to indicate that inmates would need expert legal representation. Many do not receive it, and the Rehnquist Court has ruled that even in capital cases, habeas petitioners are not constitutionally entitled to a lawyer in state postconviction proceedings: "The additional safeguards imposed by the Eighth Amendment or the Due Process Clause at the trial stage of a capital case are, we think, sufficient to assure the reliability of the process by which the death penalty is imposed."[25]

Rehnquist sought to change the law on habeas corpus not only in his opinions, but also through his administrative powers as chief justice. In 1988, he formed the Ad Hoc Committee on Federal Habeas Corpus in Capital Cases, which was chaired by retired justice Lewis F. Powell, Jr. The committee's 1989 report noted that "society is rightfully entitled to have the penalty prescribed by law carried out without unreasonable delay." Rehnquist was challenged by 14 federal judges who sat on the 27-member Judicial Conference of the United States. These judges complained that Rehnquist acted too quickly without their approval in sending the proposals in the Powell report on to the Senate Judiciary Committee.[26]

The Rehnquist Court often emphasized finality and federalism in its habeas corpus decisions. Most famously, Justice O'Connor opened her 1991 opinion in the case of *Coleman v. Thompson* with the following words: "This is a case about federalism. It concerns the respect that federal courts owe the States and the States' procedural rules when reviewing the claims of state prisoners in federal habeas corpus."[27] In that case the Court denied federal habeas review because one of Coleman's attorneys in his state postconviction proceedings mailed his notice of appeal one day too late. Three justices—Blackmun, Marshall, and Stevens—dissented. Blackmun, who a few years later would publicly announce that he no longer supported the death penalty, accused the majority of "creating a Byzantine morass of arbitrary, unnecessary and unjustifiable impediments to the vindication of federal rights."[28]

The Supreme Court's decision led to Coleman's execution the next year, in 1992. The case attracted great attention in the anti-death-penalty community as many believed the Court had ignored the possibility that Roger Coleman was an innocent man. At his execution, as his last words, Coleman uttered, "Tonight you are going to execute an innocent man."

Before condemning O'Connor and the majority of the Rehnquist Court, an important postscript recently surfaced. In 2006, Virginia governor Mark Warner ordered DNA tests for Coleman's body, which proved he in fact was the rapist and murderer.[29] The anti-death-penalty community felt that Coleman had betrayed them.

Rehnquist's vision of a limited habeas right was assisted greatly by Congress, which in 1996 passed the Antiterrorism and Effective Death Penalty Act of 1996 (AEDPA). This law imposed stricter time limits for filing federal habeas claims and imposed a stricter standard of review on petitioners who seek to overturn state court factual findings. The AEDPA provides that state factual findings are presumptively correct and the petitioner can only overcome such a presumption by clear and convincing evidence. Furthermore, the law provides that a petitioner is only entitled to relief if he can show that the state court decision "involved an unreasonable application, of clearly established Federal law." Professor Hoffman explains that "AEDPA completed the rewrite of federal habeas corpus begun by Rehnquist in the 1970s … the AEDPA gave Rehnquist almost everything he could possibly have asked for."[30]

Professor Craig Bradley, a nationally respected expert on criminal law and former Rehnquist law clerk, says that limiting habeas corpus was Rehnquist's "most successful venture, certainly in the criminal area, and probably anywhere."[31]

It should be noted, though, that even though the Rehnquist Court established high hurdles for a habeas petitioner, under an egregious set of facts, the Court would grant habeas relief to a defendant. In *Banks v. Dretke* the U.S. Supreme Court ordered a federal hearing for Delma Banks, Jr., a Texas inmate who was sentenced to death in a Texas trial court where prosecutors knowingly concealed key evidence about an informant and then continued to conceal the fact that the witness was a paid police informant with credibility issues.[32] The Court, including Chief Justice Rehnquist, ruled in favor of Banks, finding that he had met the "cause and prejudice" standard by showing that the Texas prosecutors continued to engage in a pattern of deceit by not revealing exculpatory information.

CAPITAL PUNISHMENT

Capital punishment remains intricately intertwined with habeas jurisprudence because many death row inmates file habeas petitions, desperately seeking relief from the ultimate punishment. The death penalty continues in 38 states, with a few states, such as Texas and Virginia, regularly conducting executions.

The Burger Court struggled with capital punishment, most famously in the 1972 decision *Furman v. Georgia.*[33] With all nine justices writing separately the Court in effect invalidated the death penalty nationwide, with five justices striking down several states' death penalty statutes. Justices William Brennan, Thurgood Marshall, and William Douglas invalidated the death penalty generally, while Justices Potter Stewart and Byron White wrote narrower opinions, stressing the randomness by which defendants that commit murder receive the death penalty. Stewart stressed that juries were not given adequate guidance in state law to decide the important question of ultimate punishment. He wrote that "these death sentences are cruel and unusual in the same way that being struck by lightning is cruel and unusual."[34] Justice Rehnquist wrote a short dissenting opinion, questioning the Supreme Court's ability to thwart the will of the people as expressed through their legislatures. He wrote that "this decision holding unconstitutional capital punishment is not an act of judgment, but rather an act of will."[35]

For more than four years, not a single inmate was executed in the United States. State legislatures responded to the *Furman* decision by passing new statutes that gave more guidance to jurors as to which defendants should receive the death penalty and by bifurcating the trial into separate determinations of guilt and punishment. Newly revised laws listed aggravating and mitigating factors that jurors should consider in their sentencing decisions. Then, in *Gregg v. Georgia,* the Burger Court reinstated capital punishment by voting 7–2 to uphold Georgia's revised death penalty law.[36]

The Rehnquist Court never overruled *Gregg,* banning the death penalty as a violation of the Eighth Amendment's command against "cruel and unusual punishment." Instead, the Rehnquist Court initially issued many important decisions rejecting various challenges to the death penalty. In the later years of the Rehnquist Court, however, the Court reversed course on more than one issue and began to chip away at the death penalty for certain types of defendants.

A Pro-Death-Penalty Court

Early in its tenure, the Rehnquist Court rejected an important challenge to the imposition of the death penalty. The most famous of these cases involved an African American Georgia inmate named Warren McCleskey, who was convicted of murdering a white police officer. McCleskey's lawyers mounted a serious attack on the fairness of the death penalty in Georgia during the late 1970s when McCleskey was first prosecuted.

McCleskey argued that his death sentence should be overturned because the capital punishment scheme in Georgia was infected with racial bias. His attorneys relied on the so-called Baldus study conducted by several law professors, including David C. Baldus. The study established significant race-of-the-victim discrimination in that those who killed white victims were far more likely to be charged with the death penalty than those who killed nonwhite victims. The study showed that black defendants who killed white victims—people like Warren McCleskey—were the most likely to be charged with the ultimate punishment.

The Rehnquist Court rejected McCleskey's claims by a narrow 5–4 vote in *McCleskey v. Kemp*. Justice Lewis Powell wrote for the majority that McCleskey's claims under the equal protection clause must fail because he failed to show evidence of specific discriminatory intent in his case by the prosecutors. "He offers no evidence specific to his own case that would support an inference that racial considerations played a part in his sentence," Powell wrote. "Instead, he relies solely on the Baldus study."[37]

The majority did not discredit the Baldus study but reasoned that it was legally insufficient to invalidate McCleskey's death sentence. "At most, the Baldus study indicates a discrepancy that appears to correlate with race," Powell wrote. "Apparent disparities in sentencing are an inevitable part of our criminal justice system."[38]

Justices Brennan, Marshall, Stevens, and Blackmun dissented with all but Marshall, writing opinions. In his dissenting opinion Blackmun wrote, "The Court today sanctions the execution of a man despite his presentation of evidence that establishes a constitutionally intolerable level of racially based discrimination leading to the imposition of his death sentence."[39]

The Rehnquist Court also changed American jurisprudence with respect to victims' rights in *Payne v. Tennessee*.[40] In two earlier decisions the

Rehnquist Court had disallowed victim impact testimony as a violation of a defendant's Eighth Amendment rights.[41] The Court found such a constitutional violation because it determined that the victim impact statements would "inflame the jury" and "divert it from deciding the case on the relevant evidence concerning the defendant and the crime."[42]

Chief Justice Rehnquist managed to overrule those two decisions in the capital case of defendant Pervis Tyrone Payne, convicted of murdering a woman and her two-year-old daughter. "Victim impact evidence is simply another form or method of informing the sentencing authority about the specific harm caused by the crime in question, evidence of a general type long considered by sentencing authorities," Rehnquist wrote.[43]

"*Payne v. Tennessee* was the only case in which the Court overruled a death penalty case that had favored a criminal defendant," says Kent Scheidegger, legal director for the pro-death-penalty Criminal Justice Legal Foundation.[44]

CAPITAL PUNISHMENT FOR JUVENILES AND MENTALLY RETARDED INMATES

The Rehnquist Court had ruled in *Thompson v. Oklahoma* that it violates the Eighth Amendment to execute criminal defendants who commit murder at age 15. The next year, in 1989, the Court upheld the death sentence for criminal defendants in Kentucky and Missouri who committed murder when they were 17 and 16. The Court determined 5–4 in *Stanford v. Kentucky* that juveniles who were 16 and 17 could be executed. Justice Scalia noted in his plurality opinion that a majority of the states that authorized capital punishment allowed it for defendants 16 years of age and older.[45] Because of this, the inmates were unable to establish a "national consensus" against the death penalty for juveniles. Scalia concluded that there was "neither a historical nor a modern societal consensus forbidding the imposition of capital punishment on any person who murders at 16 or 17 years of age."[46]

Justices Brennan, Marshall, Blackmun, and Stevens dissented, with Brennan writing the lead dissent. "I believe that to take the life of a person as punishment for a crime committed when below the age of 18 is cruel and unusual and hence is prohibited by the Eighth Amendment," he wrote.[47]

The same day as its *Stanford* decision, the Rehnquist Court also decided a capital case involving mentally retarded inmate John Penry in *Penry v. Lynaugh*.[48] The Court invalidated Penry's death sentence because the jury was not allowed to take proper account of Penry's mental retardation as a mitigating factor in the sentencing determination. However, a bare majority of the Court also decided that there is no categorical prohibition against executing mentally retarded inmates. The Court focused on the fact that only state, Georgia, had a statute forbidding the execution of mentally retarded inmates.

There seemed to be little hope for opponents of capital punishment as noted death penalty opponents William Brennan, Thurgood Marshall, and Harry Blackmun had left the Rehnquist Court. Over the course of his career, Blackmun underwent a complete metamorphosis on the question of the death penalty. Originally a supporter of the death penalty with his dissent in *Furman,* he often sided with Rehnquist and Burger in criminal justice cases. Over the course of his tenure, Blackmun steadily moved to the left. Though known more for *Roe v. Wade,* Blackmun attracted great attention with one of his last opinions, a dissent from a denial of certiorari in a death penalty case in 1994, *Callins v. Collins.*[49] There Blackmun publicly proclaimed his opposition to the death penalty, writing, "From this day forward, I shall no longer tinker with the machinery of death." As veteran Supreme Court reporter and Blackmun biographer Linda Greenhouse wrote, "It became one of the best-known lines ever to be attached to his name."[50]

The only remaining dissenter from *Stanford* and *Penry* was the Court's oldest justice, John Paul Stevens. Chief Justice William Rehnquist, Antonin Scalia, Sandra Day O'Connor, and Anthony Kennedy remained from the majority. Justice Clarence Thomas certainly would not vote to invalidate the death penalty. That left a seemingly solid majority of five justices to counter Stevens, Breyer, Ginsburg, and Souter.

However, in 2002 and 2005 the Rehnquist Court issued a pair of divided decisions, overruling *Stanford* and *Penry.* In *Roper v. Simmons* the Court ruled 5–4 that the Eighth Amendment forbids the execution of those who commit murder as juveniles.[51] A few years earlier, in *Atkins v. Virginia,* the Court ruled 6–3 that mentally retarded inmates could not be executed.[52] Justice O'Connor switched sides on the mentally retarded issue, while Justice Kennedy had switched sides on both the mentally retarded and juvenile issues.

In *Atkins* Justice Stevens noted a "dramatic shift in the state legislative landscape."[53] Since 1989, 16 more states had passed laws that banned the execution of mentally retarded inmates, and only five states had executed a mentally retarded inmate. To Stevens, this had created a "national consensus" against the practice. In a footnote Stevens also noted that internationally, the execution of mentally retarded inmates was a very rare practice: "Within the world community, the imposition of the death penalty for crimes committed by inmates with mental retardation is overwhelmingly disapproved."[54] He also cited the views of religious organizations and public opinion polls.

This attracted the ire of the dissenters, including Chief Justice Rehnquist, who questioned the relevance of such matters. He wrote that there are "defects" in the Court's decision to rely on such information in determining the constitutional question. He wrote that the "work product of legislatures and sentencing jury determinations … are the only objective indicia of contemporary values firmly supported by our precedents."

Justice Scalia was even more blunt in his assessment of the majority's opinion, writing, "Seldom has an opinion of this Court rested so obviously upon nothing but the personal views of its members." He accused the majority of the "miraculous extracting" of a national consensus because 18 states forbade the execution of mentally retarded inmates: "That bare number of states alone—18—should be enough to convince any reasonable person that no 'national consensus' exists."

The Court overruled another of its death penalty decisions a few terms later in the case of Christopher Simmons, a Missouri inmate who killed a couple when he was 17.[55] This time, five justices ruled that the Eighth Amendment also prohibited the execution of those who committed murders when they were under 18. Kennedy noted that since its decision in *Stanford,* five more states prohibited the execution of juvenile murderers, and there was a national and international trend toward abolishing such executions. Kennedy was more explicit in his reliance on the laws and practices of other countries. While Stevens confined such notions to a footnote in *Atkins,* Kennedy devoted a significant portion of his opinion to it.

He noted that the laws of other countries were relevant in determining whether a certain practice violated "evolving standards of decency"—long an important standard in Eighth Amendment cases since at least 1958. He cited Article 37 of the United Nations Convention on the Rights of the Child, which prohibited such executions, and added that only seven other countries—Iran, Pakistan, Saudia Arabia, Yemen, Nigeria, the Democratic Republic of the Congo, and China—had executed a juvenile since 1990. "It is proper that we acknowledge the overwhelming weight of international opinion against the juvenile death penalty," he wrote. "The opinion of the world community, while not controlling, does provide respected and significant confirmation for our own conclusions."

Kennedy noted that there were three key differences between juveniles and adults, including the fact that juveniles were less mature, more susceptible to negative influences, and had less-developed characters. "These differences render suspect any conclusion that a juvenile falls among the worst offenders," he wrote.

Scalia produced another of his memorable, stinging dissents. He took Kennedy to task for allowing the Court to exercise its subjective judgment and rely on the views of foreign nations. He wrote that the meaning of the

Eighth Amendment should not rest on the "subjective views of five members of the Court and like-minded foreigners." "Though the views of our citizens are essentially irrelevant to the Court's decision today, the views of other countries and the so-called international community take center stage," he proclaimed. Scalia thundered that the view that the United States should conform to the laws of other countries should be "rejected out of hand."

CONCLUSION

On balance, it is hard to disagree with the assessment offered by Harvard law professor Charles Ogletree: "There is little doubt that the Rehnquist Court is particularly conservative in the field of criminal law and has strongly endorsed the crime control model of criminal justice."[56]

This development was clearly shown by the Court's restriction of habeas corpus petitions by inmates. Through a series of decisions Chief Justice Rehnquist emphasized federalism and finality rather than offering inmates endless rounds of litigation to serve as a safety valve over potentially faulty procedures in state court criminal trials. Rehnquist achieved his vision partly through judicial decisions and partly through federal legislation that further limited the reach of habeas petitions.

The conservative nature of the Rehnquist Court also surfaced early through a series of decisions. "I see the lasting legacy of the Rehnquist Court as bringing the criminal law more into balance, as it had become imbalanced in favor of criminal defendants," says Scheidegger. "The Court was particularly effective in bringing more balance in the areas of habeas corpus and capital punishment."[57]

However, the later Rehnquist Court changed course and in two recent decisions invalidated the death penalty for inmates who are mentally retarded and for those who committed their crimes as juveniles. The Court majority even emphasized the laws of other countries, using those international examples as relevant in its constitutional analysis. It is an open question whether such decisions will survive the Roberts Court and its new appointees of former solicitor general Chief Justice John G. Roberts, Jr. and former federal prosecutor Samuel A. Alito, Jr.

Chapter 9

CRIMINAL LAW II: A CONSERVATIVE COURT WITH SOME SURPRISES

> So I felt that at the time I came to the Court, the boat was kind of heeling over in one direction. Interpreting my oath as I saw it, I felt that my job was, where those sort of situations arose, to kind of lean the other way.
>
> —Associate Justice William Rehnquist (1975)[1]

For much of his career William Rehnquist had railed against the excesses of the Warren Court's criminal procedure revolution. He harbored a particular distaste for that Court's controversial 1966 decision in *Miranda v. Arizona,* an opinion that arose out of the state where he had built his legal career.[2] His judicial career showed that he likely agreed with the view of President Reagan's attorney general, Edwin Meese, who termed *Miranda* an "infamous" decision in 1985, one year before Rehnquist assumed the mantle of chief justice.[3]

In *Miranda* the Warren Court invalidated the confession of Ernesto Miranda by a single vote. Phoenix police had arrested Miranda in 1963 on suspicion of robbery. During a two-hour interrogation Miranda confessed to raping and kidnapping a young woman. A jury convicted Miranda, and a judge sentenced him to 20 years in prison. However, the Supreme Court invalidated his conviction, finding that his Fifth Amendment rights against self-incrimination had been violated because he had not been informed of his constitutional rights.

Chief Justice Warren wrote that law enforcement officials could not use statements obtained from a police interrogation unless they demonstrate "the use of procedural safeguards effective to secure the privilege against self-incrimination."[4] The Court then articulated those "procedural safeguards" that became known in popular culture as the Miranda warnings. These require police to inform suspects prior to questioning (1) of their right to remain silent; (2) that any statements they make can be used against them in a court of law; (3) that they have the right to have an attorney present during questioning; and (4) that if they cannot afford an attorney, one will be provided to them. If law enforcement officials fail to provide these procedural safeguards, the Court said that evidence obtained during such interrogations cannot be used against the suspect.[5]

In dissent, Justice John Marshall Harlan warned that the decision "represents poor constitutional law" and would have harmful consequences.[6] Rehnquist believed that Justice Harlan's assessment was accurate. For much of his career Rehnquist sought to limit the *Miranda* decision. In *Michigan v. Tucker* Rehnquist wrote an opinion that described the *Miranda* rights as "prophylactic standards" rather than constitutional rules.[7] In that decision the Burger Court ruled that prosecutors could use statements made by a criminal defendant when—before the *Miranda* case was decided—he was warned of some of his rights, but not that he had a right to appointed counsel if he could not afford an attorney.

In *New York v. Quarles* Rehnquist created a "public safety" exception to *Miranda,* ruling that the police did not violate a suspect's constitutional rights when they asked him questions about a recently abandoned weapon before reading the defendant his *Miranda* rights.[8] Rehnquist wrote that *Miranda* does not "require that it be applied in all its rigor to a situation in which police officers ask questions reasonably prompted by a concern for the public safety."[9]

As an associate and chief justice, Rehnquist had presided over a Court that had created exceptions and limited the reach of the famous or infamous *Miranda* decision. Thus when the Court was asked to overrule *Miranda* in 2000, *Miranda*'s demise seemed imminent. The case arose after Charles Thomas Dickerson was charged with bank robbery and other related charges. Before trial, Dickerson contended that the Federal Bureau of Investigation had interrogated him without reading him his *Miranda* rights. A federal district court agreed with Dickerson and suppressed his statements implicating himself. On appeal the conservative Fourth U.S. Circuit Court of Appeals reversed the suppression of Dickerson's statements based on a little-used 1968 federal law that Congress had passed in response to the *Miranda* decision. The 1968 federal law provided that confessions were admissible as long as, under the totality of the circumstances, they were voluntary. This was the standard used in federal and state courts before the *Miranda* decision. In effect, Congress had passed a law that had legislatively overruled *Miranda.*

On the morning of June 26, 2000, in the Supreme Court, when Chief Justice Rehnquist announced that he was the author of the Court's majority opinion in *Dickerson v. United States,*[10] Linda Greenhouse recalled that it was "safe to assume nearly everyone in the courtroom believed they were about to hear the explanation for a decision upholding 3501 [the federal law] and in effect overruling Miranda."[11] But the courtroom audience was in for what Greenhouse termed a "surprise, to say the least" because Chief Justice Rehnquist had authored a 7–2 opinion upholding *Miranda.*[12]

Chief Justice Rehnquist ruled that Congress had overstepped its bounds in legislatively overruling a decision by the U.S. Supreme Court. He wrote that "Congress may not legislatively supersede our decisions interpreting and applying the Constitution."[13] He also rejected the temptation to overrule *Miranda,* writing that the decision "has become embedded in routine police practice to the point where the warnings have become part of our national culture."[14] While he may have disliked *Miranda,* protection of judicial supremacy was even more important to the chief justice, whose hero was John Marshall.

Only Justices Scalia and Thomas dissented. In his characteristic style Scalia warned that the Court had turned *Miranda* "from a milestone of judicial overreaching into the very Cheops' Pyramid (or perhaps the Sphinx would be a better analogue) of judicial arrogance."[15] To him, the decision represented an example of the Court imposing "extraconstitutional constraints upon Congress and the States."[16]

"I was a little surprised that Chief Justice Rehnquist not only ruled in our favor but also wrote the opinion," said attorney James W. Hundley from Fairfax, Virginia, who argued the case for Dickerson. "Rehnquist had written several opinions that had weakened some of the protections of *Miranda.* We had thought our best-case scenario was a 6–3 victory with Rehnquist in dissent."[17]

"Even though Rehnquist was a conservative jurist, he always believed in the power that came with an independent judiciary, and he was not about to write an opinion that would limit the independence of the judiciary," Hundley explained. "His point was that only the Court can overrule *Miranda.*"[18]

Critics of the Rehnquist Court reply that the chief justice did not need to overrule *Miranda* because he had, over the course of nearly three decades, already crippled the reach of the decision through a variety of exceptions and limitations. Harvard law professor Charles Ogletree wrote that "the Rehnquist Court has burdened the assertion of Miranda rights with a variety of procedural impediments."[19] Critics also point out that Rehnquist himself retreated a bit from *Dickerson* in the 2004 decision *United States v. Patane.* In that decision the Court ruled 5–4 that failure to give a suspect his Miranda warnings does not require the suppression of a pistol that was found as a result of the suspect's voluntary statements given before he was Mirandized. Rehnquist signed on to Justice Thomas's plurality opinion that once again referred to *Miranda* as dealing with "prophylactic rules" and wrote that "nothing in *Dickerson* calls into question our continued insistence that the closest possible fit be maintained between the Self-Incrimination Clause and any rule designed to protect it."[20] As respected criminal law professor Yale Kamisar writes, "In a post-Dickerson confession case, the two dissenters in Dickerson and the author of the majority opinion in Dickerson make strange bedfellows."[21] Kamisar concludes that Rehnquist's repeated "flip-flopping" on *Miranda* "has probably contributed more to the confusion over Miranda than any other member of the Court."[22]

The Rehnquist Court certainly was no friend to criminal defendants. The Court expanded the reach of numerous principles—such as harmless error and good faith exceptions to the exclusionary rule—that favored law enforcement over the accused. The Court upheld state three-strikes rules that led to life imprisonment for defendants convicted of stealing golf clubs and videotapes.[23] It rejected a host of constitutional challenges to state databases in Alaska[24] and Connecticut[25] that grouped all types of sex offenders into a general category and subjected them to restrictions years after their sentences had been served. But the Rehnquist Court was not a one-way ratchet of repression. It was far more balanced than many commentators acknowledge. A prime example is the Court's Fourth Amendment jurisprudence.

FOURTH AMENDMENT

The Fourth Amendment prohibits unreasonable searches and seizures. It generally requires law enforcement officials to obtain a warrant backed by probable cause before a search or seizure. Over the years the Court has recognized numerous exceptions to the warrant requirement, such as exigent (emergency circumstances), the plain view doctrine, consent, stop and frisk pat-downs, and numerous others. The Court also has to determine whether police conduct even constitutes a search or seizure in the first place. For example, police officers have the right to come up to citizens and ask them questions without implicating the Fourth Amendment, as long as the persons reasonably believe they are free to leave.

In many ways the Rehnquist Court curtailed Fourth Amendment freedoms. For example, the Court generally expanded the good faith exception to the exclusionary rule. The exclusionary rule provides that unlawfully obtained evidence must be excluded from a defendant's trial. It serves the primary purpose of deterring unlawful conduct by the police, but it comes with a price. In the words of Benjamin Cardozo, before he became a member of the U.S. Supreme Court, the "criminal goes free because the constable has blundered."

In 1984, the Burger Court created an exception to the exclusionary rule called the "good faith" exception. It ruled in *U.S. v. Leon* that evidence does not have to be excluded, even if courts later find a constitutional violation, if the officer reasonably relied in good faith on the search being permissibly sanctioned by a neutral magistrate.[26] The *Leon* case afforded Chief Justice Burger, a longtime critic of the exclusionary rule, to limit its reach: "The substantial social costs exacted by the exclusionary rule for the vindication of Fourth Amendment rights have long been a source of concern."[27]

The Rehnquist Court expanded the reach of the *Leon* good faith exception in several cases. In *Illinois v. Krull* the Rehnquist Court ruled that the exclusionary rule did not apply when a law enforcement official relied on a state statute that authorized warrantless searches, even though the statute was subsequently declared unconstitutional.[28] "Unless a statute is clearly unconstitutional, an officer cannot be expected to question the judgment of the legislature that passed the law," Justice Blackmun wrote for the Court.[29] He reasoned that the deterrent rationale behind the exclusionary rule has no force because the officer reasonably believes he was acting lawfully. It is not the officer's fault that a court later determines the law to be unconstitutional.

In *Arizona v. Evans* the Court ruled 6–3 that the exclusionary rule did not prohibit the introduction of evidence seized from a person after an arrest that was based on a clerical, computer error. The Court held that evidence seized in violation of the Fourth Amendment as result of clerical errors of court employees, causing incorrect computer records, fell within the *Leon* good faith exception to the exclusionary rule. The Court noted that "the exclusionary rule was historically designed as a means of deterring police misconduct, not mistakes by court employees."[30]

In other decisions the Rehnquist Court appeared to give short shrift to defendants' Fourth Amendment rights. The Court ruled in *California v. Greenwood* that police officers did not violate the Fourth Amendment in searching garbage bags placed outside a person's home.[31] The Court ruled in *Florida v. Riley* that aerial surveillance in a helicopter 400 feet above a residence does not qualify as a search.[32] In *Florida v. Bostick* the Rehnquist

Court ruled that just because police officers approached a person on a bus and asked for consent to search does not mean that the officers seized the individual within the meaning of the Fourth Amendment.[33] In *United States v. Drayton* the Rehnquist Court ruled 6–3 that police officers are not required to advise bus passengers of their right to refuse to consent to police questioning.[34]

More recently, the Court upheld a Nevada "stop and identify" law in *Hiibel v. Sixth Judicial District Court of Nevada* that permits the police to arrest someone who refuses to identify himself during a valid street stop. The Court also ruled in *Maryland v. Pringle* that the police can search all passengers in a car when they find concealed drugs where no one claims ownership. The Court also upheld, in *Illinois v. Lidster,* the right of the police to set up a roadblock to investigate a week-old hit-and-run accident. In *Illinois v. Caballes* the Rehnquist Court (without the participation of the chief justice) ruled that the random use of drug-sniffing dogs at traffic stops does not violate the Fourth Amendment. "A dog sniff conducted during a concededly lawful traffic stop that reveals no information other than the location of a substance that no individual has any right to possess does not violate the Fourth Amendment," Justice Stevens wrote for the majority.[35]

These cases show that the Rehnquist Court certainly could not be described as a Fourth Amendment–friendly forum for defendants. "The Rehnquist Court granted far more authority to the government in the Fourth Amendment realm," says criminal defense attorney Jeffrey Fisher, who has argued before the Court.[36]

However, the Rehnquist Court has pulled some surprises over the years in Fourth Amendment cases. For example, the Court ruled 5–4 in *Kyllo v. United States* that the police violated the constitutional rights of a defendant when, without a warrant, they used a thermal imager to scan a person's house to detect the presence of heat. The police suspected that Danny Kyllo might be growing marijuana in his home. They used a thermal imager to detect hot spots and then used that information to obtain a warrant, which resulted in the police finding more than 100 marijuana plants. Kyllo contended that the police engaged in an unlawful search when they used the thermal imager. The police countered that the use of a thermal imager did not even constitute a search because they never physically invaded the home.[37]

To the surprise of some experts, Justice Antonin Scalia—not exactly a criminal defense attorney's best friend—wrote the Court's majority opinion, holding that the use of "sense-enhancing technology" that obtains information that could not have been obtained without physical intrusion is a search. Scalia's libertarian impulses led he and Justice Thomas to side with the more liberal justices Breyer, Ginsburg, and Souter to form the five-member majority. Justice Stevens, in some circles considered the Court's most liberal member, authored the dissenting opinion. "Scalia has a libertarian streak that sometimes shows up in Fourth Amendment cases," Fourth Amendment expert and University of Indiana law professor Craig Bradley explains.[38]

In other decisions the Rehnquist Court—with the chief justice usually dissenting—has issued rulings favorable to criminal defendants. In *City of Indianapolis v. Edmond* the Court invalidated a city policy of instituting roadblocks to search for drug smugglers. "We cannot sanction stops justified only by the generalized and ever-present possibility that interrogation and inspection may reveal that any given motorist has committed some crime," wrote Justice O'Connor for a six-member majority.[39] The Court distinguished this type of roadblock from the sobriety checkpoints that it has approved in past decisions. Chief Justice Rehnquist, Scalia, and Thomas dissented.

In *Ferguson v. City of Charleston* the Court ruled 6–3 that a city violated the Fourth Amendment rights of pregnant women by testing them without their consent for drugs. The majority, in an opinion by Justice Stevens, reasoned that the primary purpose of the policy was a law enforcement policy that failed adequately to protect the privacy rights of the women. The city contended that it had a special needs rationale that justified its policy: to protect the health and safety of women and their children. However, the majority disagreed, finding that "the immediate objective of the searches was to generate evidence for law enforcement purposes." Once again, the three dissenters were Rehnquist, Scalia, and Thomas.

In *Bond v. United States* Chief Justice Rehnquist authored the Court's 7–2 decision that a law enforcement official violated the Fourth Amendment by squeezing a bus passenger's bag without any individualized suspicion.[40] The government argued that touching a passenger's bag that was in open view is no different than the visual inspection from a helicopter that the Court upheld in a previous decision, *Florida v. Riley.* Chief Justice Rehnquist disagreed, writing that "physically invasive inspection is simply more intrusive than purely visual inspection."[41] The two dissenters were Breyer and Scalia. Breyer wrote that the Court's decision "will lead to a constitutional jurisprudence of squeezes, thereby complicating further already complex Fourth Amendment law."[42] Professor Bradley says that *Bond* is the only decision in which Chief Justice Rehnquist voted for a criminal defendant in a Fourth Amendment decision that was not unanimous.

"Over the last 12–13 years, the Rehnquist Court has been surprisingly balanced on Fourth Amendment issues," says Bradley, editor of *The Rehnquist Legacy* (2006). "The Rehnquist Court has proven to be tough on the police with regard to police officers respecting the privacy of the home. The Court has been surprisingly balanced given that its makeup is dominated by conservative Republicans."[43]

One cause of this balance has been that some of the conservative justices rule in favor of criminal defendants when they find a textual or originalist basis for their decision. For example, Justice Scalia has been quite forceful in confrontation clause cases, such as his majority opinion *Crawford v. Washington,*[44] which limited testimonial hearsay by police officers, and his dissenting opinion in *Maryland v. Craig,*[45] which allowed an alleged child abuse victim to testify outside the direct presence of the defendant. Justice Thomas can be protective of defendants' rights if he believes that a right is properly rooted in constitutional origins. For example, he wrote the Court's opinion in *Wilson v. Arkansas,* which found that police officers often must knock before entering a person's residence.[46] Thomas explained that "the common-law knock and announce principle was woven quickly into the fabric of early American law."

A SURPRISING TURN ON SENTENCING

In the later years of the Rehnquist Court it issued a series of decisions that sent shock waves through the criminal justice field. The shock occurred because the decisions went against state and federal prosecutors. The decisions called into question the constitutionality of federal and state sentencing laws. The first foray began with a convicted carjacker named Nathaniel Jones. The federal carjacking law provided that a defendant could be sentenced to 15 years for carjacking, but the sentence could be expanded to 25 years if there is serious bodily injury. At his arraignment, Jones was informed that he faced a 15-year sentence, and his trial referenced this. However, at sentencing, a federal judge imposed a 25-year sentence. Jones contended this violated his due process and Sixth Amendment right to a jury trial. The Sixth Amendment claim was that a jury, not a judge, had to decide whether Jones committed serious bodily injury exposing him to a 25-year sentence. Five members of the Court—Souter, Stevens, Scalia, Thomas, and Ginsburg—agreed with Jones in *Jones v. U.S.* The majority implied that the jury must consider all facts that could increase a defendant's sentence.[47]

The very next year, the same five justices—an odd collection of justices, which broke ideological ranks—made themselves clearer in a New Jersey hate crime case, *Apprendi v. New Jersey.*[48] Charles Apprendi faced numerous criminal charges after he fired shots into an African American family that had recently moved into his neighborhood. Apprendi pled guilty to several charges, but prosecutors then asked the judge to increase

Apprendi's sentence by 10 years because he had committed a hate crime. The judge agreed that the penalty-enhancement statute applied because Apprendi had acted out of racial bias. New Jersey allowed a judge to apply this penalty-enhancing statute by finding by a preponderance of the evidence—a standard which simply means more likely than not—that the defendant had acted to intimidate others because of race, religion, gender, and other similar reasons.

Apprendi's attorneys appealed all the way to the Supreme Court, contending that their client's Sixth Amendment right to a jury trial was violated. They argued that their client had a constitutional right to have a jury determine whether he had violated the hate crime enhancer law by finding that he had done so beyond a reasonable doubt. The same five-member majority in *Jones* agreed with Apprendi's attorneys. Justice Stevens wrote for the majority, "Other than the fact of a prior conviction, any fact that increases the penalty for a crime beyond the prescribed statutory maximum must be submitted to a jury, and proved beyond a reasonable doubt."[49]

Four justices dissented: O'Connor, Rehnquist, Breyer, and Kennedy. O'Connor warned that the decision would threaten the constitutionality of federal and state sentencing guidelines. She wrote that "the most significant impact of the Court's decision will be a practical one—its unsettling effect on sentencing conducted under current federal and state determinate-sentencing schemes"[50] and that "our precedents did not foreordain this disruption in the world of sentencing."[51] Justice Breyer, who had helped draft the federal sentencing guidelines when he worked for the Senate Judiciary Committee, also wrote a dissenting opinion: "A sentencing scheme in which judges have discretion to find sentencing-related factors is a workable system and one that has long been thought consistent with the Constitution."[52]

Breyer's opinion engendered a harsh response from Justice Scalia in a concurring opinion over how to interpret the Constitution: "Justice Breyer proceeds on the erroneous and all-too-common assumption that the Constitution means what we think it ought to mean. It does not; it means what it says."[53]

Joseph D. O'Neill, the attorney based in Vineland, New Jersey, who argued the case for Apprendi, says the case was a landmark decision: "I've had several law professors tell me it [*Apprendi*] is one of the most significant criminal law decisions of the twenty-first century. I've also been told by representatives from Westlaw that is has been cited more than 40,000 times. I believe it is one of the most significant criminal law decisions because it protects the Sixth Amendment right to trial by a jury in a criminal case. Thomas Jefferson himself wrote that trial by jury was the most important of all the individual freedoms in the Bill of Rights."[54]

In her dissent Justice O'Connor had said that *Apprendi* represented a "watershed change in constitutional law." She was right. In June 2004, the U.S. Supreme Court invalidated Washington State's sentencing guidelines in *Blakely v. Washington.*[55] The case involved Ralph Howard Blakely, Jr., who pled guilty to kidnapping his estranged wife. A judge increased his sentence significantly, finding that Blakely had acted with "deliberate cruelty." Blakely contended on appeal that this violated his Sixth Amendment right to a jury trial.

The same five-member majority in *Jones* and *Apprendi* agreed with Blakely and invalidated the state's sentencing procedure. Justice Scalia wrote, "As Apprendi held, every defendant has the right to insist that the prosecutor prove to a jury all facts legally essential to the punishment."[56] Once again, O'Connor bitterly dissented, warning that the opinion sounded the death knell of decades of sentencing reform: "What I have feared most has now come to pass: Over 20 years of sentencing reform are all but lost; and tens of thousands of criminal judgments are in jeopardy."[57]

"The *Blakey* decision is very significant because it tells the state and the government that when you put together criminal codes, all the important factors determining the defendant's sentence exposure have to be put to the adversarial process," said Seattle-based attorney Jeffrey L. Fisher, who argued the case before the high court for Blakely. "The decision values the jury in the adversarial process."[58]

"The decision is not a wrecking ball for all sentencing guidelines, as many originally had feared," Fisher says. "Almost all the states that were affected by the ruling have added extra jury protections to their guideline systems."[59]

The *Apprendi* line of cases led to the Court's 2005 decision in *United States v. Booker,* which dealt with the federal sentencing guidelines. In another highly fractured decision the Court ruled 5–4 that *Apprendi* and *Blakely* do apply to the federal sentencing guidelines. Justice Stevens concluded his opinion with a familiar refrain: "Accordingly, we reaffirm our holding in *Apprendi:* Any fact (other than a prior conviction) which is necessary to support a sentence exceeding the maximum authorized by the facts established by a plea of guilty or a jury verdict must be admitted by the defendant or proved to a jury beyond a reasonable doubt."

Justice Breyer then wrote the Court's opinion on the question of what provisions of the guidelines were still in effect. Breyer wrote that the Court's decision "makes the Guidelines effectively advisory."

The *Apprendi-Blakely-Booker* cases were all decided by 5–4 votes with the same alignment of justices. The arrangement of justices in the majority was odd. It included the two most conservative members of the Court—Scalia and Thomas—with three more liberal members—Stevens, Ginsberg, and Souter. "The victory in *Blakely* was built on a combination of justices with judicial philosophies of originalism and legalism as opposed to pragmatism," Fisher says. "My argument appealed to those justices who favor bright-line rules as opposed to the judicial balancers."[60]

UNUSUAL ALIGNMENTS

Some of the Court's Fourth Amendment cases and the *Apprendi* line of cases show that the justices often align in different ways. The traditional conservative-liberal labels sometimes play out in criminal procedure cases, as they do in the "Federalism Five" cases of the later Rehnquist Court. For example, the Court split 5–4 on the constitutionality of controversial three-strikes laws. These laws allow prosecutors to impose life sentences on criminal defendants who have been convicted of a third felony. In *Ewing v. California* the Court ruled 5–4 that California's three-strikes law did not constitute cruel and unusual punishment under the Eighth Amendment. In that decision, and in a related one, the Court divided along the conservative-liberal lines.[61]

Other times, the Court was simply not predictable in its alignment in criminal cases. A classic example arose from *Rogers v. Tennessee,* a case with a highly unusual set of facts and an even stranger law.[62] Defendant Wilbert K. Rogers stabbed his victim with a butcher knife. The victim had surgery, but complications arising from the surgery led to his death 15 months later. The defendant was charged with murder. However, he argued that the murder charge was invalid because Tennessee common law had adopted the so-called year-and-a-day rule. This rule, which arose from England, provided that an individual was presumed not to have committed murder when the victim died more than a year and a day after the alleged assault or injury. When Rogers stabbed his victim, the year-and-a-day rule was still judge-made law in Tennessee. However, the state argued that the anachronistic rule could be retroactively abolished. A bare majority of the Supreme Court—O'Connor, Rehnquist, Kennedy, Ginsburg, and Souter—agreed. Four justices—two conservatives (Scalia and Thomas) and two liberals (Stevens and Breyer)—dissented. "The Court today approves the conviction of a man for a murder that was not murder (but only manslaughter) when the offense was committed," Scalia wrote.[63]

WAR ON TERRORISM

The Rehnquist Court also did not prove to be a rubber stamp for the Bush administration's broad attempts to restrict judicial review over executive actions during the War on Terror. In the aftermath of the cataclysmic horror of September 11, 2001, the government declared hostile individuals fighting U.S. and allied forces in Afghanistan and Iraq as "enemy combatants." This designation carries legal significance because persons classified as "prisoners of war" receive the protections of the Geneva Convention. Enemy combatants do not receive the full protection of the Bill of Rights as do regular criminal defendants. Instead, the U.S. government argued that individuals classified as enemy combatants had virtually no rights at all.

The U.S. Supreme Court disagreed in a pair of decisions: *Hamdi v. Rumsfeld* and *Rasul v. Bush.*[64] In *Hamdi v. Rumsfeld* the Court ruled that an American citizen fighting for the Taliban against the United States did have a right to contest the factual basis of his confinement before some sort of "neutral decisionmaker." Justices O'Connor, Kennedy, Breyer, and Rehnquist joined in a plurality which found that the executive branch could detain persons identified as "enemy combatants." On this question O'Connor reasoned that the executive branch had this power because the U.S. Congress authorized it in a resolution called "Authorization for Use of Military Force." However, the plurality wrote that Hamdi could challenge such confinement in the federal courts, writing that a "state of war is not a blank check when it comes to the rights of the Nation's citizens." She added that "history and common sense teach us that an unchecked system of detention carries the potential to become a means for oppression and abuse of others."[65]

Four justices—Scalia, Stevens, Ginsburg, and Souter—believed that Hamdi should be released in two separate opinions. Justices Scalia and Stevens—who often spar in opinions over constitutional interpretation—joined together in an opinion by Scalia. He wrote that Hamdi must be released unless criminal charges are promptly brought or the writ of habeas corpus is suspended. Justice Souter—in an opinion joined by Ginsburg—reasoned that Hamdi should be released because such detention is not authorized by Congress's Authorization for Use of Military Force. Only Justice Thomas agreed with the president and the executive branch. He wrote, "This detention falls squarely within the Federal Government's war powers, and we lack the expertise and capacity to second-guess that decision."[66]

In *Rasul v. Bush* the Court ruled 6–3 that even noncitizen detainees at Guantanamo Bay have the right to access U.S. courts to challenge their confinement in a federal habeas corpus proceeding. However, the Court did not explain exactly what procedure was due the detainees. Justice John Paul Stevens, in his opinion, explained that the question before the Court was "only whether the federal courts have jurisdiction to determine the legality of the Executive's potentially indefinite detention of individuals who claim to be wholly innocent of wrongdoing."[67]

Justices Scalia, Rehnquist, and Thomas dissented, with Scalia writing the opinion. "Today, the Court springs a trap on the Executive, subjecting Guantanamo Bay to the oversight of the federal courts even though it has never before been thought to be within their jurisdiction—and thus making it a foolish place to have housed alien wartime detainees," he wrote with his characteristic flair.[68]

CONCLUSION

Chief Justice Rehnquist became a U.S. Supreme Court justice with the mind-set that the Warren Court had gone too far in many of its criminal law rulings. For much of his 33 years on the Court Rehnquist voted against criminal defendants. Bradley writes, "When it comes to the Fourth Amendment, the police have had no greater friend on the Supreme Court than William Rehnquist."

To some degree, Rehnquist was able to move his Court over 19 years toward a more law enforcement–friendly model. Many rulings by the Rehnquist Court created exceptions and limitations to broad Warren Court rulings. "Without a doubt the Rehnquist Court was a pro-law enforcement Court in general," says Hundley. "They would often limit the application of defendants' rights in various procedural contexts without undermining the larger constitutional freedoms on their face."[69] Fisher agrees: "The Rehnquist Court was a quite conservative Court generally. In the realm of criminal procedure it was interested in removing what it perceived as procedural obstacles to prosecution and punishment."[70]

But that does not tell the full story and does not explain how the Rehnquist Court achieved a degree of balance. Sometimes the justices with libertarian impulses—Scalia and Thomas—sided with liberals to rule against the government, as the *Kyllo* thermal imager case showed. Sometimes defense attorneys were able to raise arguments arguing for bright-line rules that appealed to a broad coalition of justices, as the *Apprendi* line of cases showed. Fisher, who successfully argued the confrontation clause case of *Crawford v. Washington* in addition to *Blakely* before the Court, explained that in those cases, "I rooted my arguments deeply in history and tradition."

When put to its greatest challenge in the criminal arena in the War on Terror, the Supreme Court served as a key check on an executive branch that encroached on traditional boundaries of power. Chief Justice Rehnquist himself joined O'Connor's opinion in *Hamdi,* which sent a clear message to the executive branch that it violated the Constitution by denying any access to the federal courts. The Rehnquist Court may have favored law enforcement and limited constitutional protections, but it did not eviscerate them.

Chapter 10

ABORTION, GAY RIGHTS, AND AFFIRMATIVE ACTION

> The fact that a majority of the States reflecting, after all the majority sentiment in those States, have had restrictions on abortions for at least a century is a strong indication, it seems to me, that the asserted right to an abortion is not so "rooted in the traditions and conscience of our people as to be ranked as fundamental."
>
> —Associate Justice William Rehnquist, dissenting in *Roe v. Wade* (1973)[1]

"Scarcely any political question arises in the United States that is not resolved, sooner or later, into a judicial question," wrote Alexis de Tocqueville in the nineteenth century, when he traveled from France to observe America and create his famous work *Democracy in America.*[2] Three issues of social and political prominence—abortion, gay rights, and affirmative action—are no exceptions to de Tocqueville's amazing foresight. The Rehnquist Court heard numerous cases on each divisive, cultural issue that had major political ramifications.

ABORTION

Perhaps no issue has been a greater lightning rod for the U.S. Supreme Court than the abortion question. It has become a virtual litmus test for judicial appointees. The issue has led to mass protests by activists on either side and even degenerated into horrific violence as a few antiabortion activists have shed blood in the name of the unborn.

The U.S. Supreme Court first waded into the troubled waters of abortion in its historic *Roe v. Wade* decision, issued in 1973.[3] The case involved a constitutional challenge to a Texas law that criminalized abortions, except for those necessary to save the life of the mother. Several individuals, including a woman under the pseudonym Jane Roe, contended that the Texas law violated the fundamental right of personal privacy under several amendments to the Bill of Rights.

The U.S. Supreme Court ruled 7–2 against the Texas law, finding that women have a personal privacy right under the Constitution that includes a qualified right to an abortion. Justice Harry Blackmun, who had served as counsel to the prestigious Mayo Clinic, wrote that "the right of privacy ... is broad enough to encompass a woman's decision whether or not to terminate her pregnancy."[4] He reasoned that this right of privacy was "founded" in either the Fourteenth Amendment's liberty interest or on the "Ninth Amendment's reservation of rights to the people." This passage opened up Blackmun to critical commentary from both supporters and opponents of the opinion.

Blackmun relied on the Warren Court precedent *Griswold v. Connecticut,* a 1965 decision that invalidated a Connecticut law banning contraceptives.[5] Justice William Douglas determined that there was a constitutional right to privacy that emanated from various provisions of the Bill of Rights. The Constitution and the Bill of Rights do not mention the word *privacy,* but Douglas reasoned that "specific guarantees in the Bill of Rights have penumbras, formed by emanations from those guarantees that help give them life and substance" and that these "various guarantees create zones of privacy."[6] *Penumbras* ("shadows") and *emanations* ("extensions") may have been an odd way to describe a constitutional right, but it became one of the best known decisions in constitutional law. The trouble with the *Griswold* opinion was that the justices did not agree on where to place the right of privacy within the Bill of Rights: Douglas advanced his "penumbra" theory; Justice Arthur Goldberg argued that the right of privacy was grounded in the Ninth Amendment, which reserves rights not specifically listed in the Bill of Rights to the people; and Justices Byron White and John Marshall Harlan grounded the privacy right in the "liberty" interest of the Fourteenth Amendment in their separate concurrences. The different paths of legal reasoning helped establish a constitutional right of privacy, but it led to confusion as to its proper moorings.

Blackmun noted that a woman has a qualified right to an abortion, meaning that there are important state interests at play. He focused on the division of pregnancy into three periods, called "trimesters." For the first trimester, where the health risks to women are minimal, women have an unqualified right to an abortion. For the second trimester the state can regulate the abortion process "in ways that are reasonably related to maternal health," such as regulating who performs the procedure and regulating the facility where the procedure takes place. In the last trimester, after viability—the ability to live outside the mother's womb—the state can prohibit abortions, except when they are necessary to save the life of the mother.

William Rehnquist was one of two justices (the other was Byron White) who dissented in *Roe v. Wade.* Rehnquist praised Blackmun's opinion for its "extensive historical fact" and "wealth of legal scholarship." However, he disagreed with Blackmun's reasoning with regard to a right of privacy, writing, "I have difficulty in concluding, as the Court does, that the right of 'privacy' is involved in this case."[7] He thought that the case involved a more limited liberty interest in being free from "unwanted state regulation of consensual transactions." He even acknowledged that a state law that flatly prohibited all abortions, even for those essential to protect the life of the mother, would be unconstitutional. To Rehnquist, Blackmun's opinion went too far by striking down all abortions that occur during the first trimester. He considered Blackmun's opinion and its division of pregnancy into three trimesters as "judicial legislation."[8]

Roe v. Wade generated opposition from its beginnings. Some opposed it on moral and religious grounds—that it was wrong to sanction the murder of unborn life. Others believed that the issue was a matter for state legislatures and state law. Various times over the years, the Justice Department asked the U.S. Supreme Court to overrule *Roe v. Wade.* But *Roe* survived the Burger Court in cases such as *City of Akron v. Akron Center for Reproductive Health*[9] and *Thornburgh v. American College of Obstetricians and Gynecologists.*[10] In those two decisions, various state restrictions on abortion were invalidated by margins of 6–3 and 5–4, respectively. Blackmun obtained the votes of Powell, Brennan, Marshall, and Stevens in both cases and the vote of Chief Justice Burger in *Thornburgh.*

In the October 1986 term Justice Rehnquist became chief justice, and Antonin Scalia took Rehnquist's associate justice position. In 1988, Anthony Kennedy filled the seat previously filled by Powell. Kennedy, a friend of President Ronald Reagan and Attorney General Edwin Meese, was considered a solid conservative vote. The question became whether Rehnquist could obtain enough votes to tilt the Court in his direction on the abortion issue.

The test came in a case out of Missouri. The state had enacted several regulations limiting abortion, including a ban on abortions in public hospitals, a ban on public employees performing or assisting with abortions, and a requirement that medical tests be performed on fetuses that are thought to be at least 20 weeks old. The Court upheld these requirements in *Webster v. Reproductive Health Services* in a plurality, rather than a majority, opinion by Chief Justice Rehnquist.[11] The difference between a plurality and majority opinion can have great significance as to the viability of an opinion as future precedent because a plurality opinion is not signed on to by a majority (five justices) of the Court. Justices Kennedy and White, the Court's other dissenter in *Roe,* joined Rehnquist's plurality opinion. Justices Scalia and O'Connor wrote separate concurring opinions. Scalia argued for a full-scale reversal, while O'Connor disappointed the conservative movement with her cautious concurrence that advocated judicial restraint when it came to analyzing *Roe.*

Rehnquist's opinion did not call for a formal overruling of *Roe,* but it chipped away at it with consistency. "Nothing in the Constitution requires States to enter or remain in the business of performing abortions," wrote the chief justice of the ban on abortions in public hospitals.[12] He reasoned that women did not suffer any loss of their Fourteenth Amendment liberty rights because they could still seek abortions in private hospitals.

The Court also upheld the testing requirement for fetuses, finding that the measure was "reasonably designed to ensure that abortions are not performed where the fetus is viable—an end which all concede is legitimate—and that is sufficient to sustain its constitutionality."[13] In his analysis Rehnquist took aim at much of Blackmun's majority opinion in *Roe,* noting that the terms "trimesters and viability are not found in the text of the Constitution."[14]

Justice Antonin Scalia wrote separately and argued that the Court should have explicitly overruled *Roe v. Wade.* He called Rehnquist's plurality opinion "a triumph of judicial statesmanship," and he did not mean this as a compliment.[15] Rather, Scalia believed that the Court danced around the issue and should have squarely overruled *Roe v. Wade.* Scalia's ire was directed particularly at Justice O'Connor, who did not provide the crucial fifth vote formally needed to overrule *Roe v. Wade.* O'Connor, in her concurring opinion, urged for judicial restraint, saying that "there will be time enough to reexamine Roe" carefully in the near future.[16] Scalia retorted that O'Connor's warning about not reexamining *Roe* "cannot be taken seriously."[17]

Justice Blackmun dissented with a spirited defense of his *Roe v. Wade* opinion. He criticized the Rehnquist plurality for its "proposed revolutionary revision in the law of abortion" that "invites charges of cowardice and illegitimacy to our door."[18] He sounded an ominous tone: "I fear for the future. I fear for the liberty and equality of the millions of women who have lived and come of age in the 16 years since Roe was decided. I fear for the integrity of, and public esteem for, this Court."[19] Justices Brennan and Marshall joined Blackmun in dissent, while the very independent Stevens filed an opinion characterized as partial concurrence and partial dissent.

After *Webster, Roe* survived, but many believed that it was on life support. The *New York Times* authored an editorial entitled "A Women's Right, Barely Viable."[20] Expert *Times* Supreme Court reporter Linda Greenhouse wrote that a majority of the Court no longer considered abortion to be a "fundamental constitutional right."[21] The die appeared cast for *Roe v. Wade,* and Blackmun's warnings appeared prescient. The change in the Court's membership only heightened speculation that *Roe v. Wade* would fall into the judicial graveyard. Justices Brennan and Marshall, Blackmun stalwarts in this area, were replaced by President George H. W. Bush appointees David Souter and Clarence Thomas.

The Court's lineup appeared to signal a demise for *Roe v. Wade* as six justices seemed to be friendly to a full-scale assault on the 1973 decision. Rehnquist and White were the original *Roe* dissenters, Scalia abhorred *Roe* and wrote as such in *Webster,* Kennedy had joined Rehnquist's plurality in *Webster,* and Thomas appeared to be a solid conservative vote.

In 1992, the justices heard the case of *Planned Parenthood of Southeastern Pennsylvania v. Casey,* which involved challenges to several provisions of the Pennsylvania Abortion Control Act of 1982.[22] The provisions included requiring information be given to women seeking abortions 24 hours before the procedure, a requirement of informed consent, a parental notice requirement, reporting requirements on abortion facilities, and a spousal notification requirement. The United States intervened, arguing for the reversal of *Roe v. Wade.*

Four justices—Rehnquist, Scalia, White, and Thomas—voted to overrule *Roe v. Wade.* However, they could not obtain the votes of O'Connor, Souter, and Kennedy, who joined forces in an unusual per curiam opinion. The three justices had met privately and decided jointly to draft an opinion that would not overrule *Roe.*[23] These three justices wrote that "the essential holding of Roe v. Wade should be retained and once again reaffirmed."[24] This "essential holding" included "the right of a woman to choose to have an abortion before viability and to obtain it without undue interference from the State."[25]

Instead of applying strict scrutiny, as Justice Blackmun called for, the troika advocated O'Connor's undue burden test: "Only where a state regulation imposes an undue burden on a woman's ability to make this decision does the power of the State reach into the heart of the liberty protected by the Due Process Clause."[26] The plurality defined a regulation causing an undue burden as one that places a "substantial obstacle in the path" of a woman seeking an abortion.[27]

Applying this standard, the plurality upheld all the provisions of the Pennsylvania law, except for the spousal notification provision. According to the plurality, the notification provision would constitute an undue burden for millions of abused and battered women. The plurality rationally concluded that these victims of physical and psychological abuse may have very valid reasons for not informing their spouses.[28]

The plurality rejected Blackmun's trimester analysis from *Roe* and applied a standard that was a form of intermediate scrutiny between Blackmun's strict scrutiny and Rehnquist's rational basis test. However, the plurality refused to go all the way and overrule *Roe v. Wade.* In an extended discussion on the virtues of stare decisis (adherence to precedent), the plurality emphasized judicial restraint, consistency, and public reliance on a decision that impacted millions of families and women. Ken Starr, who argued for the reversal of *Roe* in the case as solicitor general, wrote in his book on the Court many years later of the *Casey* plurality: "Their theory was novel. It centered on public expectations, not on the internal strength of the precedent itself in law and logic. This was an overtly political and cultural approach toward constitutional interpretation."[29]

Rehnquist and Scalia authored opinions critical of the plurality opinion. Rehnquist called the plurality's approach an "unjustified constitutional compromise."[30] He said that *Roe* continued to survive "but only in the way a storefront on a western movie set exists: a mere façade to give the illusion of reality."[31] He criticized the plurality's new "undue burden" standard, which he wrote was "created largely out of whole cloth" and "plucked from nowhere."[32] Scalia was even more critical, comparing the plurality opinion to the infamous Dred Scott decision by quoting from Justice Benjamin Curtiss, who had dissented in that infamous 1857 decision, and by warning the plurality of what happened to Chief Justice Roger Brooke Taney, whose great judicial career was tarnished because he embroiled the Court in the slavery question.[33] "We should get out of this area, where we have no right to be, and where we do neither ourselves nor the country any good by remaining," he concluded.[34]

While Chief Justice Rehnquist and Scalia were disappointed, Justice Blackmun expressed relief in his separate opinion that *Roe v. Wade* survived. "All that remained between the promise of Roe and the darkness of the plurality was a single, flickering flame," he wrote. "But, now just when so many expected the darkness to fall, the flame has grown bright."[35] He referred to the decision of the plurality to retain the "essential holding" of *Roe v. Wade* as "an act of personal courage and constitutional principle."[36] He then proceeded to reaffirm his view that a state's abortion restrictions can only be constitutional if they pass "the strictest of judicial scrutiny."[37] Blackmun biographer and longtime Supreme Court reporter Linda

Greenhouse summed up the justice's connection with *Roe* well when she wrote that "he locked Roe in a tight embrace and never let it go."[38] Blackmun certainly embraced *Roe* tightly in his concluding words in *Casey:* "I am 83 years old. I cannot remain on this Court forever, and when I do step down, the confirmation process for my successor well may be exactly where the choice between the two worlds will be made."[39]

In 1993 and 1994, Democratic president Bill Clinton made his only two nominations for the Court in Ruth Bader Ginsburg, who replaced original *Roe* dissenter Byron White, and Stephen Breyer, who replaced Blackmun. Ginsburg and Breyer both told the Senate during the confirmation process that they believed in a constitutional right to abortion.[40] The selection of Ginsburg had initially concerned some *Roe* supporters, despite her ACLU background, because she had voiced criticisms of the decision in the past for focusing on privacy rather than on women's equality. However, both new justices appeared to insure the safety of *Roe.*

The Rehnquist Court returned to the abortion controversy eight years later in *Stenberg v. Carhart,* which involved a Nebraska law banning "partial-birth" abortions.[41] Partial birth abortions are those in which the physician partially delivers vaginally a living, unborn child before killing it and completing the procedure. A Nebraska physician who performed such procedures challenged the law in court. The lower federal courts had invalidated the law, in part because it failed to provide a general health of the mother exception.

The U.S. Supreme Court upheld the lower courts and invalidated the law by a narrow 5–4 vote. Justices Breyer, Ginsburg, Souter, Stevens, and O'Connor voted in the majority, while Chief Justice Rehnquist, Scalia, Thomas, and Kennedy dissented. Breyer reasoned that because partial-birth abortions were sometimes the safest form of abortion for certain women, a complete ban posed an undue burden to a woman's fundamental constitutional right to reproductive health choices. He wrote that "we believe the law requires a health exception."[42]

Predictably, Chief Justice Rehnquist, Scalia, and Thomas dissented. Scalia compared the majority's decision to *Korematsu v. United States,* the case that sanctioned the internment of American citizens of Japanese ancestry during World War II, and Dred Scott, the ruling that upheld slavery. "I am optimistic enough to believe that, one day, Stenberg v. Carhart will be assigned its rightful place in the history of this Court's jurisprudence beside Korematsu and Dred Scott."[43] The most interesting dissent came from Justice Kennedy, who had been a member of the plurality in *Casey.* Kennedy wrote that the *Casey* analysis had been misapplied and that the majority had shown a "basic misunderstanding" of the *Casey* decision. "The *Casey* plurality seems to have unraveled a bit," explains constitutional law professor Thomas Baker. "Kennedy was upset enough with how the analysis was applied in the partial-birth abortion case, *Stenberg v. Carhart,* to file a separate opinion saying as far as he was concerned, the others had gone back on the deal he thought he was making. O'Connor since has left the Court, of course, so that vote is undetermined."[44]

Roe v. Wade survived the Rehnquist Court—but barely. Chief Justice Rehnquist, as in other areas of broad social concern, was not able flatly to overrule Warren and Burger Court precedents, but he managed to chip away at them or, at the very least, to curtail their reach. Abortion was no exception. The Rehnquist Court upheld many state regulations on abortion in *Casey* and other decisions.

"He did move the Court in the abortion area as he pulled the Court away from *Roe,*" Baker says of Rehnquist. "The undue burden test is not as rigorous as the previous strict scrutiny analysis that Blackmun preferred. I refer to the undue burden test as less-strict, strict scrutiny. *Casey* allows some regulations of abortion that would not have passed strict scrutiny under the Blackmun approach."[45]

Obviously, the abortion debate is not likely to die down anytime soon. The U.S. Supreme Court justices understand this phenomenon, as Justice Breyer confirmed in his opinion in the partial-birth abortion case: "We understand the controversial nature of the problem."[46] Whether the Supreme Court will change its mind on this issue will rest with the Roberts Court justices.

GAY RIGHTS

Another emerging area of social concern that has reached the hallowed halls of the Supreme Court concerns gay rights. The Rehnquist Court was not the first Court to address the issue. In its last term the Burger Court ruled 5–4 in *Bowers v. Hardwick* that a Georgia sodomy law did not violate the Constitution.[47] Michael Hardwick, a gay man, challenged the constitutionality of the law, which on its face did not single out same-sex acts of sodomy. Hardwick contended that the law violated the fundamental right of privacy protected by the due process clause. The case arose after Hardwick, a bartender from Atlanta, failed to pay a ticket for public drinking. A police officer went to Hardwick's home with a warrant, saw him engaged in sex with another man, and arrested him. Hardwick sued the state, even though the charges were dropped. He wanted a judgment from the courts declaring that the law was unconstitutional.

A bare majority of the Court, in an opinion by Justice Byron White, rejected Hardwick's claims and upheld the statute. The Court ruled that there was no fundamental right to engage in homosexual sodomy, focusing on the fact that many states criminalized such conduct. Because there was no fundamental right, the Georgia law had only to survive the deferential rational basis standard. The majority determined that the law furthered the state's rational basis in protecting morality through its criminal laws.

Four justices—Blackmun, Brennan, Marshall, and Stevens—dissented, with opinions by Blackmun and Stevens. The dissenting justices reasoned that the law invaded individual privacy. Justice Lewis Powell, often the swing vote on the Burger Court, changed his mind on the case. Initially, he expressed his intention in conference to vote against the law. He later circulated a memo to the other justices, informing them of his change.[48] He eventually wrote a short concurring opinion that shifted the Court. Years later, Powell admitted that he regretted his vote in the case and that it may have been wrongly decided.

At the time of *Bowers v. Hardwick* an ACLU attorney declared that *Bowers* was "the opening shot of the Rehnquist Court,"[49] even though the decision was at the end of Chief Justice Burger's career. *Bowers v. Hardwick* may have been the "opening shot" of the Rehnquist Court, but it certainly was not the final flurry of gunfire.

The Rehnquist Court took a turn on the issue of gay rights, eventually overruling *Bowers v. Hardwick* in 2003. The path may have begun in the case of an unknown electronics technician in the Central Intelligence Agency who alleged that he was fired in part for his sexual orientation. In *Webster v. Doe* the Rehnquist Court ruled 6–2 that national security laws do not automatically prevent federal employees from suing for violation of their constitutional rights.[50] Chief Justice Rehnquist wrote that "we believe that a constitutional claim based on an individual discharge may be reviewed by the District Court."[51] Justices Antonin Scalia and Sandra Day O'Connor dissented.

Employment and gay rights activists praised the decision as a victory for employees in general and for gay rights.[52] However, the decision did not lead to a significant advance for gay rights.

Those advances came later, particularly with the Court's 1996 decision in *Romer v. Evans*.[53] The case involved an amendment to the Colorado Constitution prohibiting cities and counties from passing laws protecting homosexuals. The amendment began with the words "No Protected Status Based on Homosexual, Lesbian or Bisexual Orientation." The state argued that the amendment did not discriminate against gays and lesbians but merely denied them special rights or preferential treatment. Six members of the U.S. Supreme Court disagreed, characterizing this reading of the amendment and its history as "implausible."[54]

Justice Anthony Kennedy wrote that the Colorado amendment displayed class animus that failed even the deferential rational basis standard. "We must conclude that Amendment 2 classifies homosexuals not to further a proper legislative end but to make them unequal to everyone else," he wrote. "A State cannot so deem a class of persons a stranger to its laws."[55]

Interestingly, Kennedy failed to cite *Bowers* in his majority opinion. The notice was conspicuous, particularly to Justice Antonin Scalia, who dissented vigorously with purple prose: "The case most relevant to the issue before us today is not even mentioned in the Court's opinion."[56] He accused the majority of intruding into a Kulturkampf, or culture war. Scalia reasoned that the U.S. Supreme Court should not interfere with the "normal democratic means, including the democratic adoption" of Amendment 2.[57]

Romer laid the groundwork for a wholesale attack on *Bowers*. "*Romer* unofficially overruled *Bowers* without saying so at the time," says Baker. "Only later, in *Lawrence,* did we find out, when Kennedy (the author of both opinions) came out and admitted it."[58] Baker refers to the Court's historic 2003 decision in *Lawrence v. Texas,* in which Justice Kennedy led the Court in striking down a state sodomy law that singled out gays and lesbians.[59]

Lawrence v. Texas began when police were called to the residence of John Geddes Lawrence on a false weapons disturbance complaint. On arrival the police discovered Lawrence having sexual relations with Tyron Garner. The two were charged with "deviate sexual intercourse, namely anal sex, with a member of the same sex (man)."[60]

Lawrence and Garner lost in the Texas courts based on *Bowers* but appealed to the U.S. Supreme Court. Kennedy began his opinion with a salvo on the importance of privacy and liberty in the home: "Liberty protects the person from unwarranted government intrusions into a dwelling or other private places."[61] Kennedy noted that *Romer* and *Casey,* in particular, called into question the validity of *Bowers.* He also pointed out that far fewer states were criminalizing sodomy laws. Even in those states that still had sodomy laws on the books, a pattern of nonenforcement prevailed.

Kennedy then took dead aim at *Bowers:* "Bowers was not correct when it was decided, and it is not correct today. It ought not to remain binding precedent. *Bowers v. Hardwick* should be and now is overruled."[62] The justices split down the exact same 6–3 alignment as in *Romer.* O'Connor authored a narrow concurring opinion, finding an equal protection violation because the state singled out same-sex sodomy acts.

Once again, Justice Scalia was left to inject his purple prose in dissent. He jabbed Kennedy for the disconnect between his concurring opinion in *Casey,* which emphasized the importance of stare decisis, and his opinion in *Lawrence,* which overruled *Bowers.* According to Scalia, the difference in treatment of *Roe v. Wade* and *Bowers* "exposed Casey's extraordinary deference to precedent for the result-oriented expedient that it is."[63]

He questioned the majority's analysis as "an unheard-of form of rational basis"[64] and warned that the decision "effectively decrees the end of all morals legislation."[65] According to Scalia, a whole host of laws banning bigamy, fornication, prostitution, incest, and bestiality were called into question.

To a certain extent, Scalia was prescient. The Court's decision in *Lawrence* paved the way for the invalidation of other laws, including same-sex marriage. In November 2003, the Supreme Judicial Court of Massachusetts ruled in *Goodridge v. Department of Public Health* that the state of Massachusetts could not deny marriage licenses to same-sex couples.[66] The Virginia Supreme Court invalidated a state law prohibiting fornication based on *Lawrence.* A federal district judge in Pennsylvania went so far as to cite *Lawrence* as his primary precedent in invalidating federal obscenity laws, though an appeals court later reversed his decision.

AFFIRMATIVE ACTION

The Rehnquist Court also entered the fray on another pressing social issue that continues to divide Americans: affirmative action. The term, chosen by African American attorney Hobart Taylor, Jr. in 1961 for its alliterative effect, reflects a positive commitment to equality and diversity to its supporters. President Lyndon B. Johnson expressed the rationale behind affirmative action in a 1965 speech he delivered at Howard University: "You do not take a person who for years has been hobbled by chains and liberate him, bring him up to the starting line of a race and then say, 'You are free to compete with all the others,' and still justly believe you have been completely fair."[67]

Others contend that affirmative action, with its explicit focus on racial classifications, offends the basic principle of equal protection and amounts to a form of reverse discrimination. During the administration of Lyndon Johnson and the early years of Richard Nixon the federal government actively pursued a policy of affirmative action. However, during the presidency of Ronald Reagan, affirmative action policies were attacked as unfair quota systems that divide Americans based on race.

The U.S. Supreme Court first addressed the constitutionality of affirmative action in its 1978 decision *Regents of University of California v. Bakke.*[68] The case began after medical school officials at the University of California, Davis denied admission to Allan Bakke, a white male. Bakke, who had standardized test scores higher than minority applicants accepted to the program, contended that the university violated his equal protection rights. The admissions program set aside 16 of its 100 seats specifically for minority candidates. Bakke asserted that admission should go to the best applicants, regardless of race.

The Court ruled 5–4 in favor of Bakke and against the university. It ruled that the school could not show that it would have rejected Bakke but for its "unlawful special admissions program."[69] Justice Lewis Powell explained for the majority that "the guarantee of equal protection cannot mean one thing when applied to one individual and something else when applied to a person of another color."[70] In dissent, Harry Blackmun countered, "In order to get beyond racism, we must first take account of race. There is no other way. And in order to treat some persons equally, we must treat them differently."[71]

However, Powell—the model of moderation—refused to rule that affirmative action programs were per se unlawful and could never take account of race. In fact, he recognized the value of diversity for universities and said that universities could take race into account as one factor in their selection decisions. The highly fractured nature of the *Bakke* decision insured that the controversy would not die down. These controversies continued throughout virtually the entire Rehnquist Court period.

In 1989, the Rehnquist Court examined an affirmative action policy in *Richmond v. J.A. Croson Co.*[72] The city of Richmond, Virginia, had adopted a program mandating that 30 percent of its contracting work should be designated to minority-owned businesses. The city had adopted the policy in 1983, noting that minority-owned businesses in Richmond received less than 1 percent of city contracts in a city that was 50 percent African American. The city contended that there should be a less rigorous standard of review for "benign" or "remedial" discrimination that is designed to redress past instances of societal discrimination.

Justice O'Connor wrote the Court's plurality opinion that invalidated the city's set-aside program. In her opinion O'Connor reasoned that all racial classifications should be subject to strict scrutiny. She wrote that "the standard of review under the Equal Protection Clause is not dependent on the race of those burdened or benefited by a particular classification." She determined that the city had not justified its policy by showing that it resulted in actual individual discrimination. She reached this conclusion because the city had not shown evidence of actual qualified minority businesses in the local construction market that were available to perform the work in question. Only three justices dissented: the familiar liberal troika of Brennan, Marshall, and Blackmun.

The very next year, the Rehnquist Court reversed course in *Metro Broadcasting, Inc. v. FCC,* upholding two Federal Communications Commission

(FCC) policies designed to increase minority ownership in the television and radio broadcast arena. The Court upheld the measures by a 5–4 vote, as Justices Stevens and White switched sides from the *Richmond* case a year earlier. Justice Brennan, in his last opinion for the Court, emphasized that the FCC minority ownership programs were authorized by Congress. He cited a 1980 Burger Court decision, *Fullilove v. Klutznick,* in which the Court did not apply strict scrutiny to a race-based effort at increasing diversity in the broadcast area.[73] Brennan said that instead of strict scrutiny, the Court would apply a form of intermediate scrutiny, that the measures are "constitutionally permissible to the extent that they serve important governmental objectives within the power of Congress and are substantially related to achievement of those objectives."[74] The Court's opinion left O'Connor to write in dissent that the Court had "departed" from the *Richmond* opinion and the principle that race-based classifications are subject to the highest form of judicial review.

O'Connor managed to regain control over the Court on this issue in the 1995 decision *Adarand Constructors, Inc. v. Pena.*[75] The case involved a federal policy that awarded more money to contractors if they employed minority-owned subcontractors. Because of this policy, a contractor selected a minority subcontractor for the product of guardrails over Adarand Constructors, a white-owned business that had submitted the lowest bid. The Court ruled 5–4 that the federal policy violated Adarand's constitutional rights.

O'Connor wrote that "all racial classifications, imposed by whatever federal, state or local governmental actor, must be analyzed by a reviewing court under strict scrutiny."[76] She overruled *Metro Broadcasting*, saying that the Court was restoring basic principles of equal protection jurisprudence developed for the past 50 years. Justices Scalia and Thomas authored separate concurring opinions establishing their strong views that affirmative action policies are per se unconstitutional.

"In my view, government can never have a 'compelling interest' in discriminating on the basis of race in order to 'make up' for past racial discrimination in the opposite direction," Scalia wrote.[77] Thomas, criticized by civil rights groups for his position opposing affirmative action, did not back down an inch from his previous writings and speeches on the subject. He said such policies based on "racial paternalism … can be as poisonous and pernicious as any other form of discrimination." He warned that such programs stamp minorities with badges of inferiority and create a mentality of entitlement.[78] The familiar bloc of four liberal justices in the later era of the Rehnquist Court—Stevens, Ginsberg, Souter, and Breyer—dissented.

The Court returned to the affirmative action debate eight years later in the same context that it began: the university. The Court examined affirmative action policies from the University of Michigan law and undergraduate schools in *Grutter v. Bollinger*[79] and *Gratz v. Bollinger*.[80] The law school policy sought a "critical mass" of minority students but did not mandate a specific numerical quota. Instead, the law school used race as a "plus" factor that was evaluated along with many other factors. The undergraduate policy added 20 extra points to the raw admission score of minority applicants.

The Court split the difference, ruling 5–4 in favor of the law school policy and 6–3 against the undergraduate policy. Four justices—Rehnquist, Kennedy, Scalia, and Thomas—voted against both policies. Three justices—Stevens, Souter, and Ginsburg—voted to uphold both affirmative action policies. That left Justices O'Connor and Breyer as the key swing votes. After watching oral arguments, Adam Cohen authored an editorial in the *New York Times* predicting that O'Connor could be "affirmative action's unlikely savior."[81] Cohen proved prescient, as O'Connor provided the key fifth vote that upheld the law school's affirmative action policy.

O'Connor found, like her friend Justice Powell in *Bakke,* that achieving a diverse student body is a compelling governmental interest. She further found that the particular characteristics of the law school's program were narrowly tailored and based on individualized assessment. "Unlike the program at issue in Gratz v. Bollinger, the Law School awards no mechanical, predetermined diversity 'bonuses' based on race or ethnicity," O'Connor wrote.[82]

The *Grutter* case showed how powerful Justice O'Connor was on the Rehnquist Court. She managed to maintain the middle ground on the Court and served as the key swing vote on a divisive issue. It was cases like these that have caused many experts to label the later Rehnquist Court as the "O'Connor Court." "From the beginning, there was a widespread perception that Justice O'Connor's vote would be crucial and would determine the Court's position in the case," said Kent Syverud, a law school dean who served as an expert witness in the case in the lower court decision in *Grutter*.[83]

"Rehnquist could never move the Court all the way to his position in this area, primarily because of O'Connor, who was influenced greatly by her feelings and intellectual bonds with Lewis Powell," says Baker. "Indeed, his *Bakke* concurring opinion is the inspiration and wellspring of ideas for her affirmative action jurisprudence."[84]

"The Court's decision in *Gratz* and *Grutter* provided some additional guidance on the permissible uses of race, insofar as it is now quite clear that large mechanical or automatic preferences based on race/ethnicity (such as those that were at issue in *Gratz*) will not likely survive strict scrutiny," said attorney Kris Kolbo, who represented Barbara Grutter and Jennifer Gratz. "This aspect of the decisions probably explains why many educational institutions shortly after the decisions abandoned scholarship programs set up exclusively for members of specified racial minorities."[85]

O'Connor remained troubled by the concept of preference and then made an unusual remark toward the end of her opinion. She noted that it had been 25 years since the *Bakke* decision, and she hoped that "in 25 years from now, the use of racial preferences will no longer be necessary to further the interest approved today."[86] "I think O'Connor's 25-year-old comment was an effort to give a wake-up call to academic institutions," Syverud, who used to clerk for Justice O'Connor, says. "I read the sentence as essentially a message to universities that if you can't accomplish your goals, then it is not worth the costs."[87]

This statement of 25 years in the future prompted a sharp retort from Justice Thomas in dissent, who wrote that "the Constitution means the same thing today as it will in 300 months."[88] *Grutter* was another O'Connor opinion that also earned the wrath of Scalia, who criticized the law school's "mythical 'critical mass' justification" as a sham. The chief justice also authored a dissenting opinion, in which he characterized the law school policy as a "naked effort to achieve racial balancing."[89]

"Overall, the Rehnquist Court adopted legal standards making it more difficult to justify the use of race under the requirements of the equal protection clause, even if the Court did not always apply those standards consistently," said Kolbo. "Prior to the Rehnquist Court, it was not always clear what tests the Court or justices would use to evaluate racial preferences and whether the same standard should apply to 'benign' discrimination, like affirmative action. The decisions of the Rehnquist Court have now decisively established that all racial classifications will be evaluated under 'strict scrutiny,' the most stringent standard that the Court applies."[90]

But it is also true that the Rehnquist Court sometimes would uphold laws even under a strict scrutiny standard, as O'Connor's opinion in *Grutter* establishes. "The Rehnquist Court recalibrated strict scrutiny," says Baker. "It used to be that strict scrutiny was outcome-determinative in that if a law was subject to strict scrutiny, it was struck down. The government lost. But when the Rehnquist Court hit its stride, it showed that just because the analysis is strict scrutiny, it doesn't necessarily mean that the government loses. Strict doesn't mean automatically unconstitutional. This was part and parcel of O'Connor's judicial philosophy, which embraced judicial balancing and minimal case-by-case decisionmaking."[91]

CONCLUSION

Three of the most divisive social issues of the past 30 years have been abortion, gay rights, and affirmative action. The Rehnquist Court—whether it wished to or not—had to face serious constitutional questions on each of these topics. In all three areas Chief Justice Rehnquist, in the end, was not able to command a majority of the Court. He managed to limit *Roe v. Wade* by upholding various state regulations through the years, but he could never extinguish the light, as Justice Blackmun warned. At key moments Rehnquist could not obtain the vote of Justices Sandra Day O'Connor, David Souter, or even Anthony Kennedy.

In the area of gay rights the Rehnquist Court directly overruled *Bowers,* though it should be mentioned that Bowers only lost by one vote when Justice Powell changed his mind. In this area, Justice Kennedy proved to be more liberal than social conservatives had hoped he would be. As in the area of abortion, Rehnquist's vision of a right of privacy did not extend as far as the majority of his colleagues. "In *Lawrence,* Rehnquist lost again in a constitutional battle over the right of privacy," Baker says.[92]

In the area of affirmative action Rehnquist managed to move the Court toward employing strict scrutiny for all race-based classifications—a major step in his direction from the Burger Court years, when William Brennan and Thurgood Marshall exercised important influence. However, he once again could not control Justice O'Connor, who proved to be the pivotal vote in the *Grutter* decision.

Chapter 11

LEGACIES OF THE CHIEF JUSTICE AND HIS COURT

> William Rehnquist's independent, impartial, and dedicated leadership of the Supreme Court has been an inspiration to those of us privileged to serve with him—and to the entire Nation as well.
>
> —Associate Justice John Paul Stevens (September 4, 2005)[1]

> William Rehnquist will go down in history as one of the great Chief Justices of the Supreme Court of the United States.
>
> —Associate Justice Sandra Day O'Connor (September 4, 2005)[2]

> The Chief is a towering figure in American law, one of a handful of great Chief Justices.
>
> —Chief Justice John G. Roberts, Jr.[3]

William Rehnquist presided over the Supreme Court as chief justice for 19 years—longer than 12 of his 15 predecessors. Only his judicial hero John Marshall as well as Roger Taney and Melville Fuller served longer terms as chief justice. He served on the Court for a period of more than 33 years from 1972 to 2005. He survived two brutal confirmation hearings and earned praise from even liberal senators who had excoriated him decades earlier. The man labeled an extremist had earned praise for his defense of judicial independence, his fairness as an administrator, and his skilled judicial performance over the Clinton impeachment trial in the U.S. Senate.

During that time from 1986 to 2005, the Rehnquist Court decided countless landmark decisions involving freedom of expression, freedom of religion, abortion, the death penalty, affirmative action, the allocation of power between federal and state governments, and even a presidential election. It reversed itself on issues involving the criminalization of same-sex sodomy, the death penalty for the mentally retarded and juveniles, the use of victim impact testimony in criminal cases, and affirmative action. Many of the Court's decisions were controversial. Some, like *Bush v. Gore,*[4] were blasted as blatantly political and misguided. But the Court survived, and even thrived. Its public opinion numbers remained well above that of the other branches of government.

Many of its members, in addition to William Rehnquist, will go down in history as great justices. Justice William Brennan is often celebrated as one of the greatest justices in Supreme Court history. Justice Thurgood Marshall is revered as a civil rights hero in addition to his historic appointment to the Court. Justice Sandra Day O'Connor, like Marshall, will forever be linked with her trailblazing role as the first female justice. Justice John Paul Stevens, who has now served 30 years, looks like he could break the Court's all-time record for service if his health continues to improve. He could become only the second Supreme Court justice—with Oliver Wendell Holmes—to serve on the bench while he is at least 90 years old. Antonin Scalia will not go quietly as his purple prose and fiery temperament insure he will be remembered. Clarence Thomas will be remembered for more than his most contentious confirmation hearings as he is proving to be a unique constitutional thinker. Others on the Court may well achieve lasting fame.

The last 11 years of the Rehnquist Court witnessed a stability in membership that was nearly unsurpassed in the annals of Supreme Court history. It was a Court composed of many different judicial philosophies, personalities, and predilections. However, the Court was, by and large, a collegial place that shoved aside its disagreements to fulfill its functions efficiently. This was largely the result of William Rehnquist, who did not allow philosophical disagreements to cloud his management skills. As Ruth Bader Ginsburg said on his death, "Chief Justice William H. Rehnquist was the fairest, most efficient boss I have ever had."[5] Nearly every member of the Rehnquist Court had nothing but the most effusive of praise for Chief Justice Rehnquist—even if they were often ideologically opposed to many of his positions. Justice Brennan referred to Rehnquist as the "most all-around successful" chief justice he had worked with[6] and a "magnificent" chief justice.[7] Thurgood Marshall called him a "great chief justice." Lewis Powell said, "Rehnquist is a strong chief justice and all of us knew it."[8]

COURT ADMINISTRATOR

Not only was Rehnquist an efficient and fair boss, but he guided the federal judicial system with a firm and steady hand. Many legal experts say that Rehnquist was one of the greatest judicial administrators. "There is no doubt that the chief was a very skilled administrator," says attorney Jeffrey Bleich, a former law clerk to Rehnquist. "He had reasonable and well-developed expectations, he let you know exactly what he expected, and he was rigorously consistent in applying those rules across the board."[9] When asked by Charlie Rose how he would most like to be remembered, Rehnquist replied as a good administrator, as one who had tried to run "a relatively smoothly functioning Court."[10]

"He also had a broad range of interests, a refreshing candor about his views, and a very good sense of humor," Bleich recalled. "As a result of these administrative and personal skills, he had an uncanny ability to win people over and get them to work together. To a person, I felt that all of his colleagues genuinely liked and respected him."[11]

Another notable mark of Chief Justice Rehnquist's guiding hand was the reduced caseload of the Court. As an associate justice, Rehnquist had been one of at least six justices to complain about the Court's heavy workload. When he became chief justice, Rehnquist did something about the problem: He reduced the number of cases the Court took. The numbers were a dramatic drop from the number of cases taken by the Burger Court each year.

"Truly, the Rehnquist Court pursued his constitutional agenda in the way it managed the docket and granted cases," said Thomas Baker, who was Rehnquist's acting administrative assistant when Rehnquist first replaced Chief Justice Burger. "The change in the actual granting of cases was profound. In the Burger era, the Court granted review in more than 150 cases per year. With the Rehnquist Court, the number was around 80 per year. There also was a huge change in the way the Court saw itself. William Rehnquist got the other justices to see the Court as a kind of Olympian Court that didn't have to resolve every legal dispute or every conflict in the law. It could take fewer cases. It could be more of a supreme court and less of a court of errors or a supervisory court."[12]

Rehnquist's skills as an administrator were shown in how he guided the federal judiciary as a whole, overseeing the Federal Judicial Conference. "He was good without regard to ideology," said federal appeals court judge Gilbert S. Merritt. "He did a good job in broadening the participation among the federal judiciary."[13]

"I never felt that my own views had to coincide with his," says the well-regarded, Democratic-appointed Merritt, whom Rehnquist selected for several positions in federal judicial administration.[14]

AN ACTIVE BENCH

The Rehnquist Court will be known in the annals of history as a Court that actively questioned attorneys arguing cases before it. Veteran Supreme Court reporter Tony Mauro says that the Rehnquist Court is "probably the most active bench in recent Supreme Court history."[15]

"Except for Clarence Thomas, they are all quite active," Mauro says. In the Burger Court, there were several justices—Brennan, Blackmun, and Powell—who did not ask many questions. However, on the Rehnquist Court, in later years, Scalia, Ginsburg, Souter, Kennedy, O'Connor, Rehnquist, and Stevens were all fairly active. Of all the active questioners, Scalia is the most active. After Scalia fired off a series of questions at a hapless attorney, Lewis Powell once asked a colleague, "Does he know the rest of us are even here?"[16]

FEDERALISM

Rehnquist also managed to articulate a consistent, conservative judicial philosophy from his time as the "Lone Ranger" on the Burger Court to majority positions when he was chief justice. As Texas solicitor general Ted Cruz, a former Rehnquist law clerk, writes, "Indeed, there are few clearer legal arcs than the path from Rehnquist dissent to Court majority over these three decades."[17]

In an interview Cruz explained, "This was a Court with famously different personalities and views often difficult to predict. One of the chief's subtle and underappreciated abilities was to guide and lead the Court to the very best possible legal outcome given the personal predilections of his eight colleagues."[18]

Perhaps no clearer arc can be identified than Rehnquist's positions on federalism. He staked out the lonely position as the lone dissenter on the Burger Court. When he became chief justice, and with a few key appointments, Rehnquist managed to unleash what many called a federalism revolution that breathed life into the Tenth and Eleventh Amendments, questioned the extremely broad reach of Congress's commerce clause powers, and energized the autonomy of state governments.

JUDICIAL INDEPENDENCE

Rehnquist and his Court will also be remembered for its commitment to judicial independence. "He understood that part of his role as chief justice was to stand up for judicial independence," Merritt says. "He had a strong philosophical view on the authority and independence of the federal judiciary."[19] He advocated for better pay for federal judges, argued that

Congress needed to speed up the confirmation process to fill vacancies, urged Congress to create new judgeship positions, and stressed that the federal judiciary must be independent.

He was not afraid to express his displeasure with Congress if he felt that it improperly encroached on or ignored the judicial branch. In his annual year-end address in 2003, he chastised Congress for passing the PROTECT Act, dealing with federal sentencing, without any consultation with the judiciary.

"During the last year, it seems that the traditional interchange between the Congress and the Judiciary broke down when Congress enacted what is known as the PROTECT Act, making some rather dramatic changes to the laws governing the federal sentencing process," he said. "Obtaining the views of the Judiciary before the PROTECT Act was enacted would have given all members of Congress the benefit of a perspective they may not have been aware of on this aspect of the legislation and other aspects that deal with a delicate process that judges understand very well. Congress may well have enacted these provisions of the PROTECT Act in any event. But at least judges would have known that the process included a meaningful opportunity to have their views heard."[20] He concluded that "consultation with the Judiciary will improve both the process and the product."[21]

In his next year-end address Rehnquist took aim at the problem of members of Congress criticizing federal judges as activists and attempts to limit the jurisdiction of the courts in certain types of case. Rehnquist explained that "Congress's authority to impeach and remove judges should not extend to decisions from the bench."[22] He recounted the impeachment of Supreme Court Justice Samuel Chase in the early 1800s. The precedent from that process—Chase was acquitted in the Senate—was that "a judge's judicial acts may not serve as a basis for impeachment."[23] According to Rehnquist, "any other rule would destroy judicial independence—instead of trying to apply the law fairly, regardless of public opinion, judges would be concerned about inflaming any group that might be able to muster the votes in Congress to impeach and convict them."[24]

THE END OF THE REHNQUIST COURT

In October 2004, it was revealed to the public that Chief Justice Rehnquist had been diagnosed with thyroid cancer. He underwent radiation and chemotherapy and had to miss many weeks of work at the Court. However, Rehnquist managed to give President George W. Bush his oath of office for his second term in January 2005. Rehnquist even returned to work in March 2005 and asked questions from the bench, as he did throughout his over 30 years on the bench.

Rehnquist managed to finish the 2004–2005 term, but his health regressed again over the summer and fall. He died at the age of 80 on September 4, 2005. On his death his Supreme Court colleagues and various government officials praised his character, work, intellect, and career. "He was extremely well-respected for his powerful intellect," President Bush said. "He was respected for his deep commitment to the rule of law and his profound devotion to duty. He provided superb leadership for the federal court system, improving the delivery of justice for the American people and earning the admiration of his colleagues throughout the judiciary."[25]

Members of Congress from both major political parties paid their respects. The entire Senate joined in a resolution that praised Rehnquist for his years of service on the Court and his masterful guidance of the federal courts in an administrative capacity. The resolution included the following statement: "Whereas William H. Rehnquist will be remembered as one of the greatest Chief Justices of the United States."[26] Republican Senate majority leader Bill Frist from Tennessee gave a long speech in the chief's honor on September 7, 2005. He stated, in part,

> Many feel that history will remember the Chief for presiding over the Senate during impeachment trials, for his participation in landmark decisions, for his perseverance in fulfilling his duties through ailing health. I believe William Rehnquist will be most remembered for his magnificent leadership and management, his ability to build consensus, his compassion and respect for others, and his fair and impartial review of each and every case that came before the Court. The imprint of William Rehnquist's gavel will not fade fast. No, it is indelibly stamped upon the face of American history and the legacy of the law we uphold. America was blessed to have William Rehnquist as Chief Justice and today he enters the history books as one of the greatest Chief Justices ever to serve on the Supreme Court of the United States.[27]

African American Democratic senator Barrack Obama from Illinois also offered praise of the chief justice: "Justice Rehnquist also engaged directly with many of the toughest constitutional controversies of the twentieth century. Although I often disagreed with his decisions, Justice Rehnquist's opinions have been the source of important scholarship and litigation. Like the Chief Justice he followed, the late Chief Justice Earl Warren [Rehnquist actually followed Chief Justice Warren Burger], Justice Rehnquist will be remembered as an important historical figure whose legacy will impact generations of Americans."[28]

Even some of his ideological opponents in the U.S. Senate praised him posthumously. Senator Edward Kennedy stated, "Chief Justice Rehnquist served this country with the greatest distinction, and I respected his leadership of the federal judiciary and his strong commitment to the integrity and independence of the courts."[29]

Senator John McCain introduced the William H. Rehnquist Center Act of 2005 in the Senate on December 16, 2005, which would provide federal funds for the creation of the William H. Rehnquist Center on Constitutional Structures and Judicial Independence at the University of Arizona Law School.[30] On January 3, 2006, the House passed a joint resolution calling for federal funds "to procure a marble bust" of Rehnquist that will be placed in the Supreme Court building in his honor.[31]

It perhaps was fitting that Rehnquist died while still serving as chief justice—a job he enjoyed and relished. Ironically, the last Supreme Court justice to die in office was none other than Justice Robert Jackson—Rehnquist's former boss when he clerked at the Court in the early 1950s.

CONCLUSION

The Rehnquist Court and its chief have often been criticized in certain circles for conservative rulings. Many saw its federalism cases as a dangerous trend that would result in the diminution of federal protection for individual rights. Others believed that it had curtailed habeas corpus so much that it increased the possibility of executing inmates innocent of their crimes. The Court was excoriated for its 2000 decision in *Bush v. Gore,* which effectively ensured that the presidential election would go to Republican candidate George W. Bush instead of Democratic candidate Albert Gore, Jr. But the Court—as it has done largely throughout its 215-year existence—has survived, and even thrived. A Gallup poll in 2004 revealed that William Rehnquist received a favorable rating of 53 percent and an unfavorable rating of only 20 percent.

"The Rehnquist Court really was William H. Rehnquist's Court," says Professor Thomas Baker. "We often use the last name of chief justices to mark eras in Court history. But the Rehnquist Court really was the court of William Rehnquist in style and substance. Yet, at the same time, he did not dominate his colleagues. He ranks with the greatest of chief justices, with John Marshall and Earl Warren."[32]

History generally regards Rehnquist's hero, John Marshall, as the nation's finest chief justice. History may not place William H. Rehnquist very far behind.

NOTES

CHAPTER 1

1. George Lardner, Jr. and Saundra Saperstein, "A Chief Justice-Designate with Big Ambitions," *Washington Post,* April 6, 1986, p. A1.

2. William H. Rehnquist, *The Supreme Court* (New York: Vintage Books, 2002), p. 4.

3. 347 U.S. 483 (1954).

4. Richard West, "Rehnquist Backed by Liberals in Hometown," *Los Angeles Times,* October 30, 1971, p. 16.

5. "Justice Dept. Backs Change to Nonunanimous Jury System," *Chicago Tribune,* September 15, 1971, p. A9.

6. *Ibid.*

7. John H. Averill, "Rehnquist Gentle but Staunch Conservative," *Los Angeles Times,* October 22, 1971, p. A15.

8. Jules Witover and Ronald J. Ostrow, "Chronology of Justice Department's Pentagon Papers Battle," *Washington Post,* July 4, 1971, p. 12.

9. Richard G. Kleindienst, *Justice: The Memoirs of Attorney General Richard Kleindienst* (Ottawa, IL: Jameson Books, 1985), pp. 121–22.

10. *Ibid.*, p. 119.

11. "Administration Firmly Defends Justice Lillie's Judicial Record," *Los Angeles Times,* October 20, 1971, p. A1.

12. John W. Dean, *The Rehnquist Choice: The Untold Story of the Nixon Appointment That Redefined the Supreme Court* (New York: Free Press, 2001), p. 127.

13. Dean, p. 86.

14. Saundra Saperstein and George Lardner, Jr., "Rehnquist: Nixon's Long Shot for a Law and Order Court," *Washington Post,* July 7, 1986, p. A1.

15. "President's Text on Nominees," *Los Angeles Times,* October 22, 1971, p. A16.

16. Philip Warden, "Surprise Choices for Court," *Chicago Tribune,* October 22, 1971, p. 1.

17. Philip Warden, "Liberals Aim at Rehnquist," *Chicago Tribune,* October 23, 1971, p. 1.

18. Roy Wilkins, "Sentiments against Rehnquist," *Los Angeles Times,* November 22, 1971, p. B7.

19. Vernon E. Jordan, Jr., "To Be Equal," *Chicago Daily Defender,* December 4, 1971, p. 28.

20. West, "Rehnquist Backed."

21. Leroy F. Aarons and Ken W. Clawson, "Rehnquist: Admired Yet Decried," *Washington Post,* November 3, 1971, p. A1.

22. "Judiciary Unit Majority Report Hails Rehnquist," *Los Angeles Times,* December 1, 1971, p. A25.

23. John P. MacKenzie, "Minority Report Hits Rehnquist," *Washington Post,* December 1, 1971, p. A33.

24. "Texts of Rehnquist Letter to Senator Eastland and Memo of 1952 on Rights Cases," *New York Times,* December 9, 1971, p. 26.

25. Anthony Lewis, "Ex-Colleague Says Rehnquist Opposed Segregation," *New York Times,* December 10, 1971, p. 28.

26. Fred P. Graham, "Rehnquist Says 52 Memo Outlined Jackson's Views," *New York Times,* December 9, 1971, p. 26.

27. "Brooke Says He's Opposed to Rehnquist," *Washington Post,* December 3, 1971, p. A23.

28. "Rehnquist Confirmed by Senate, 68–26," *New York Times,* December 11, 1971, p. 1.

29. "William Rehnquist," *Chicago Daily Defender,* December 16, 1971, p. 23.

30. "Powell, Rehnquist Take Supreme Court Seats," *Los Angeles Times,* January 8, 1972, p. A15.

31. "Two New High Court Justices," *Los Angeles Times,* December 12, 1971, p. 15.

CHAPTER 2

1. Quoted in John A. Jenkins, "The Partisan: A Talk with Justice Rehnquist," *New York Times,* March 3, 1985, p. SM28.

2. Bernard Schwartz, *A History of the Supreme Court* (New York: Oxford University Press, 1993), p. 263.

3. 347 U.S. 483 (1954).

4. 376 U.S. 254 (1964).

5. 370 U.S. 421 (1962).

6. 372 U.S. 335 (1963).

7. 384 U.S. 436 (1966).
8. 369 U.S. 186 (1962).
9. 367 U.S. 643 (1961).
10. Kenneth W. Starr, *First among Equals: The Supreme Court in American Life* (New York: Warner Books, 2002), p. 176.
11. *Ibid.*, p. 177.
12. 407 U.S. 25 (1972).
13. 408 U.S. 238 (1972).
14. Jim Mann, "Rehnquist: At High Court Cutting Edge," *Los Angeles Times,* September 6, 1981, p. 1.
15. Schwartz, *A History,* p. 364.
16. Harold J. Spaeth, "Chief Justice Rehnquist: 'Poster Child' for the Attitudinal Model," *Judicature* 89 (November–December 2005): 110.
17. 413 U.S. 189 (1973).
18. *Id.* at 208.
19. *Id.* at 254–55 (J. Rehnquist, dissenting).
20. 419 U.S. 522 (1975).
21. *Id.* at 532.
22. *Id.* at 537.
23. *Id.* at 538–39 (J. Rehnquist, dissenting).
24. *Hoyt v. Florida,* 368 U.S. 57 (1961).
25. *Taylor,* 419 U.S. at 540.
26. *Id.* at 543.
27. 406 U.S. 164 (1972).
28. *Id.* at 175.
29. *Id.* at 185 (J. Rehnquist, dissenting).
30. *Id.* at 182.
31. 411 U.S. 619 (1973).
32. *Id.* at 621.
33. *Id.* at 622 (J. Rehnquist, dissenting).
34. 442 U.S. 95 (1979).
35. *Id.* at 97.
36. *Id.* at 98 (J. Rehnquist, dissenting).
37. *Id.*
38. 470 U.S. 68 (1985).
39. *Id.* at 74.
40. *Id.* at 87 (J. Rehnquist, dissenting).
41. *Id.*
42. 405 U.S. 319 (1972).
43. *Id.* at 322.
44. *Id.* at 326 (J. Rehnquist, dissenting).
45. 425 U.S. 748 (1976).
46. *Id.* at 781 (J. Rehnquist, dissenting).
47. 436 U.S. 412 (1978).
48. *Id.* at 422.

49. *Id.* at 440 (J. Rehnquist, dissenting).

50. 448 U.S. 555 (1980).

51. *Id.* at 580.

52. *Id.* at 581.

53. *Id.* at 604 (J. Rehnquist, dissenting).

54. *Id.* at 605.

55. *Id.* at 606.

56. 420 U.S. 469 (1975).

57. *Id.* at 496.

58. 444 U.S. 620 (1980).

59. *Id.* at 637.

60. *Id.* at 639 (J. Rehnquist, dissenting).

61. *Id.* at 644.

62. 447 U.S. 557 (1980).

63. *Id.* at 570.

64. *Id.* at 584 (J. Rehnquist, dissenting).

65. *Id.* at 587.

66. 459 U.S. 116, 127 (1982).

67. *Id.* at 127–28 (J. Rehnquist, dissenting).

68. *Id.* at 130 (J. Rehnquist, dissenting).

69. 428 U.S. 153 (1976).

70. 410 U.S. 113 (1973).

71. Linda Greenhouse, "Justice Rehnquist: Firm Ways, Witty Means," *New York Times,* July 12, 1981, p. E22.

72. Warren Weaver, Jr., "Mr. Justice Rehnquist, Dissenting," *New York Times,* October 13, 1974, p. 312.

73. 409 U.S. 824 (1972).

74. *Id.* at 831.

75. David L. Shapiro, "Mr. Justice Rehnquist: A Preliminary View," *Harvard Law Review* 90 (1976): 294.

76. William H. Rehnquist, "The Notion of a Living Constitution," *Texas Law Review* 54 (1976).

77. 477 U.S. 57, 64 (1986).

78. *Id.* at 66.

79. 418 U.S. 153, 161 (1974).

80. 439 U.S. 410 (1979).

81. *Id.* at 413.

82. *Id.* at 415–16.

83. David L. Hudson, Jr., "Teacher Taught Miss. Schools a Free-Speech Lesson," First Amendment Center, http://www.firstamendmentcenter.org/analysis.aspx?id=16992 (accessed June 8, 2006).

84. Bob Woodward and Scott Armstrong, *The Brethren: Inside the Supreme Court* (New York: Simon and Schuster, 1979), p. 267.

85. Weaver, "Mr. Justice Rehnquist."

86. Mann, "Rehnquist," p. 5.

CHAPTER 3

1. Stanley Mosk, "A Liberal for Rehnquist; His Federalism Served the Cause of Individual Rights," *Los Angeles Times,* July 30, 1986, Metro, part 2, p. 5.

2. Michael Putzel, "Choices of Rehnquist, Scalia Followed Methodological Selection Process," Associated Press, June 18, 1986.

3. Associated Press, "Chief Justice Burger Quits; Rehnquist to Succeed Him; D.C. Judge Picked for Vacancy; Both of the Appointees Staunch Conservatives," *Los Angeles Times,* June 17, 1986, p. 1.

4. *Ibid.*

5. William Rehnquist, interview by Sam Donaldson, *World News Tonight,* ABC News, June 17, 1986.

6. George Lardner, Jr. and Al Kamen, "Kennedy Calls Rehnquist 'Too Extreme,'" *Washington Post,* July 30, 1986, p. A1.

7. Robert Dole of Kansas, *Congressional Record,* 99th Cong., 2d sess. (July 30, 1986): 18043.

8. *Ibid.*

9. 447 U.S. 74 (1980).

10. Associated Press, "Rehnquist's View on Memos Disputed by Aide to Jackson," *New York Times,* August 11, 1986, p. A14.

11. George Lardner, Jr., "Rehnquist Said Backer of '50s Racial Tenet; Ex-Colleague Recounts Stance on Segregation," *Washington Post,* July 22, 1986, p. A8.

12. John W. Dean, *The Rehnquist Choice: The Untold Story of the Nixon Appointment That Redefined the Supreme Court* (New York: Free Press, 2001), p. 284.

13. Stuart Taylor, Jr., "4 Rebut Testimony of Rehnquist on Challenging of Voters in 60s," *New York Times,* August 2, 1986, p. 1.

14. Stuart Taylor, Jr., "Rehnquist Says He Didn't Deter Voters in 1960s," *New York Times,* July 31, 1986, p. A1.

15. Linda Greenhouse, "Senate Unit Backs Rehnquist, 13 to 5," *New York Times,* August 15, 1986, p. A1.

16. Letter from Gillers to Metzenbaum, September 4, 1986, published in *Congressional Record,* 99th Cong., 2d sess. (September 10, 1986): 22592–93.

17. Stuart Taylor, Jr., "Rehnquist's Critics Press Charges That He Was Unethical on Court," *New York Times,* September 11, 1986, p. B15.

18. Christopher Pyle, "The Case Rehnquist Shouldn't Have Decided," *New York Times,* September 9, 1986, p. A26.

19. Letter to U.S. Senate from American Law Professors, published in *Congressional Record,* 99th Cong., 2d sess. (September 10, 1986): 22602–03.

20. Associated Press, "ABA Boosts Rehnquist Cause as Partisan Scrap Continues," *Chicago Tribune,* July 31, 1986, p. 4.

21. Greenhouse, "Senate Unit."

22. "Rights Leaders Say Senate Could Reject Rehnquist," *New York Times,* September 5, 1986, p. A22.

23. Robert Dole of Kansas, *Congressional Record,* 99th Cong., 2d sess. (September 11, 1986): 23033.

24. Paul Sarbanes of Maryland, *Congressional Record,* 99th Cong., 2d sess. (September 16, 1986): 23552.

25. *Ibid.*

26. Howard Heflin of Alabama, *Congressional Record,* 99th Cong., 2d sess. (September 17, 1986): 23718.

27. Associated Press, "Rehnquist's Civil Rights View Spurs Heckling at Indiana U.," *New York Times,* September 13, 1986, p. 10.

28. Linda Greenhouse, "Senate, 65 to 33, Votes to Confirm Rehnquist as 16th Chief Justice," *New York Times,* September 18, 1986, p. A1.

29. Linda Greenhouse, "Reporter's Notebook: Senators v. Rehnquist," *New York Times,* September 19, 1986, p. A24.

30. Greenhouse, "Senate, 65 to 33."

31. Al Kamen, "Rehnquist Confirmed in 65–33 Senate Vote," *Washington Post,* September 18, 1986, p. A1; Stuart Taylor, Jr., "Rehnquist Seeks 'to Be a Good Chief Justice,'" *New York Times,* September 19, 1986, p. A24.

32. Al Kamen, "For Rehnquist, Aftermath of Confirmation Is Routine," *Washington Post,* September 19, 1986, p. A3.

33. Crystal Patterson, "Senator Kennedy on the Passing of William Rehnquist," TedKennedy.com, http://www.tedkennedy.com/journal/222/senator-kennedy-on-the-passing-of-chief-justice-william-rehnquist.

CHAPTER 4

1. Linda Greenhouse, "The Last Days of the Rehnquist Court: The Rewards of Patience and Power," *Arizona Law Review* 45 (2003): 267.

2. William H. Rehnquist, *The Supreme Court* (New York: Vintage Books, 2002), p. 227.

3. 369 U.S. 186 (1962).

4. 376 U.S. 254 (1964).

5. 374 U.S. 398 (1963).

6. Thomas Baker, personal communication, May 16, 2006.

7. "White's Law; A Justice Who Avoided Grand Pronouncements," *Pittsburgh Post-Gazette,* April 17, 2002, p. A24.

8. 384 U.S. 486 (1966).

9. 408 U.S. 665 (1972).

10. 484 U.S. 260 (1988).

11. 478 U.S. 186 (1986).

12. Juan Williams, *Thurgood Marshall: American Revolutionary,* 1st. ed. (New York: Times Books, 1998), p. 401.

13. *Callins v. Collins,* 510 U.S. 1141, 1145 (1994) (J. Blackmun, dissenting from denial of certiorari).

14. 410 U.S. 113 (1973).

15. *Id.* at 228.

16. 438 U.S. 265 (1978).

17. Tony Mauro, "Supreme Court's Moderate 'Gentleman' Powell Dies at 90," *USA Today,* August 26, 1998, p. 1A.

18. Jim Mann, "Stevens' Role: Junior Justice a Maverick in Liberal Wing," *Los Angeles Times,* May 18, 1980, p. 1.

19. Jerald terHorst, "Justice Stevens Faces Toughest Test," *Chicago Tribune,* December 28, 1975, p. A6.

20. "Justice Stevens, in Dissents, Gives a Hint of Some Liberal Views," *New York Times,* March 9, 1976, p. 17.

21. Stuart Taylor, Jr., "Justice Stevens, in Rare Criticism, Disputes Meese on Constitution," *New York Times,* October 26, 1985, p. 1.

22. Stuart Taylor, Jr., "Justice Stevens, in Unusual Move, Praises Bork as Nominee to Court," *New York Times,* August 1, 1987, p. 1.

23. 438 U.S. 726 (1978).

24. 521 U.S. 844 (1997).

25. Jeffrey Fisher, personal communication, May 25, 2006.

26. Joan Biskupic, *Sandra Day O'Connor: How the First Woman on the Supreme Court Became Its Most Influential Justice,* 1st ed. (New York: ECCO, 2005), p. 42.

27. *Ibid.*, p. 47.

28. Linda Greenhouse, "Court Dropping Mr. Justice," *New York Times,* November 19, 1980, p. A16.

29. Biskupic, *Sandra Day O'Connor,* p. 77.

30. *Ibid.*, p. 85.

31. Rehnquist, *Supreme Court,* p. 229.

32. Ruth Marcus, "Judge a Favorite with Conservative Lawyers, Activists," *Washington Post,* June 18, 1986, p. A1.

33. *Ibid.*

34. Thomas Baker, personal communication, May 26, 2006.

35. Howard Kurtz and Al Kamen, "First Day of Questioning Leaves Scalia Unscathed," *Washington Post,* August 6, 1986, p. A6.

36. Thomas Baker, personal communication, May 26, 2006.

37. Antonin Scalia, *A Matter of Interpretation: Federal Courts and the Law: An Essay* (Princeton, NJ: Princeton University Press, 1997).

38. *Ibid.*, p. 23.

39. *Ibid.*, p. 45.

40. Associated Press, "Scalia Says Constitution Still Has Most Answers," April 11, 2003.

41. Thomas Baker, personal communication, May 26, 2006.

42. *Apprendi v. New Jersey,* 530 U.S. 466, 499 (2000) (J. Scalia, concurring).

43. Frank J. Murray, "Irate Scalia Lashes Out at Resignation Rumors; Attacks Article As 'Gossipy, Titillating,'" *Washington Times,* October 3, 2000, p. A1.

44. Tony Mauro, personal communication, June 2, 2006.

45. Kenneth L. Zimmerman, letter to the editor, *Los Angeles Times,* November 12, 1987, Metro, part 2, p. 6.

46. Al Kamen, "Kennedy Moves Court to Right," *Washington Post,* April 11, 1989, p. A1.

47. Linda Greenhouse, "The Year the Court Turned Right," *New York Times,* July 7, 1989, p. A1.

48. 539 U.S. 558 (2003).

49. 125 S.Ct. 1183 (2005).

50. Quoted in Carl M. Cannon, "Anthony Kennedy," *California Journal,* November 1, 1997.

51. Adam Cohen, "Anthony Kennedy Is Ready for His Close-Up," *New York Times,* April 3, 2006, p. A16.

52. Ruth Marcus and Michael Isikoff, "Souter Declines Comment on Abortion," *Washington Post,* September 14, 1990, p. A1.

53. Linda Greenhouse, "Souter Anchoring the Court's New Center," *New York Times,* July 3, 1992, p. A1.

54. Tinsley E. Yarbrough, *David Hackett Souter: Traditional Republican on the Rehnquist Court* (New York: Oxford University Press, 2005), p. 149.

55. "Excerpts from Senate's Hearings on the Souter Nomination," *New York Times,* September 18, 1990, p. B6.

56. *Planned Parenthood of Southeastern Pennsylvania v. Casey,* 505 U.S. 833 (1992).

57. 501 U.S. 560 (1991).

58. 529 U.S. 277 (2000).

59. *Id.* at 316–17 (J. Souter, concurring in part and dissenting in part).

60. 531 U.S. 98 (2000).

61. Yarbrough, *David Hackett Souter,* p. 259.

62. Associated Press, "Ten Years Later, Sununu Admits to Disappointment in Souter," March 2, 2000.

63. Ken Foskett, *Judging Thomas: The Life and Times of Clarence Thomas* (New York: William Morrow, 2004), p. 177.

64. *Ibid.*, p. 248.

65. Kenneth W. Starr, *First among Equals: The Supreme Court in American Life* (New York: Warner Books, 2002), p. xxi.

66. 514 U.S. 549 (1995).

67. *Id.* at 585 (J. Thomas, concurring).

68. David L. Hudson, Jr., "Justice Clarence Thomas: The Emergence of a Commercial-Speech Protector," *Creighton Law Review* 35 (2002): 485.

69. *44 Liquormart v. Rhode Island,* 517 U.S. 484, 522 (1996) (J. Thomas, concurring).

70. Foskett, *Judging Thomas,* pp. 12–3.

71. Associated Press, "Supreme Court Justice Ruth Bader Ginsburg Touches on Roe v. Wade during Kansas Visit," March 11, 2005.

72. Thomas Baker, personal communication, May 26, 2006.

73. Linda Greenhouse, "Supreme Court Roundup; Opening Term, Court Will Ponder Sign on a Home," *New York Times,* October 23, 1993, p. B10.

74. Jeffrey Rosen, "The New Look of Liberalism on the Court," *New York Times,* October 5, 1997, p. SM60.

75. 518 U.S. 515 (1996).

76. *Van Orden v. Perry,* 545 U.S. 677 (2005); *McCreary County v. ACLU of Kentucky,* 545 U.S. 844 (2005)

77. Linda Greenhouse, "The Competing Visions of the Role of the Court," *New York Times,* July 7, 2002, p. C3.

78. Stephen Breyer, *Active Liberty: Interpreting Our Democratic Constitution,* 1st ed. (New York: Alfred A. Knopf, 2005).

79. *Ibid.*, p. 127.

80. *Ibid.*, p. 132.

CHAPTER 5

1. *Fry v. United States,* 421 U.S. 542, 559 (1975) (J. Rehnquist, dissenting).

2. Eric R. Claeys, "Raich and Judicial Conservatism at the Close of the Rehnquist Court," *Lewis and Clark Law Review* 9 (2005): 791.

3. 392 U.S. 183 (1968).

4. *Fry,* 421 U.S. at 543 (J. Rehnquist, dissenting).

5. *Id.* at 558.

6. *Id.* at 559.

7. 426 U.S. 833 (1976).

8. *Id.* at 852.

9. *Id.* at 854.

10. 469 U.S. 528 (1985).

11. *Id.* at 531.

12. *Id.* at 580 (J. Rehnquist, dissenting).

13. 456 U.S. 742 (1982).

14. *Id.* at 777 (J. O'Connor, concurring in part and dissenting in part).

15. 514 U.S. 552.

16. 301 U.S. 1, 36–8 (1937).

17. 317 U.S. 111, 125 (1942).

18. *Lopez,* 514 U.S. at 556.

19. *Id.* at 558–9.

20. *Id.* at 560.

21. *Id.* at 567.

22. *Id.* at 581 (J. Kennedy, concurring).

23. *Id.* at 585 (J. Thomas, concurring).

24. *Id.* at 602 (J. Stevens, dissenting).

25. *Id.* at 604, 608 (J. Souter, dissenting).

26. *Id.* at 625–30 (J. Breyer, dissenting).

27. 529 U.S. 598 (2000).

28. *Id.* at 613.

29. *Id.* at 616.

30. *Id.* at 626.

31. *Id.* at 654–5 (J. Souter, dissenting).

32. 545 U.S. 1 (2005).

33. 505 U.S. 144 (1992).

34. *Id.* at 176.

35. 521 U.S. 898 (1997).

36. *Id.* at 932.
37. *Id.* at 944 (J. Stevens, dissenting).
38. 517 U.S. 44 (1996).
39. *Id.* at 100 (J. Souter, dissenting).
40. 528 U.S. 62 (2000).
41. *Id.* at 91.
42. 531 U.S. 356 (2001).
43. Martin Garbus, *Courting Disaster: The Supreme Court and the Unmaking of American Law,* 1st ed. (New York: Times Books, 2002), p. 155.
44. *Fitzpatrick v. Bitzer,* 427 U.S. 445, 456 (1976).
45. 538 U.S. 721 (2003).
46. *Id.* at 738.
47. 541 U.S. 509 (2004).
48. Ilya Somin, "Rehnquist's Federalist Legacy," Fox News.com, http://www.cato.org/pub_display.php?pub_id=4689&print=Y.
49. Mark Tushnet, "William Rehnquist's Federalism," in *The Rehnquist Legacy,* ed. Craig M. Bradley (New York: Cambridge University Press, 2006), pp. 187–204.
50. Marci Hamilton, "The Supreme Court's Federalism Cases This Term: A String of Decisions Upholding Federal Power Show the Portrayal of the Court as Extreme Is a Caricature," Findlaw.com, http://writ.news.findlaw.com/hamilton/20040603.html.

CHAPTER 6

1. *Mueller v. Allen,* 463 U.S. 388, 392 (1983).
2. *Employment Division v. Smith,* 494 U.S. 872, 877 (1990).
3. See *Cutter v. Wilkinson,* 125 S.Ct. 2113, 2125 (2005).
4. *Everson v. Board of Education,* 330 U.S. 1, 16 (1947).
5. 370 U.S. 421, 424 (1962).
6. *Wallace v. Jaffree,* 472 U.S. 38, 92 (1985) (J. Rehnquist, dissenting).
7. *Id.* at 107.
8. Douglas Laycock, personal communication, May 11, 2006.
9. *Ibid.*
10. 496 U.S. 226 (1990).
11. *Elk Grove Unified School District v. Newdow,* 542 U.S. 1 (2005).
12. 403 U.S. 602 (1971).
13. *Id.* at 110.
14. *Lamb's Chapel v. Center Moriches Union Free School District,* 508 U.S. 384, 398 (1993).
15. *Lynch v. Donnelly,* 465 U.S. 668, 687–94 (1984) (J. O'Connor, concurring).
16. Douglas Laycock, personal communication, May 11, 2006.
17. *County of Allegheny v. ACLU Greater Pittsburgh Chapter,* 492 U.S. 573, 659 (1989) (J. Kennedy, dissenting).
18. 505 U.S. 577 (1992).
19. *Id.* at 592.
20. *Id.* at 577.

21. *Id.* at 593.
22. *Id.* at 631 (J. Scalia, dissenting).
23. *Id.* at 644.
24. *Id.* at 646 (J. Scalia, dissenting).
25. *Santa Fe Independent School Dist. v. Doe,* 530 U.S. 290 (2000).
26. *Id.* at 320.
27. *Id.* at 320 (C. J. Rehnquist, dissenting).
28. *County of Allegheny v. American Civil Liberties Union Greater Pittsburgh Chapter,* 492 U.S. 573 (1989).
29. *Lynch v. Donnelly,* 465 U.S. 668 (1984).
30. 449 U.S. 39 (1980).
31. 545 U.S. 677, 125 S.Ct. 2854 (2005).
32. 545 U.S. 844, 125 S.Ct. 2722.
33. *Van Orden*, 125 S.Ct. at 2863.
34. *Id.* at 2870–71 (J. Breyer, concurring).
35. 463 U.S. 388, 397 (1983).
36. 474 U.S. 481 (1989).
37. 509 U.S. 1 (1993).
38. 536 U.S. 639 (2002).
39. *Id.* at 652.
40. *Id.* at 662.
41. Douglas Laycock, personal communication, May 11, 2006.
42. 374 U.S. 398 (1963).
43. 406 U.S. 205 (1972).
44. 494 U.S. 872 (1990).
45. *Id.* at 886.
46. *Id.* at 891 (J. O'Connor, concurring).
47. Charles Haynes, "Religious Freedom: Inherent Right or Gift of the State?" First Amendment Center, http://www.firstamendmentcenter.org//commentary.aspx?id=16578.
48. 521 U.S. 507 (1997).
49. *Lassiter v. Northampton County Bd. of Elections,* 360 U.S. 45 (1959).
50. *South Carolina v. Katzenbach,* 383 U.S. 301 (1966).
51. *Id.* at 519.
52. *Id.* at 524.
53. Douglas Laycock, personal communication, May 11, 2006.
54. *Cutter v. Wilkinson,* 1256 S.Ct. 2113 (2005).
55. *Van Orden,* 125 S.Ct. at 2866 (J. Thomas, concurring).
56. 542 U.S. 1 (2004).

CHAPTER 7

1. *Boy Scouts of America v. Dale,* 530 U.S. 640, 660 (2000).
2. Kevin O'Neill, "A First Amendment Compass: Navigating the Speech Clause with a Five-Step Analytical Framework," *Southwestern University Law Review* 29 (2000): 223, 225.

3. *Jacobellis v. Ohio,* 378 U.S. 184, 197 (1964) (J. Stewart, concurring).

4. *City of Los Angeles v. Alameda Books, Inc.*, 535 U.S. 425, 455 (2002) (J. Souter, dissenting).

5. Wendy Zentz, "The Jerry and Larry Show," United Press International, December 3, 1987.

6. *Hustler Magazine v. Falwell,* 485 U.S. 46, 53 (1988).

7. *Id.* at 55.

8. Robert O'Neil, personal communication, May 11, 2006.

9. Jane Kirtley, personal communication, February 16, 2006.

10. Alex Brummer, "Supreme Court Backs Porno King Appeal against Moral Majority," *Guardian,* February 25, 1988.

11. "Courageous Stand by Supreme Court," *Chicago Tribune,* February 26, 1988, p. 18C.

12. "Outrageous Speech? Yes, and Free," *New York Times,* February 26, 1988, p. 34A.

13. *Texas v. Johnson,* 491 U.S. 397, 412 (1989).

14. *Id.* at 420 (J. Kennedy, concurring).

15. *Id.* at 432 (C. J. Rehnquist, dissenting).

16. *Id.* at 438 (J. Stevens, dissenting).

17. 529 U.S. 803 (2000).

18. *Id.* at 826.

19. *Id.* at 830 (J. Thomas, concurring).

20. 530 U.S. 640, 659 (2000).

21. *Id.* at 679 (J. Stevens, dissenting).

22. 536 U.S. 765 (2002).

23. Ronald K. L. Collins, "Recent Trends Go against Free Speech: The Free-Speech Record of the Rehnquist II Court," First Amendment Center, http://www.firstamendmentcenter.org/analysis.aspx?id=13985.

24. Eugene Volokh, "How the Justices Voted in Free Speech Cases, 1994–2002," http://www.law.ucla.edu/volokh/howvoted.htm. On his Web site, Professor Volokh explains that this article is an updated version of Eugene Volokh, "How the Justices Voted in Free Speech Cases, 1994–2000," *UCLA Law Review* 48 (2001): 1191.

25. David L. Hudson, Jr., "Justice Thomas Emerges as Court's Champion of Commercial Speech," *Commercial Speech Digest,* Fall 1997, http://www.mediainstitute.org/digest/97fall/hudson.html.

26. *McConnell v. FEC,* 540 U.S. 93 (2003) (J. Thomas, dissenting).

27. 505 U.S. 377 (1992).

28. *Id.* at 391.

29. *Rosenberger v. Rector and Visitors of the University of Virginia,* 515 U.S. 819 (1995).

30. *Legal Services Corp. v. Velazquez,* 531 U.S. 533 (2001).

31. *Young v. American Mini Theatres,* 427 U.S. 50, 81 at n. 4 (1976).

32. *Renton v. Playtime Theatres,* 475 U.S. 41 (1986).

33. Interview with John Weston as quoted in David L. Hudson, Jr., "Adult Entertainment and the Secondary-Effects Doctrine: How a Zoning Regulation May Affect

First Amendment Freedoms," FreedomForum.org, http://www.freedomforum.org/templates/document.asp?documentID=16466.

34. 529 U.S. 277 (2000).

35. *Id.* at 317 (J. Souter, dissenting).

36. 485 U.S. 312, 321 (1988).

37. David L. Hudson, Jr., "The Secondary Effects Doctrine: The Evisceration of First Amendment Freedoms," *Washburn Law Journal* 37 (1997): 55; David L. Hudson, Jr., "Justice Brennan's Significant Departure and Warning of an Evisceration," *Nexus Journal* 10 (2005): 93–97.

38. 500 U.S. 173, 193 (1991).

39. 544 U.S. 550 (2005).

40. 521 U.S. 844 (1997).

41. David L. Hudson, Jr., "First Amendment Triumphs Mark Attorney's Supreme Court Record," First Amendment Center, http://www.firstamendmentcenter.org/news.aspx?id=8583.

42. *Ashcroft v. ACLU,* 542 U.S. 656 (2004).

43. *Valentine v. Chrestensen,* 316 U.S. 52, 54 (1942).

44. *Virginia Pharmacy Board v. Virginia Consumer Council,* 425 U.S. 748 (1976).

45. *Id.* at 770.

46. *Bates v. Arizona,* 433 U.S. 350 (1977).

47. *Central Hudson Gas & Elec. Corp. v. Public Service Comm'n of N.Y.*, 447 U.S. 557 (1980).

48. *Ohralik v. Ohio,* 436 U.S. 456 (1978).

49. 517 U.S. 484, 503 (1996).

50. *Greater New Orleans Broadcasting Ass'n v. U.S.*, 527 U.S. 173 (1999).

51. *Lorillard Tobacco Co. v. Reilly,* 533 U.S. 525 (2001).

52. *Thompson v. Western States Medical Center,* 535 U.S. 357 (2002).

53. 484 U.S. 260 (1988).

54. 393 U.S. 503 (1969).

55. *Hazelwood,* 484 U.S. at 273.

56. 482 U.S. 78 (1987).

57. *Id.* at 84.

58. Collins, "Recent Trends."

59. 391 U.S. 563 (1968).

60. 461 U.S. 138 (1983).

61. 483 U.S. 378, 389 (1987).

62. 511 U.S. 661, 679 (1994).

63. *Board of County Commissioners v. Umbehr,* 518 U.S. 668 (1996).

64. Robert Van Kirk, personal communication, May 16, 2006.

65. Burt Neuborne, "Free Expression and the Rehnquist Court," in *The Rehnquist Court: A Retrospective,* ed. Martin H. Belsky (New York: Oxford University Press, 2002), p. 15.

66. Jamin B. Raskin, "The First Amendment: The High Ground and the Low Road," in *The Rehnquist Court: Judicial Activism on the Right,* ed. Herman Schwartz (New York: Hill and Wang, 2002), p. 117.

CHAPTER 8

1. *Coleman v. Balkcom,* 451 U.S. 949, 958 (1981) (J. Rehnquist, dissenting from denial of certiorari).
2. *Atkins v. Virginia,* 536 U.S. 304, 353 (2002).
3. *Id.* at 374 (J. Scalia, dissenting).
4. 384 U.S. 436 (1966).
5. 372 U.S. 335 (1963).
6. Stephen F. Smith, "The Rehnquist Court and Criminal Procedure," *University of Colorado Law Review* 73 (2002) 1337–1361, 1338.
7. 442 U.S. 95 (1979).
8. *Id.* at 97.
9. *Id.* at 98 (J. Rehnquist, dissenting).
10. 450 U.S. 288 (1981).
11. *Malloy v. Hogan,* 378 U.S. 1 (1964); *Griffin v. California,* 380 U.S. 609 (1965).
12. *Malloy,* 378 U.S. at 309–10, citing *Griffin,* 380 U.S. 609, 623 (J. Stewart, dissenting).
13. 436 U.S. 499 (1978).
14. 451 U.S. 949, 956 (1981) (J. Rehnquist, dissenting from denial of certiorari).
15. *Id.* at 958.
16. Joseph L. Hoffman, "Narrowing Habeas Corpus," in *The Rehnquist Legacy,* ed. Craig M. Bradley (New York: Cambridge University Press, 2006), pp. 156–7.
17. 433 U.S. 72 (1977).
18. *Id.* at 91.
19. 489 U.S. 288 (1989).
20. *Id.* at 309.
21. *Id.* at 310.
22. 507 U.S. 619 (1993).
23. 506 U.S. 390 (1993).
24. *Id.* at 400.
25. *Murray v. Giarratano,* 492 U.S. 1, 10 (1989).
26. Linda Greenhouse, "Judges Challenge Rehnquist's Role on Death Penalty," *New York Times,* October 6, 1989, p. A1.
27. 501 U.S. 722 (1991).
28. *Id.* at 759 (J. Blackmun, dissenting).
29. Maria Glod and Michael Shear, "DNA Tests Confirm Guilt of Executed Man," *Washington Post,* January 13, 2006, p. A1, http://www.washingtonpost.com/wp-dyn/content/article/2006/01/12/AR2006011201210.html.
30. Hoffman, "Narrowing Habeas Corpus," p. 181.
31. Craig Bradley, personal communication, May 11, 2006.
32. 540 U.S. 668 (2004).
33. 408 U.S. 238 (1972).
34. *Id.* at 239 (J. Stewart, concurring).

35. *Id.* at 468 (J. Rehnquist, dissenting).
36. 428 U.S. 153 (1976).
37. *Id.* at 292–3.
38. *Id.* at 312.
39. *Id.* at 345 (J. Blackmun, dissenting).
40. 501 U.S. 808 (1991).
41. *Booth v. Maryland,* 482 U.S. 496 (1987); *South Carolina v. Gathers,* 400 U.S. 805 (1989).
42. *Booth,* 482 U.S. at 508.
43. *Payne,* 501 U.S. at 825.
44. Kent Scheidegger, personal communication, May 15, 2006.
45. 492 U.S. 361 (1989).
46. *Id.* at 378.
47. *Id.* at 382 (J. Brennan, dissenting).
48. 492 U.S. 302 (1989).
49. 530 U.S. 1141, 1145 (1994) (J. Blackmun, dissenting from denial of certiorari).
50. Linda Greenhouse, *Becoming Justice Blackmun: Harry Blackmun's Supreme Court Journey,* 1st ed. (New York: Times Books, 2005), p. 178.
51. 543 U.S. 551 (2005).
52. 536 U.S. 304 (2002).
53. *Id.* at 310.
54. *Id.* at 347, n. 21.
55. *Roper v. Simmons,* 543 U.S. 551 (2005).
56. Charles Ogletree, "Rehnquist Revolution in Criminal Procedure," in *The Rehnquist Court: Judicial Activism on the Right,* ed. Herman Schwartz (New York: Hill and Wang, 2002), p. 58.
57. Kent Scheidegger, personal communication, May 15, 2006.

CHAPTER 9

1. Quoted in John A. Jenkins, "The Partisan: A Talk with Justice Rehnquist," *New York Times,* March 3, 1985, p. SM32.
2. 384 U.S. 436 (1966).
3. Bob Sector, "Meese Raps Court for 'Infamous' Rulings," *Los Angeles Times,* August 26, 1985, p. A4.
4. *Miranda,* 384 U.S. at 444.
5. *Id.* at 444–5, 479.
6. *Id.* at 504 (J. Harlan, dissenting).
7. 417 U.S. 433, 446 (1974).
8. 467 U.S. 649 (1984).
9. *Id.* at 656.
10. 530 U.S. 428 (2000).
11. Linda Greenhouse, "The Last Days of the Rehnquist Court: The Rewards of Patience and Power," *Arizona Law Review* 45 (2003): 252.

12. *Ibid.*

13. *Dickerson,* 530 U.S. at 437.

14. *Id.* at 443.

15. *Id.* at 465 (J. Scalia, dissenting).

16. *Id.*

17. James W. Hundley, personal communication, May 15, 2006.

18. *Ibid.*

19. Charles Ogletree, "Rehnquist Revolution in Criminal Procedure," in *The Rehnquist Court: Judicial Activism on the Right,* ed. Herman Schwartz (New York: Hill and Wang, 2002), p. 63.

20. *United States v. Patone,* 542 U.S. 630, 640 (2004).

21. Yale Kamisar, "Dickerson v. United States: The Case That Disappointed Miranda's Critics—and Then Its Supporters," in *The Rehnquist Legacy,* ed. Craig M. Bradley (New York: Cambridge University Press, 2006), p. 125.

22. *Ibid.*, p. 128.

23. *Ewing v. California,* 538 U.S. 11 (2003); *Lockyer v. Andrade,* 538 U.S. 63 (2003).

24. *Smith v. Doe,* 538 U.S. 84 (2003).

25. *Connecticut Dept. of Public Safety v. Doe,* 538 U.S. 1 (2003).

26. 468 U.S. 897 (1984).

27. *Id.* at 906.

28. 480 U.S. 340 (1987).

29. *Id.* at 349–50.

30. 514 U.S. 1 (1995).

31. 486 U.S. 35 (1988).

32. 488 U.S. 445 (1989).

33. 501 U.S. 429 (1991).

34. 536 U.S. 194 (2002).

35. *Hiibel v. Sixth Judicial District Court of Nevada,* 542 U.S. 177 (2004); *Maryland v. Pringle,* 540 U.S. 366 (2003); *Illinois v. Lidster,* 540 U.S. 419 (2004); *Illinois v. Caballes,* 543 U.S. 405 (2005); *Id.* at 410.

36. Jeffrey L. Fisher, personal communication, May 25, 2006.

37. 533 U.S. 27 (2001).

38. Craig M. Bradley, personal communication, May 23, 2006.

39. 531 U.S. 32 (2000).

40. 529 U.S. 334 (2000).

41. *Id.* at 337.

42. *Id.* at 342 (J. Breyer, dissenting).

43. Craig M. Bradley, personal communication, May 23, 2006.

44. 541 U.S. 36 (2004).

45. 497 U.S. 836 (1990).

46. 514 U.S. 927 (1995).

47. 526 U.S. 227 (1999).

48. 530 U.S. 466 (2000).

49. *Id.* at 491.

50. *Id.* at 551 (J. O'Connor, dissenting).
51. *Id.* at 552.
52. *Id.* at 559 (J. Breyer, dissenting).
53. *Id.* at 499 (J. Scalia, concurring).
54. Joseph D. O'Neill, personal communication, May 16, 2006.
55. 542 U.S. 296 (2004).
56. *Id.* at 313.
57. *Id.* at 326 (J. O'Connor, dissenting).
58. Jeffrey L. Fisher, personal communication, May 25, 2006.
59. *Ibid.*
60. *Ibid.*
61. *Ewing v. California,* 538 U.S. 11 (2003).; *Lockyer v. Andrade,* 538 U.S. 63 (2003).
62. 532 U.S. 451 (2001).
63. *Id.* at 467 (J. Scalia, dissenting).
64. 542 U.S. 507 (2004); 542 U.S. 466 (2004).
65. *Hamdi v. Rumsfeld,* 542 U.S. at 530.
66. *Id.* at 579 (J. Thomas, dissenting).
67. *Rasul v. Bush,* 542 U.S. at 563.
68. *Id.* at 497 (J. Scalia, dissenting).
69. James W. Hundley, personal communication, May 15, 2006.
70. Jeffrey L. Fisher, personal communication, May 25, 2006.

CHAPTER 10

1. 410 U.S. 113, 174 (1973) (J. Rehnquist, dissenting).
2. Alexis de Tocqueville, *Democracy in America,* Vol. 1 (Philips Bradley ed.) (New York: A. Knopf, 1945 [1835]), p. 280.
3. 410 U.S. 113 (1973).
4. *Id.* at 153.
5. 381 U.S. 479 (1965).
6. *Id.* at 484.
7. *Id.* at 172 (J. Rehnquist, dissenting).
8. *Id.* at 174 (J. Rehnquist, dissenting).
9. 462 U.S. 416 (1983).
10. 476 U.S. 747 (1986).
11. 492 U.S. 490 (1989).
12. *Id.* at 510.
13. *Id.* at 520.
14. *Id.* at 518.
15. *Id.* at 532 (J. Scalia, concurring).
16. *Id.* at 526 (J. O'Connor, concurring).
17. *Id.* at 532 (J. Scalia, concurring).
18. *Id.* at 559–60 (J. Blackmun, dissenting).
19. *Id.* at 540 (J. Blackmun, dissenting).

20. "A Woman's Right, Barely Viable," *New York Times,* July 4, 1989, p. 28.
21. Linda Greenhouse, "Change in Course," *New York Times,* July 4, 1989, p. 1.
22. 505 U.S. 833 (1992).
23. James F. Simon, "Politics and the Rehnquist Court," *New York School Law Review* 40 (1996): 863–875, 870.
24. *Casey,* 505 U.S. at 846.
25. *Id.*
26. *Id.* at 874.
27. *Id.* at 877.
28. *Id.* at 893.
29. Kenneth W. Starr, *First among Equals: The Supreme Court in American Life* (New York: Warner Books, 2002), p. 134.
30. *Casey,* 505 U.S. at 945 (J. Rehnquist, concurring in part and dissenting in part).
31. *Id.* at 954.
32. *Id.* at 964–5.
33. *Id.* at 1002.
34. *Id.*
35. *Id.* at 922 (J. Blackmun, concurring in part and dissenting in part).
36. *Id.* at 923.
37. *Id.* at 926.
38. Greenhouse, *Becoming Justice Blackmun,* pp. 250–1.
39. *Casey,* 505 U.S. at 943.
40. Neil A. Lewis, "Ginsburg Affirms Right of a Woman To Have Abortion," *New York Times,* July 22, 1993, p. A1; David Hess, "Breyer Has Easy First Day before Senate Committee," *Philadelphia Inquirer,* July 13, 1994, p. A03.
41. 530 U.S. 914 (2000).
42. *Id.* at 937.
43. *Id.* at 952 (J. Scalia, dissenting).
44. Thomas Baker, personal communication, May 24, 2006.
45. *Ibid.*
46. *Stenberg,* 530 U.S. at 920.
47. 478 U.S. 186 (1986).
48. Al Kamen, "Powell Changed Vote in Sodomy Case," *Washington Post,* July 13, 1986, p. A1.
49. Al Kamen, "Court Upholds State Law Prohibiting Sodomy, 5–4," *Washington Post,* July 1, 1986, p. A1.
50. 486 U.S. 592 (1988).
51. *Id.* at 603–4.
52. Al Kamen, "High Court Rules Gay Man Can Sue CIA on Firing," *Washington Post,* June 16, 1988, p. A1.
53. 517 U.S. 620 (1996).
54. *Id.* at 626.
55. *Id.* at 635.
56. *Id.* at 640 (J. Scalia, dissenting).

57. *Id.* at 636 (J. Scalia, dissenting).

58. Thomas Baker, personal communication, May 24, 2006.

59. 539 U.S. 558 (2003).

60. *Id.* at 563.

61. *Id.* at 562.

62. *Id.* at 578.

63. *Id.* at 592 (J. Scalia, dissenting).

64. *Id.* at 586 (J. Scalia, dissenting).

65. *Id.* at 599 (J. Scalia, dissenting).

66. 798 N.E.2d 941 (Mass. 2003).

67. Howard Ball, *The Bakke Case: Education and Affirmative Action* (Lawrence: University Press of Kansas, 2000), p. 12 (quoting President Johnson's speech).

68. 438 U.S. 265 (1978).

69. *Id.* at 320.

70. *Id.* at 288.

71. *Id.* at 406 (J. Blackmun, dissenting).

72. 488 U.S. 469 (1989).

73. 448 U.S. 448 (1980).

74. *Richmond,* 488 U.S. at 564.

75. 515 U.S. 200 (1995).

76. *Id.* at 227.

77. *Id.* at 239 (J. Scalia, concurring).

78. *Id.* at 241 (J. Thomas, concurring).

79. 539 U.S. 306 (2003).

80. 539 U.S. 244 (2003).

81. Adam Cohen, "Why Justice O'Connor Could Be Affirmative Action's Unlikely Savior," *New York Times,* April 6, 2003, p. WK12.

82. *Grutter,* 539 U.S. at 337.

83. Kent Syverud, personal communication, June 5, 2006.

84. Thomas Baker, personal communication, May 24, 2006.

85. Kris Kolbo, personal communication, May 22, 2006.

86. *Grutter,* 539 U.S. at 343.

87. Kent Syverud, personal communication, June 5, 2006.

88. *Id.* at 351 (J. Thomas, dissenting).

89. *Id.* at 379 (C.J. Rehnquist, dissenting).

90. Kris Kolbo, personal communication, May 22, 2006.

91. Thomas Baker, personal communication, May 24, 2006.

92. *Ibid.*

CHAPTER 11

1. Supreme Court of the United States, "Statements from the Supreme Court Regarding the Death of Chief Justice William H. Rehnquist," news release, September 4, 2005, http://www.supremecourtus.gov/publicinfo/press/pr_09–04–05b.html.

2. *Ibid.*

3. John G. Roberts, Jr., "In Memoriam: William H. Rehnquist," *Harvard Law Review* 119 (2005): 2.

4. 531 U.S. 98 (2000).

5. *Ibid.*

6. Jeffrey Rosen, "Rehnquist the Great?" *Atlantic Monthly,* April 2005, http://www.theatlantic.com/doc/200504/rosen.

7. John C. Jeffries, Jr., *Justice Lewis F. Powell, Jr.* (New York: Charles Scribner's Sons, 1994), p. 533.

8. Henry J. Reske, "Powell Praises Rehnquist," United Press International, August 8, 1987.

9. Jeffrey Bleich, personal communication, November 4, 2005.

10. Rosen, "Rehnquist the Great?"

11. *Ibid.*

12. Thomas Baker, personal communication, May 24, 2006.

13. Judge Gilbert S. Merritt, personal communication, November 8, 2005.

14. Judge Gilbert Merritt, personal communication, November 8, 2005.

15. Tony Mauro, personal communication, June 2, 2006.

16. Margaret Talbot, "Supreme Confidence: The Jurisprudence of Justice Antonin Scalia," *New Yorker,* March 28, 2005, http://www.newamerica.net/publications/articles/2005/supreme_confidence.

17. R. Ted Cruz, "In Memoriam: William H. Rehnquist," *Harvard Law Review* 119 (2005): 11.

18. Ted Cruz, personal communication, November 2005.

19. Judge Gilbert Merritt, personal communication, November 8, 2005.

20. Supreme Court of the United States, "2003 Year-End Report on the Federal Judiciary," http://www.supremecourtus.gov/publicinfo/year-end/2003year-endreport.html.

21. *Ibid.*

22. Supreme Court of the United States, "2004 Year-End Report on the Federal Judiciary," http://www.supremecourtus.gov/publicinfo/year-end/2004year-endreport.pdf.

23. *Ibid.*

24. *Ibid.*

25. President's Statement on the Death of Chief Justice William Rehnquist, September 4, 2005, http://www.whitehouse.gov/news/releases/2005/09/20050904.html.

26. *A Resolution Relative to the Death of William H. Rehnquist, Chief Justice of the United States,* S Res. 234, 109th Cong., 1st sess.

27. "Statement of Senator Frist," *Congressional Record,* 109th Cong. (September 7, 2005): S9695.

28. "Statement of Senator Obama," *Congressional Record,* 109th Cong. (September 7, 2005): S9707.

29. Senator Edward M. Kennedy, "Statement on the Passing of Chief Justice Rehnquist," news release, September 4, 2005, http://kennedy.senate.gov/newsroom/press_release.cfm?id=849b9d23-a90a-40a0-83bc-4a6c19ea9b28.

30. *William H. Rehnquist Center Act of 2005,* S 2136, 109th Cong., 1st sess.

31. *To Memorialize and Honor the Contribution of Chief Justice William H. Rehnquist,* H.J. Res. 83, 109th Cong., 1st sess.

32. Thomas Baker, personal communication, May 22, 2005.

BIBLIOGRAPHY

Abraham, Henry Julian. *Justices, Presidents, and Senators: A History of the U.S. Supreme Court Appointments from Washington to Clinton.* Lanham, MD: Rowman and Littlefield, 1999.

Adair, Bill. "William Rehnquist I: 1924–2005; Supreme Court Loses Leader." *St. Petersburg Times,* September 4, 2005, p. 1A.

American Bar Association. "Hail to the Chief: Former Law Clerks for William Rehnquist Recall What They Learned and How He Touched Their Lives." *American Bar Association Journal* 91 (2005): 42–48.

Baum, Lawrence. *The Supreme Court.* 8th ed. Washington, DC: CQ Press, 2004.

Belsky, Martin H., ed. *The Rehnquist Court: A Retrospective.* New York: Oxford University Press, 2002.

Biskupic, Joan. *Sandra Day O'Connor: How the First Woman on the Supreme Court Became Its Most Influential Justice.* 1st ed. New York: ECCO, 2005.

Blasi, Vincent, ed. *The Burger Court: The Counter-Revolution That Wasn't.* New Haven, CT: Yale University Press, 1983.

Bleich, Jeff. "Lessons from the Chief: Remembering William Rehnquist." *Oregon State Bar Bulletin* 66 (2005): 15–18.

Bradley, Craig M., ed. *The Rehnquist Legacy.* New York: Cambridge University Press, 2006.

Breyer, Stephen. *Active Liberty: Interpreting Our Democratic Constitution.* 1st ed. New York: Alfred A. Knopf, 2005.

Brisbin, Richard A., Jr. *Justice Antonin Scalia and the Conservative Revival.* Baltimore: John Hopkins University Press, 1997.

Cray, Ed. *Chief Justice: A Biography of Earl Warren.* New York: Simon and Schuster, 1997.

Cruz, R. Ted. "In Memoriam: William H. Rehnquist." *Harvard Law Review* 119 (2005): 10–16.

Cushman, Clare, ed. *The Supreme Court Justices: Illustrated Biographies, 1789–1995.* 2nd ed. Washington, DC: Congressional Quarterly, 1995.

Davis, Sue. *Justice Rehnquist and the Constitution: The Quest for a New Federalism.* Princeton, NJ: Princeton University Press, 1989.

Dean, John W. *The Rehnquist Choice: The Untold Story of the Nixon Appointment That Redefined the Supreme Court.* New York: Free Press, 2001.

Duff, James C. "In Memoriam: William H. Rehnquist." *Harvard Law Review* 119 (2005): 16–20.

Elgo, Tim. "Roots and Branches: The Collegial Intellect of Chief Justice." *Arizona Attorney* 42 (2005): 12–15.

Foskett, Ken. *Judging Thomas: The Life and Times of Clarence Thomas.* New York: William Morrow, 2004.

Friedman, Leon, and Fred L. Israel, eds. *The Justices of the United States Supreme Court, 1789–1968: Their Lives and Major Opinions.* 5 vols. New York: Chelsea House, 1968–1978.

Garbus, Martin. *Courting Disaster: The Supreme Court and the Unmaking of American Law.* 1st ed. New York: Times Books, 2002.

Garnett, Richard W. "In Memoriam: William H. Rehnquist: Chief Justice Rehnquist's Enduring, Democratic Constitution." *Harvard Journal of Law and Public Policy* 29 (2006): 395–400.

Greenhouse, Linda. *Becoming Justice Blackmun: Harry Blackmun's Supreme Court Journey.* 1st ed. New York: Times Books, 2005.

Greenhouse, Linda. "The Last Days of the Rehnquist Court—The Rewards of Patience and Power," *Arizona Law Review* 45 (2003): 251–67.

Hall, Kermit L., James W. Ely, Jr., and Joel B. Grossmann, eds. *The Oxford Companion to the Supreme Court of the United States.* 2nd ed. New York: Oxford University Press, 2005.

Hutchinson, Dennis J. *The Man Who Once Was Whizzer White: A Portrait of Justice Byron R. White.* New York: Free Press, 1998.

Irons, Peter. *Brennan vs. Rehnquist: The Battle for the Constitution.* New York: Alfred A. Knopf, 1994.

Jenkins, John A. "The Partisan: A Talk with Justice Rehnquist." *New York Times,* March 3, 1985, p. SM28.

Kleindienst, Richard G. *Justice: The Memoirs of Attorney General Richard Kleindienst.* Ottawa, IL: Jameson Books, 1985.

Kyl, Jon. "William H. Rehnquist: Tribute to Chief Justice William H. Rehnquist," *Yale Law Journal* 115 (2006): 1857–60.

Lazarus, Edward. *Closed Chambers: The Rise, Fall, and Future of the Modern Supreme Court.* New York: Penguin Books, 1999.

Lieberman, Jethro Koller. *A Practical Companion to the Constitution: How the Supreme Court Has Ruled on Issues from Abortion to Zoning.* Rev ed. Berkeley: University of California Press, 1999.

O'Connor, Sandra Day. *The Majesty of the Law: Reflections of a Supreme Court Justice.* New York: Random House, 2003.

Pacelle, Richard. *The Role of the U.S. Supreme Court in Politics: The Least Dangerous Branch.* Boulder, CO: Westview Press, 2002.

Paddock, Lisa. *Facts about the Supreme Court of the United States.* New York: H. W. Wilson, 1996.

Rehnquist, William H. *The Supreme Court.* New York: Vintage Books, 2002.

Rosen, Jeffrey. "Rehnquist the Great?" *Atlantic Monthly,* April 2005, http://www.theatlantic.com/doc/200504/rosen.

Savage, David G. *Turning Right: The Making of the Rehnquist Supreme Court.* New York: Wiley, 1992.

Scalia, Antonin. *A Matter of Interpretation: Federal Courts and the Law: An Essay.* Princeton, NJ: Princeton University Press, 1997.

Schwartz, Herman, ed. *The Rehnquist Court: Judicial Activism on the Right.* New York: Hill and Wang, 2002.

Selya, Bruce. "Remembering William Rehnquist: October 1, 1924–September 3, 2005." *Rhode Island Bar Journal* 54 (2005): 13.

Starr, Kenneth W. *First among Equals: The Supreme Court in American Life.* New York: Warner Books, 2002.

Tomlins, Christopher, ed. *The United States Supreme Court: The Pursuit of Justice.* Boston: Houghton Mifflin, 2005.

Tushnet, Mark. *A Court Divided: The Rehnquist Court and the Future of Constitutional Law.* New York: W. W. Norton, 2005.

Williams, Juan. *Thurgood Marshall: American Revolutionary.* 1st ed. New York: Times Books, 1998.

Woodward, Bob, and Scott Armstrong. *The Brethren: Inside the Supreme Court.* New York: Simon and Schuster, 1979.

Yalof, David Alistair. *Pursuit of Justices: Presidential Politics and the Selection of Supreme Court Nominees.* Chicago: University of Chicago Press, 1999.

Yarbrough, Tinsley E. *The Rehnquist Court and the Constitution.* New York: Oxford University Press, 2000.

Yarbrough, Tinsley E. *David Hackett Souter: Traditional Republican on the Rehnquist Court.* New York: Oxford University Press, 2005.

INDEX

About the Author

DAVID L. HUDSON JR. is a research attorney with the First Amendment Center at Vanderbilt University. Hudson also teaches classes at the Nashville School of Law and Middle Tennessee State University. He serves as a First Amendment contributing editor to the American Bar Association's *Preview of United States Supreme Court Cases.* He has written about the First Amendment jurisprudence of a number of Supreme Court Justices, including Clarence Thomas, William Brennan, John Paul Stevens, David Souter, and Samuel Alito. He is the author or co-author of 15 book.